Hocking Valley Community Residential Center
111 West Twenty-Nine Drive
Nelsonville, Ohio   45764

How to Keep the Children You Love Off Drugs

How to Keep the Children You Love Off Drugs

A Prevention and Intervention Guide for Parents of Preschoolers, School-agers, Preteens, and Teens

by Ken Barun and Philip Bashe

THE ATLANTIC MONTHLY PRESS
NEW YORK

Grateful acknowledgment is made to the following for the right to adapt previously published material:
Bantam Books, for "In an Emergency" from *The Little Black Pill Book*, 1983.
The National Association of State Alcohol and Drug Abuse Directors, for "Coverage for Alcoholism and/or Drug Dependency Treatment Services: Summary of State Health Insurance Statutes as of January 1, 1986 (Exhibit I)," from its January/February 1986 Special Report.

Published simultaneously in Canada
Printed in the United States of America
FIRST EDITION

Library of Congress Cataloging-in-Publication Data

Barun, Ken.
    How to keep the children you love off drugs.

    1. Children—United States—Drug use. 2. Teenagers
—United States—Drug use. 3. Drug abuse—United
States—Prevention. I. Bashe, Philip. II. Title.
HV5824.C45B37   1988   649'.4   88-3376
ISBN 0-87113-180-3

Design by Laura Hough

The Atlantic Monthly Press
19 Union Square West
New York, NY 10003

FIRST PRINTING

This book is dedicated to my wife, Maria, a partner in my accomplishments past, present and future, and to my sons, Seth, Adam, and Max, the inspiration for this book. It is also dedicated to Sarah and Dawn, who together inspired me to live.

—Ken Barun

Acknowledgments

Ken Barun would like to thank: my close childhood friends Howie Sorkin, Barry Galvin, Alan Miller, Jim Neri, and the late John Sutton, who made life a storybook. Also my parents, Elayne and Sam Barun, my grandmother, Gertrude Goldstein, my in-laws, Gene and Helen Heard, and my assistant mother-in-law, Aldean Harper.

Everyone at the Cenikor Foundation but especially Ed and Lynda Fresquez, without whose help I would not be alive today.

A very special thanks to President Ronald Reagan and First Lady Nancy Reagan for their faith and confidence in me, and to my associates at the White House, with whom I shared one of my life's greatest experiences: Marty Coyne, Elaine Crispen, Jane Erkenbeck, Gahl Hodges-Burt, Linda Faulkner, Deborah Balfour, Frank McKay, Fred Ryan, Jim Manning, and the rest of the First Lady's staff.

Also, thanks to the late Ray Kroc, his wife, Joan Kroc, and to everyone in the great McDonald's family, but mostly to Gerry and Bobbi Newman, Ed Rensi, Fred Turner, Mike Quinlan, Irv Klein, Don Lubin, Dick Starmann, Al Golin, and the rest of the board of trustees of Ronald McDonald Children's Charities. More thank yous to Linda and Angel Wiltz and the kids in this country that make up the Just Say No clubs. They are our future.

Finally, very special thanks to Stacy and Malgosia Keach, Larry Gatlin, Otto and Connie Moulton, William T. (Tom) Adams, Bob Sutter, Fred Wolf, Glen and Bonnie Christ, Al and Lydia Dugan, Jim Stansill, and to my closest friend, Don Pinson.

Acknowledgments

Philip Bashe would like to thank the following people for their contributions to the creation of this book.

First, the following persons and organizations for their input and for supplying materials:

Abraxas Foundation, Inc., Al-Anon, Alateen, Alcohol, Drug Abuse and Mental Health Administration, Alcoholics Anonymous, American Association for Marriage and Family Therapy, American Cancer Society, American Psychiatric Association, American Psychological Association, Bantam Books, Behavioral Health Services, Peter Bell, Beth Israel Medical Center Methadone Maintenance Treatment Program, The Bridge, William Butynski, California Office of the Attorney General, Diane M. Canova, Cenikor Foundation, Charter Medical Corporation, Children's Health Program, Cocaine Anonymous, Commission of Accreditation of Rehabilitation Facilities, Committees of Correspondence, Comprehensive Health Education Foundation, Connecticut Mental Health Center/APT Foundation, Connecticut Renaissance, Crossroads, DARE, Daytop Village, Delancey Street Foundation, Department of Health and Human Services, Drug Abuse Programs of America, Drugs Anonymous, E.L.A. Alcoholism Council, Fair Oaks Hospital, Fairview Treatment Program, Families Anonymous, Families in Action National Drug Information Center, Family Service America, Henry Ford Hospital, Guadenzia, HART, Hazelden Foundation, Help Is Possible, Impact Drug and Alcohol Treatment Center, Integrity, Intergovernmental Health-Policy Project, Joint Commission on Accreditation of Hospitals, Just Say No Foundation, Liberation Programs, Magdala Foundation, Marathon House, Matrix Community Services, Mayo Clinic, Medicaid, C. E. Mendez Foundation, The Menninger Foundation, Meridian House, Minnesota Institute on Black Chemical Abuse, Mothers Against Drunk Driving, Narcotics Anonymous, National Adolescent Suicide Hotline, National Association of State Alcohol and Drug Abuse Directors, National Clearinghouse for Alcohol and Drug Information, National Council on Alcoholism, National Federation of Parents for Drug-Free Youth, National Institute on Drug Abuse, National Parents' Resource Institute for Drug Education, National Self-Help Clearinghouse, New Horizons Child and Adolescent Services, New York State Office of Alcoholism and Alcohol Abuse, New York State Office of Substance Abuse, Odyssey House, Odyssey House Louisiana, Palmview Hospital, Parents' Association to Neutralize Drug and Alcohol Abuse, Pathfinder, Phoenix House Foundation, Poison Control, Project Star, Quest International, Renaissance West, St. Joseph

Acknowledgments

Hospital, St. Luke's Behavioral Center, St. Patrick Hospital, Second Genesis, Shalom et Benedictus, Sierra Family Services, Spectrum Programs, Starz, Straight, Students Against Driving Drunk, Tarzana Treatment Center, Therapeutic Communities of America, Toughlove, Turning Point, University of Alabama at Birmingham Substance Abuse Programs, U.S. Department of Education, U.S. National Center for Health Statistics, and Youth to Youth.

Special thanks to Barbara Arnold, Dr. Robert Newman, Marion C. H. Pines, Patricia Puritz, Carol Rubiano, Richard Sackett, Barbara Schuford, Ira Schwartz, and Dr. Charles Shuster. Also to John Danowsky, Lisa Freitag, Carlos Gonzalez, Joseph Johnson, Olga Kelly, James Massimillo, Ronald Roberg, John Vero, and Quintin Wallace for their honesty and their willingness to share.

Very special thanks to Mr. and Mrs. Robert Bashe, the late Evelyn Bashe, and to Patty Romanowski Bashe for her great ideas, as usual.

Ken Barun and Philip Bashe would like to thank our editor, Ann Godoff; her assistant, Nancy Lewin; copy editor Ed Sedarbaum; designer Laura Hough; our agents, Jed Mattes and Sarah Lazin, respectively; and their assistants, Adeena Karsseboom and Gila Sand, respectively.

Contents

Contents

Prevention

Chapter One

The Wily Beast Drug Abuse

Just ask the kids.

With wide-eyed innocence or rebellious sarcasm they reveal the severity of America's adolescent and preadolescent substance-abuse problem. Perhaps few of them confide in their parents, but they are disarmingly candid when replying anonymously to polls about drug use among them and their peers. The results are disturbing, and for parents, frightening:

According to the National Institute on Drug Abuse (NIDA) and the National Council on Alcoholism (NCA),

- the average age of first drug use is now thirteen, and of first alcohol use, twelve;
- over half (57%) of high-school seniors have tried an illicit drug, and over one-third (36%) have tried an illicit drug other than marijuana;
- nearly one-third of all high-school seniors claim that most or all of their friends get drunk at least once a week;
- nearly one in six seniors has tried cocaine or its powerfully addictive derivative, crack;
- high-school senior girls ingest more stimulants and tranquilizers than boys, and come close to matching boys' levels of alcohol, marijuana, sedative, barbiturate, inhalant, hallucinogen, cocaine, crack, and opium use;
- a *Weekly Reader* survey of fourth-graders found that nearly one-third were already being pressured by their peers to try alcohol and marijuana.

3

However, ask these same kids' parents, and you're likely to get a contrasting, soft-pedaled assessment of how far-reaching the problem is. When Atlanta's Emory University queried six hundred high-school seniors and their parents about alcohol use, only 35% of the adults believed their sons and daughters had consumed beer, wine, or liquor within the last month; yet according to their kids, the actual figure was nearly double that.

In a midwestern school district, while four out of five parents considered marijuana use to be a problem among seventh- through twelfth-graders, only one in five thought his or her child was involved. In reality, over half the students had tried it, and nearly one-third admitted smoking pot regularly.

Youthful drug abuse is a wily, unpredictable beast. It may be snarling right outside their door, ready to carry off their children into the darkness, yet many mothers and fathers choose to ignore its ominous presence. How could they be so blind? many of us ask, hastily judging them as unfit, uncaring, or plain incompetent. But it is just not that simple.

Parents feel unequal to the responsibility of protecting their kids for a multitude of reasons. Some believe that admitting to a child's drug problem is conceding failure or neglect, while others are incapacitated by the crisis, unable to respond sensibly. Many are ignorant of substance abuse's signs and fail to notice the secretive behavior, or the conspicuous red eyes, or the paraphernalia stashed in an upstairs dresser drawer. But most parents simply cannot believe that such a terrible thing could happen to their child. It is literally beyond their comprehension. And while they pray fervently, "Please don't let it happen to me, please don't let it happen to my kid," the beast snatches the child in its jaws.

Perhaps these parents misinterpret the much-heralded statistics suggesting drug use has stabilized to mean this national cancer is in remission and that we can now all breathe a sigh of relief. Hardly. Although overall levels have decreased since 1979—except for an upsurge in 1985—the United States still has the highest unlawful-drug-use rate of any industrialized country. Generating yearly sales of roughly $100 billion, the illicit-drug industry ranks right up there with General Motors, AT&T, and Exxon. And the economic cost to the country from alcohol abuse and alcoholism is well in excess of that amount.

In the words of Dr. Lloyd Johnston, project director of an annual survey of high-school seniors conducted for NIDA by the University of Michigan Institute for Social Research, yes, youthful drug abuse has stalled, "but very high up on the mountain"—one from which many kids will surely plummet before they are rescued.

National Institute on Drug Abuse director Dr. Charles Shuster acknowledges that although the percentage of high-school seniors who smoke marijuana daily dropped from a high of 11% in 1978 to 4% in 1986, "that still means four out of every one hundred use it regularly, which is far too high." The real figure is certainly higher, since habitual pot smokers are twice as likely as nonusers to drop out of school and therefore may be excluded from the University of Michigan study. For that reason, we refer frequently to the survey of drug and alcohol use among students in grades seven, nine, and eleven commissioned by California Attorney General John K. Van De Kamp. It held that nearly twice as many—seven out of one hundred—high-school juniors smoked grass at least once a day.

Now, enough statistics.

How to Keep the Children You Love Off Drugs will not inundate you with figures and charts. To you, the concerned parent of a youngster either in or entering what we call the drug-vulnerable years between twelve and twenty, it doesn't matter if one, one thousand, or one million kids are mired in drugs. All that matters is your child and what steps you can take to prevent him from becoming a victim. (For brevity's sake, *he, him,* and *his* will apply to both genders.) Or, if you suspect he is presently handling substances, you want to know how to get him off. And there's no time to waste.

I believe you'll find much valuable information and applicable plans of action in this practical guide. We offer no scientific systems, diagrams, or models but examples drawn from real-life situations. No impenetrable psychological, sociological, or medical jargon but straight talk. *How to Keep the Children You Love Off Drugs* is written to and for mothers and fathers, not for my colleagues in the drug-treatment field.

My involvement with drugs goes back almost a quarter century. During the first six of those years I was drug dependent and didn't expect to see my twenty-fifth birthday, strung out on a potpourri of substances including marijuana, pills, hallucinogens, cocaine, and heroin. Since recovering at one of the country's oldest, most respected drug-rehabilitation facilities, Cenikor, I have worked extensively with drug-dependent young people— first as a Cenikor counselor, then as its chief executive officer. Our program attracted such national attention that, after a visit by President Ronald Reagan and later Mrs. Reagan, I assumed the position of director

5

of projects and policy for the First Lady at the White House. From 1985 to 1987 I helped to implement her antidrug campaign. Today I am vice-president and executive director of Ronald McDonald Children's Charities, which funds projects that benefit children, including drug-prevention and drug-treatment programs, and am a member of the National White House Conference for a Drug-Free America.

I am neither a psychiatrist, a psychologist, nor an M.D. To tell the truth, I've never really considered myself to be a health-care professional. I acquired my substance-abuse education the hard way, nearly dying in the process. Though it has been more than a decade and a half since I cleaned up my act, and the scars on my arms have faded, the anguish and despair of those years remain eternally embedded in my memory. I'll never forget the desperate desire to fit in with other teenagers that led to my experimenting with drugs, the self-loathing I felt as an addict, and the life-affirming exuberance I discovered once I finally stopped using chemicals and began pulling others from the same fire. Despite my many years in the drug-rehabilitation profession, as the father of three boys ages five, eight, and eleven and a seventeen-year-old daughter, I harbor the same concerns about my kids as you do about yours. Accordingly, *How to Keep the Children You Love Off Drugs* is written from one parent to another.

Along with other similarities we have as parents, many of us came of age during the 1960s, one of the most tumultuous decades in American history. Fueling the fires of cultural and social upheaval were drugs, and during that period their use soared as precipitously as the *Apollo 11* moon shot from its launchpad. We so-called Baby Boomers are an interesting bunch, perhaps the first generation of mothers and fathers to hold the dubious distinction of having some personal involvement in drugs; according to a National Institute on Drug Abuse poll, one in five persons thirty-five and older has used an illegal substance in his lifetime. Yet those of you who once skinny-dipped in Lake Drug Culture can actually benefit from your inglorious past: Tapping into your memory can aid you in identifying the physical and behavioral signs of substance abuse that, based on National Parents' Resource Institute for Drug Education (PRIDE) findings, typically evade parents for at least a year.

However, you cannot rely solely on what may be outdated, inaccurate drug information, for not only have the drugs of choice changed, their chemical compositions may differ radically from years ago. A case in point is today's marijuana, up to twenty times stronger than the *Cannabis sativa* harvested a decade ago. Furthermore, it has been substantiated that pot has more cancer-causing agents than tobacco. (And what did those of us who used grass always reply impertinently to our objecting parents? "Oh yeah? Well, it's a lot safer than those cigarettes *you* smoke!") No longer is marijuana the harmless vice many renowned researchers once thought it to be. Clearly, parents must keep abreast of the dangers, a tall order when you consider how often new research contradicts established studies.

My unconditional message to parents is that *no* drugs are harmless and none is acceptable, including alcohol and cigarettes. As the distinguished former White House drug chief Dr. Robert L. DuPont, Jr., wrote in the *Journal of the American Medical Association:* "The earlier in life a child starts using any dependence-producing drug, the more likely he or she is to experience dependence and other health problems and go on to other dependence-producing drugs." Most kids become drug dependent through cigarettes, alcohol, and marijuana.

Here is one instance where cold, hard facts speak volumes. According to Dupont, cigarette-smoking twelve-to-seventeen-year-olds are

- twice as likely to use alcohol;
- nine times as likely to ingest depressants and stimulants;
- ten times as likely to smoke marijuana;
- fourteen times as likely to use cocaine, hallucinogens, and heroin.

If you cling stubbornly to antiquated attitudes such as "I used drugs 'responsibly' as a teenager, and they didn't do me any irreparable harm," or "Drug experimentation is just a phase of growing up," I hope to change them before you put this book down. Certainly not every kid who takes a hit off a joint or drains a bottle of booze winds up as I did: an addict destroying his life and the lives of his loved ones. But *one in ten* does develop substance dependency, and no one can say who it will be until it's too late. Whenever youngsters plunge into an affair with drugs, there are no assurances they won't become members of that 10% group: wed through physical or psychological addiction till death—or treatment, if caught in time—do them part.

Let's put the drug problem in perspective: The odds that your child will be a homicide victim are 1 in 90 for boys and 1 in 275 for girls. Naturally you take every precaution to safeguard him, instructing him never to get in cars with strangers, to keep doors locked when alone at home, and so on. The likelihood of alcohol and drugs threatening him is so much greater. Are you willing to bet his health, his happiness, maybe even his life? Of course not.

The first section of *How to Keep the Children You Love Off Drugs* is **Prevention**. Parents, educators, and politicians often react to a drug crisis only after it has manifested itself beyond the shadow of a doubt. I advocate *pre*action instead of *re*action. Indoctrinate your children against drugs at the earliest possible age, and hopefully you will never need to read the chapters on intervention. As asserted by Dr. Dupont, relatively few persons are introduced to drugs after age twenty, so if you can protect your child until then, he has an excellent chance of growing into a drug-free adult.

Prevention's chapters detail
- the reasons why America's young people turn to drugs;
- how to guide your youngster toward alternatives to chemicals;
- how to create an atmosphere at home that is more conducive to raising a drug-free child;
- how to educate him about drugs.

Intervention's chapters encompass
- what you need to know about each drug and its effects;
- how to identify evidence of substance abuse;
- what steps to take and ironclad rules to establish once you've verified an existing problem;
- how and where to seek the best professional treatment, including a comprehensive listing of personally approved programs around the country;
- what to expect in the aftermath of treatment;
- what course to follow in the event that all else fails.

Although prevention and intervention strategies are presented throughout, I am mindful that a single approach is not going to apply to all kids. One of this book's goals is to sharpen your sensitivity in determining what will work best for your child. Another is to develop your communication skills. To that end we've included sample blueprints—scripts, if you will—enabling you to more effectively convey drug education to an eyeball-rolling youngster who takes the misinformation he gets from his friends to be gospel. Or to calmly yet productively confront a suspected drug abuser.

Yet another aim of *How to Keep the Children You Love Off Drugs* is to enhance your attunement to your kids' world, so strikingly different from, yet so similar to, the one in which we grew up. Certainly today's adolescents face more pressures than did previous generations, and they deserve—no, demand—pragmatic answers from their parents. Especially where drugs are concerned. So, for example, if your child asks you how he can refuse friendly offers of drugs without alienating his peers, merely telling him to decline politely does him a grave disservice. Because no matter how good your intentions, he may be easily won over by a persuasive adolescent proffering drugs or drink. Saying "no" is a start, but truly building a youngster's refusal skills requires a much more intensive effort. As you will see, though this book proposes solutions, they are seldom simple.

Because youthful substance abuse is such a complex problem, each chapter is appended with a summary of key points. Also included are lists of recommended resources that I encourage you to utilize: from organizations that publish free drug-education information, to alternative-activity groups for kids, to treatment referral agencies.

At times in *How to Keep the Children You Love Off Drugs* I'm going to exhort you to get tough with your kids. But too tough? You can never be too tough when it comes to drugs and the children you love. Perhaps this sounds ironic coming from a member of the sixties generation, but it was our parents' vacillation from a staunchly antidrug posture that contributed greatly to the current epidemic. What other conclusion can be reached from the appalling figures about kids and substance abuse? Further, it's an opinion shared by Dr. Shuster, who contends:

> Parents must assume responsibility for their children's conduct. In the sixties and seventies parents abdicated that responsibility, believing falsely all you had to do was to teach kids how to think about problems and they would come up with the appropriate answers. That approach served only to confuse children and exacerbate their insecurities, which in turn led to a further escalation of drug abuse.

I admit I'm frequently hard on kids, but I'm equally hard on parents about their obligations; it may often seem that the responsibilities I place on your shoulders are overwhelming. Believe me, I sincerely empathize with you; I know that a child's drug problem can seem like an interminable ordeal testing every ounce of your resolve. Too, it is natural to fear that you will not be able to persevere with your sanity, your marriage, or your family intact. But you will, because you love your child so deeply. Your refusal to let drugs wrest him away from you provides a remarkable inner strength and tenacity.

* * *

It is naïve to believe drugs will ever be banished entirely from our society. They won't. But even in the face of such seemingly staggering odds, it can be within your power to keep drugs out of your family. The best way to arm yourself in this battle to save your kids is with early, accurate education and by instilling positive values they can fall back on when they are out of your sight and are being cajoled by friends to take a hit off a joint behind the bleachers or to snort a line of cocaine at a party. Having picked up this book, you've already taken your first step.

That's the good news. The not-so-good news is that *How to Keep the Children You Love Off Drugs* does not come with a money-back guarantee. Only if we kept our kids permanently corralled at home could we rest reasonably assured they would never touch alcohol or drugs. (But imagine the phone bills.) The reality, of course, is that our youngsters spend the majority of their waking hours in a world where temptations and pressures to imbibe, to conform, to be accepted confront them constantly, like land mines in a war zone.

You've probably heard this said a million times, but before you can deal effectively with your kids and drugs, you must believe it: Drug abuse can happen to anyone's children, regardless of the parents' socioeconomic group, how strict or lenient they are, and how loving and nurturing they are. Just ask my mom and dad.

I NEVER SMILED—THE STORY OF A DRUG USER

It was a scene that has been reenacted time and time again: A sixteen-year-old boy playing basketball in a deserted playground is motioned over to the sidelines by another kid holding up a marijuana cigarette. "Hey, ever try this before?" Curious, and anxious to fit in with the other teenagers passing around the joint, the boy takes one tentative puff—not an innocent experimentation but the first step of an unwitting descent into the shadowy world of drugs.

The neighborhood was not a decaying urban slum but a sleepy, middle-class New York suburb. The year was 1964, with American society on the threshold of a substance-abuse proliferation that continues unabated to this day. The typical teenager was me.

Like most adolescents I was plagued by insecurities, but I excelled in sports and played on the football team despite a fear of physical pain. I also enjoyed basketball, which was what a dozen or so of us were doing when this heavyset kid named Irving, with a ruddy complexion and jet black, short-cropped hair, came ambling onto the court, dragging on a cigarette.

"You know what this here is?"

I shook my head.

"This here's a joint. Marijuana."

"Oooooh," I said, shaking my head disapprovingly, "that's bad stuff." All I had heard about pot was the old story that a lot of musicians smoked it and it was dangerous.

But he persisted. "Aw, c'mon, try some. It won't hurt you."

So I took a puff or two, felt nothing, and left the schoolyard that night thinking, *Marijuana? What's the big deal?* My only intoxication was derived from the peer approval that accompanied merely toking on a sweet-smelling cigarette.

When I was seventeen I transferred to a private military school in upstate New York and, keen on fitting into my new environment, adapted to the rigid regulations. Surrounded by straight arrows—or so they seemed—I began acting like one. But whenever I saw the old gang I felt awkward in my severe buzz haircut and sharply creased uniform. Adding to my discomfort was my generation's growing resistance to the Vietnam War; at home my military outfit made me feel like a pariah. And liberalized mores pertaining to sex and drugs only confused me. I felt like the rope in a tug-of-war.

One weekend back in White Plains I smoked pot at a party. The music—probably Bob Dylan, the Beatles, the Rolling Stones—was abrasively but wonderfully loud, and I drifted off into a corner feeling, in the words of a Pink Floyd song, comfortably numb. Worries and confusion about the future and conflicts with my parents seemed to dissipate into the air along with the smoke. *I like this feeling,* I thought. No feeling. In retrospect I understand a child's fear of getting hurt and the fear of experiencing emotional pain. And I realized at that early stage that drugs blocked out emotional pain.

Increasingly, grass became integral to my social life. On weekends my friends and I would drive into Manhattan to listen to rock groups and artists such as the Mothers of Invention, Richie Havens, and the Paul Butterfield Blues Band at the East Village cafés. We were, without fail, stoned. Now that I was out of military school, jeans and sandals replaced navy blue trousers and spit-shined shoes as my uniform. I grew my hair

11

and a beard to conform to my new "nonconformist" friends. We were a very real part of the burgeoning hippie generation, and everything was "cool."

Except that months of habitual marijuana use had made me extremely paranoid and apathetic. I was attending a liberal college in affluent Southampton, Long Island, where I mixed with students dedicated mainly to smoking grass and skipping classes. Parties were the rule, even during the week. One night as I tried futilely to. ignore the tumult in the dormitory, studying bleary-eyed for a test, my door swung open and a head appeared.

"Can't stay awake? Here." In the palm of his hand were several pills. I looked up at him quizzically.

"Amphetamines," he explained. "Try some." I did, and in a few minutes it was like I had ingested rocket fuel. I felt wide awake and completely alert. Also wide-eyed and wired. I managed to complete my studying (although getting to class for the test was another story). And when I needed to come down for sleep just as the sun was coming up, someone else fed me barbiturates to counteract the previous pills. Drugs seemed so mathematical: One up plus one down equaled zero. How simple. How precise. For someone who felt his life spinning out of control, the notion that I could regain the upper hand by swallowing pills was seductive. In reality drugs began to gradually snatch authority over my life from me, but I didn't—and couldn't—see it that way. Only now do I appreciate the irony that at the same time many members of the sixties generation objected strenuously to oppressive governmental and corporate powers, we willed our minds and bodies to chemicals.

My enthusiasm for pot and pills was tempered by the innate conviction that taking them was wrong. Although the issue of drugs and alcohol was never raised at home, my parents instilled in me decent values, and so every time I got high I experienced guilt and distress. To anesthetize those feelings I smoked more pot or gulped more downs, which only generated more guilt, more distress, and more of that emotional pain I was trying so hard to avoid. It became a perpetual cycle.

With my older brother and me out of the nest, my parents sold our White Plains home and moved to New York City. Presumably, not yet ready to forsake any chance of glimpsing some greenery, they bought a small cottage in Montauk, on the tip of Long Island. For my friends and me the tiny bungalow became a resort-town opium den. We'd catch lobsters in the Atlantic Ocean, then, on our way home, trail behind one of the local produce trucks to scavenge for the potatoes that fell off the back as it bounced along the bumpy, winding roads. Virtually every night we'd feast on lobster and baked potatoes, with grass, uppers, and downers comprising the final course. Because the area was quiet and desolate during off-season, we never worried about the police—not with car headlights visible from nearly a mile away. So we got more daring.

One night one of the guys turned up at the front door, grinning wickedly. "Guess what," he said, "I scored us some smack." He'd boasted previously about using heroin and had tantalized us with vivid accounts of its exquisite high. From his pocket he withdrew a cellophane envelope, which he passed around for inspection. Then he brandished a homemade syringe consisting of an eyedropper and a stainless-steel needle, and prepared to shoot up. The rest of us—six men and two women—were already high and looked on transfixed, as if observing some sacred rite: his gently shaking the white powder into a spoon and charily adding drops of tap water, all the while working as meticulously as a laboratory chemist. Next a lit match was held to the bottom of the spoon, the mixture boiling and dissolving almost immediately.

Finally, we drew in our breaths as he drew the clear liquid into the syringe, rolled up his shirtsleeve, strapped a belt tightly around his arm, probed for a vein, and injected the drug. His eyes rolled back in his head, which lolled precariously, before he lapsed into semiconsciousness. When he came to, he held the needle aloft as if asking for volunteers. His narcose gaze found me.

"Oh, no," I said, laughing nervously, "no way am I going to stick a needle in my arm." I meant it, as since childhood I had been terrified by the mere prospect of receiving polio vaccinations from the family doctor.

"Don't worry," he purred, trying to soothe me, "I won't stick it in your vein." It was called skin popping. As usual, desiring acceptance, not wanting to appear chicken, I agreed impetuously. *If the needle doesn't pierce a vein,* I figured, *how dangerous could it be?* and he shot me up. The sensation was nearly beyond description: nausea, then a charge of euphoria that raced through my body like electricity through copper wire. Warmth, serenity. It was as if I were a musical instrument able to harmonize with itself, and I knew at once that heroin was the drug for me.

All I remember from the balance of that evening is a bunch of very high people sprawled about the cottage, babbling incessantly, incoherently. Sometimes a person would begin a sentence, nod off for several minutes before awakening, and then resume the conversation in the middle of the very same sentence.

Afraid of becoming addicted, I refrained from further use for a time but soon ached to know the warmth and serenity again. Several of my friends' drug use had snowballed in tandem with mine, so that they too were now heroin users. Instead of raising glasses in toasts to our friendship, we'd celebrate in someone's dank apartment with syringes and powder. Curiously, it all seemed romantic and exciting.

However, it didn't take long for that idyll to deteriorate just like the rest of my life. If there's one image I have of myself as an addict, it is that I never smiled. No exaggeration. I *never* smiled. It was certainly no laughing matter when I came down with hepatitis and had to drop out of college because I'd already missed so many classes. Had it been fifteen years later, instead of hepatitis I almost certainly would have contracted the AIDS virus from shared needles. The liver inflammation turned my skin a ghastly yellow, but once I recovered it was back to frequenting shooting galleries: usually vacant, dilapidated buildings inhabited by prostitutes, pushers, and punks. One room would be reserved for shooting up; in others girls turned tricks. When I think back, it's a wonder I didn't die, not just from the drugs but from the dangerous and scary element with which I associated as part of my new life-style. Some life, some style.

Incredibly, during all this time my parents didn't seem to have a clue about what was wrong with their son, the onetime military-school cadet and athlete. Like so many of their generation, they had no awareness of drugs. Only recently had the media begun covering the substance-abuse menace among what it called the Woodstock Generation, of which I was a card-carrying member. I certainly looked the part, with shoulder-length hair and unkempt clothes. No photographs of me from that period exist because my parents destroyed them. Out of embarrassment, I suppose.

They were mortified by my physical appearance and baffled by my erratic behavior. Their way of dealing with the problem, however, was not to deal with it, just as *I* chose not to handle my troubles and get wasted instead. There was the time at Thanksgiving when, soporific from heroin, I fell face first into my plate of turkey, yams, and gravy. My parents' reaction to their son snoring into his dinner? "He's just tired," my mother said impassively. Tired? I didn't work, I didn't go to school. From what could I possibly be tired?

There was the time when I decided to get out of New York and start over again at a college in Florida, where my parents had purchased a retirement home. I was determined to get clean but, the day before leaving, stalked the Manhattan streets for some fixes for the road. *As soon as I get down there, I'll quit,* I lied to myself. Never today, always tomorrow. And at regular intervals during the trip south I'd pull into gas stations, head to the rest room, and fix—then continue driving, my body traveling south and my brain traveling in space.

Within weeks of having arrived in Hollywood, Florida, I was already consorting with the city's drug population. There was no need to ferret them out; we just seemed to cluster together instinctively. I rented a shabby one-room apartment in which I spent most of my time, getting stoned. Sometimes in a burst of ambition I'd cook a meal—pancakes, always pancakes—but it was usually so unpalatable I'd toss it in the sink to languish for eternity. Who needed food anyway? I had heroin.

I did, however, need money, and after depleting my own sources I started on my parents', which is how they finally learned about—or, should I say, opened their eyes to—my habit.

"What is going on down there?" my father demanded angrily, calling from New York.

"Dad," I said indifferently, devoid of conscience, "I'm strung out on drugs. I'm addicted to heroin." I can see now that my cold confession was actually a desperate cry for help.

I thought he was going to collapse and could hear him gasp for breath. Regaining his composure, he said sternly, "Stay there and don't do anything." He and my mother were on the next plane to Florida and took me to a hospital. Their reaction, after denying the obvious for so long, was, "How could you do this to us?" I had no answer, since I couldn't even comprehend how I could do such a thing to myself.

After ten days of detoxification by way of the synthetic narcotic called methadone and some psychiatric mumbo jumbo, I was pronounced cured. Everyone believed it, even me. But with drug treatment still in its infancy at that time, few professionals and patients truly grasped what it took to get clean and stay clean, and just days after strolling out of the hospital into the warm Florida sunshine, I was back to my old ways again. Addiction became like a possessive, spiteful lover refusing to set me free.

Eventually, I was injecting up to ten times a day and suffering through the torment of withdrawal at least once a week when dope was hard to come by or I didn't have enough cash for a deal. In spite of my enslavement, I was clearheaded enough to realize that continuing like this would kill me. So I impulsively went traveling cross-country with a Vietnam-veteran friend, in a scene right out of the period-piece film *Easy Rider*. Environment and social network can indeed conspire against a drug user wishing to go straight, but my believing that a change of milieu was the answer epitomized a junkie's self-delusion. It wouldn't have mattered if I had journeyed to the remote Australian Outback, I still would have gotten my hands on heroin somehow. Addicts can be remarkably resourceful.

Instead of Down Under, I wound up down and out in Dallas, which is where I met my first wife. Sarah was a beautiful nineteen-year-old girl who was completely sober. I found employment in Texas, but with a cocaine dealer; he was the wholesaler, I was the retailer. Like any good salesman I sampled my wares to make sure they were of the highest quality, until my entire inventory had disappeared up my nose. When my supplier heard about this he came looking for me, presumably to speed me to the grave for which I seemed destined anyway. Sarah, pregnant at the time, stood defiantly between me and certain death. Not so heartless that he could kill an expectant mother, he turned on his heel and left.

A few days before we married I pleaded with Sarah not to marry me. Too young to comprehend what she was getting into, she went ahead anyway. Like many spouses and relatives of substance abusers she probably hoped that her positive influence, as well as impending nuptials and fatherhood, would straighten me out. They didn't. I would vanish for days at a time, running with a new drug crowd. After my disappearing acts my wife would accuse me of philandering. What she didn't understand was that while I did indeed have a mistress, her name was heroin. Sex didn't hold half the allure of plunging a needle into my arm, losing consciousness, and coming to in filthy back alleys and flophouses subleased by roaches.

In fact, the day our daughter, Dawn, was born, I was stoned. And when I lurched into the delivery room to squeeze Sarah's hand, she looked at me with a combination of hurt and hate in her eyes. I felt so guilty that I bolted from the hospital, proceeded to get even more loaded, and wrecked the car.

Believe me, I was not proud of what I'd become; every day I woke up with a gnawing in the pit of my stomach and wished I were dead. But heroin kills remorse the way penicillin kills bacteria. The difference was that my medicine no longer made me feel good; it barely kept me from feeling bad. Being strung out was *normal* for me. Finally, both my parents and my wife had enough of watching me destroy my life.

This was the last straw for them: I'd fled Texas for Florida, taking Sarah and Dawn with me. I was so paranoid from all the drugs and from the constant fear of arrest that one sultry night I raced through the streets of Miami in a rented Cadillac at ninety miles per hour dead certain two FBI agents were on my tail. For several hours I led my imaginary pursuers on a chase up and down one street after another, glancing frantically in the rearview mirror and flooring the accelerator. In retrospect I'm convinced that no one was following me at all.

When I screeched to a halt in front of a friend's house, my frustrated father was there waiting for me with my wife and daughter. In his hand were clutched two hundred dollars and two airplane tickets, which he gave to Sarah; a wise move. "Get out of here," he said disgustedly. "I never want to see you again."

My reaction? Elation. After all, I was being hounded by the authorities and needed to skip town. His timing couldn't have been more perfect.

Shortly after we slipped away to Houston, where my wife's brother lived, I developed a coronary embolism, which is a sudden blocking of the arteries that lead to the heart. Small wonder considering how I'd been abusing my body with heroin, Quaaludes, Ritalin, and so on. I was in the hospital for weeks, and the doctors told me that at one point I had died in the emergency room. They placed me in intensive care with a dozen other patients, half of whom didn't make it.

It was then Sarah decided she, too, could tolerate no more, and one afternoon while convalescing I looked out the hospital window to glimpse her and my one-year-old daughter waving good-bye. I would see them again only once in the next ten years. Never have I blamed my wife for leaving; she gave up on me only when I had given up on myself. But neither her returning to Dallas nor my parents' throwing me out seemed to faze me. Even when I learned that one of my closest friends had died of an overdose, I rationalized, "He screwed up. That'll never happen to me, I'm too smart." Yes, I was really smart.

The lowest point of all came after my release from the hospital. Others my age were two years out of college, establishing careers and raising families. Me? I'd ruined a marriage, my relationship with my family and, irrevocably, it seemed, my future. I lived in squalor beneath a bridge, heating tins of beans over a Sterno can and looking like a vagrant. I was disheveled and dirty. Having physically deteriorated to a gaunt 150 pounds, my skin had taken on a ghostly pallor. When I panhandled for spare change on street corners, pedestrians stared right through me, even those who seemed to recognize me.

At long last, I said to myself, *You've got to do something*. Though I'd long ago lost the will to live, I didn't have the guts to die, so I went to see a Catholic nun named Sister Amelia, who ran the methadone program in which I was enrolled. I pleaded with her to help me, "even though," I said apologetically, "I'm not a Christian." That very day I began a week and a half of torturous detoxification. It was analogous to undergoing an exorcism, since in relation to my life the deadly powder was the devil incarnate. But even emancipated from drugs physically, I was an absolute wretch emotionally, petrified of having to function without chemicals.

I was discharged to a halfway house, which is where formerly dependent people in the transitional stages of drug detoxification or rehabilitation live, work, and receive therapy. The place was called Who Cares, a large Cape Cod–style house painted chocolate brown. I remember trudging up the front steps, littered with newspapers, and peering at a posted Day-Glo sign that read, "If you're carrying anything, stash it outside." For a change I wasn't and went inside.

While a resident there, I heard about a successful drug-treatment program called Cenikor, which had been launched in Lakewood, Colorado, in 1967, with plans under way for a Houston facility. Accepted into Lakewood, I was told I'd have to pay my own way out there. So I remained temporarily at the halfway house and worked as a housepainter, for which I was paid one hundred dollars—the first legitimate money I'd earned in years.

As I stepped off the airplane in Denver, I thought about the commitment I was about to make. Treatment usually took up to a year and a half, but I intended to complete it in two, three months at the most. *I'll put one over on these people*, I thought, so accustomed to deceiving those around me. Two, three months stretched into two years of rigorous therapy, every day of which was necessary to undo the considerable damage of the previous half decade.

I found comfort at Cenikor, both from the staff and the thirty or so other residents. I had been searching for people like these all my life: men and women with the same experiences, the same drug dependencies, the same kinds of feelings. I could talk to them, no nonsense, just be painfully honest, and they understood. I learned a great deal about myself from listening to them, and the fact that they were clean now—working, laughing—started me believing that if the program could work for them, perhaps it could work for me.

Things began to get better. I began looking and feeling better, even though I was doing nothing more than menial labor around the facility: washing dishes and mopping floors. One day my face broke out in a grin, and I remember thinking, *What a strange feeling*. I wasn't used to it.

After I graduated from the program, two years later, I remarried, to Maria, a young woman I had met while in treatment. And from there my life took on a completely different, brighter hue. Out of my newfound self-perception came the realization that I possessed a natural flair for business and for coordinating, motivating people. Rising through the corporate ranks at Cenikor, in 1980 I became its chairman of the board, president, and chief executive officer.

The events since then are something of a blur. In 1983, I was standing in front of the Houston facility waiting for the presidential motorcade to pull up to the curb. Ronald Reagan had heard of our work and wanted to observe it personally. A short time later I had joined First Lady Nancy Reagan in the White House. If there is a title to my story, it's *From the Outhouse to the White House*.

Admittedly, it all sounds improbable, so much so that I deliberately underplay the drama lest people think I have an overactive imagination. Whenever I tell it, it's as if this Ken Barun character is someone else. And believe me, it is embarrassing. I recount it here not to shock you but to prove a point: that drug abuse can happen to anyone, from any background. My case may have been extreme, but kids don't have to inject heroin into their veins for drugs to be ruinous; today I hear similarly painful accounts from parents whose sons and daughters are using alcohol, crack, pills, PCP.

Drug addiction "shouldn't" have happened to me; I didn't fit the popular profile of a substance abuser. But it did. And all along my mother and father had no idea why a seemingly well-adjusted boy was drawn to drugs' siren song. For many parents—and especially for their children—there lies the root of the problem.

Chapter Two

Drugs and Your Child's World

It is not the most original analogy, perhaps, but true: Raising a drug-free child is like nurturing a flower. For a youngster to bloom, physically and emotionally, his needs must be attended to until he can sustain himself with only periodic maintenance.

However, before any conscientious gardener plants a seed he surveys the patch of land, weighing factors such as the fertility of the earth and the amount of sunlight the flower will receive. Even once it begins growing, the gardener keeps as much watch on the environment as on the plant itself.

You, the parent of a child in or entering the drug-vulnerable years, are that gardener. It is your responsibility to protect your precious flower from encroaching weeds—kids pressuring him to drink or drug—and from heavy winds—those of changing, and in recent years diminishing, standards of right and wrong.

Promoting a youngster's development and well-being demands that you participate in and come to know his universe: home, school, extracurricular activities, and his social network. You must research and observe all of its attendant customs, culture, uniforms, and language. If this sounds like venturing to a foreign country, in some respects it is. Another dimension, perhaps. But be prepared to experience a great deal of déjà vu, for the world of today's kids is not so alien from the one in which you grew up. The difficult part is gaining entrée, since most kids—especially adolescents—rarely welcome parental involvement in their lives.

In the next two chapters we explore the world of today's child, one that is frequently cloistered behind a shut bedroom door plastered with rock-group posters. Once you appreciate the intense pressures he faces to drink and to take drugs, the insecurities that can drive him to seek acceptance through wrongful behavior, and his confusion over our culture's contradictory values about drugs, you can more effectively guide him, discipline him, and provide him with a solid moral foundation. Now, before I analogize kids as wee acorns from whence spring mighty oaks, let us move on.

The question on every parent's mind is, "Where did our children ever learn to use substances?"

From us.

The popular image of a youngster's introduction to drugs is that of an unsavory pusher lurking by the schoolyard gate, hissing, "Psst! Hey kid!" and dispensing funny cigarettes. If only it manifested itself so conspicuously, as an external presence we could rally against.

A youngster's attitudes about drugs are often shaped by those of his parents; expressed verbally and, more profoundly, through their actions. So before you can hope to impress upon your kid drugs' dangers, you need to carefully—and honestly—take stock of your own position and addictions.

Do you see yourself or your spouse in the following example? A parent straggles home after a thoroughly exasperating day at work, collapses into a chair, and sighs wearily, "I need a drink." He goes to the bar, fixes himself a cocktail, drains the glass, and exclaims, "Now I feel better." His five-year-old or fifteen-year-old, meanwhile, is in the same room, absorbed in a television program.

We sometimes forget that kids observe us as acutely as we do them. But unlike adults, who process information through a series of filters acquired by way of experience, children analyze our actions literally and cannot always place them in context. So although on the surface this fictitious parent merely unwound with a drink, he actually relayed to his youngster a detrimental precedent for handling stress. As examined later in this chapter, kids' lives can be every bit as pressured as adults'. Those who never learn stress management are more inclined to ease their anxieties with alcohol and drugs. The parent also erred in judgment by conveying that alcohol is an antidote to the blues.

As an isolated incident perhaps the damage done is not grave. But multiply it over an extended period of time, and kids begin equating Dad's liquor or Mom's pills with feeling better. And we *all* want to feel better, whether to elevate ourselves from the doldrums or to scale the heights of euphoria.

The next time you reach for a bottle of beer, a headache remedy, even a container of ice cream, be cognizant of the subliminal message you transmit. Is it "I'm doing this because I want to," which is acceptable in moderation, or "because I need to"? Eliminate "I need" from your vocabulary. Think of your youngster's developing mind as a computer filling up rapidly with impressions and see to it you input only those that are antidrug and antidependency. Because he will one day call up that information—received not only from you but from other, possibly less trustworthy sources—when forming an opinion about alcohol and drugs. If he is a preteen or older, that day may be right around the corner.

Bear in mind constantly that until children reach adolescence, you are the sun of their universe. All they want is to be "like Mommy" or "like Daddy." Unquestionably, having your kid imitate you is a wonderful feeling. It is also a sober reminder of how it is your responsibility to furnish him a positive role model. Even once a kid acts out in search of his self-identity through what is called oppositional behavior—rejecting, to various degrees, adult values and codes of acceptable conduct—his parents still wield great influence over him. Based on a family study published by the Pacific Institute for Research and Evaluation, children are more prone to drug abuse if their parents

- smoke cigarettes;
- abuse alcohol or are alcoholics;
- take illicit drugs;
- use any substance to help master stress;
- impart an ambivalent or positive attitude toward drugs.

National Institute on Drug Abuse research shows that 20.5 million adults thirty-five and older have had some illicit-drug experience. Alarmingly, 6.6 million continue to get high. Further evidence is provided by a survey of California eleventh-graders, who claimed that of the adults they knew,

- one in three smoked marijuana or hashish on occasion, and nearly one in five regularly;
- more than one in five ingested cocaine occasionally, and one in ten regularly;

- nearly one in three took pills occasionally, and more than one in ten regularly.

PARENTAL USE OF DRUGS, TOBACCO, AND ALCOHOL

Becoming a parent is much like joining the army. If you detest the sound of reveille and cringe at the very idea of a military crew cut, the solution is simple: Don't join the army.

So it is with parenthood. Most mothers and fathers realize at least intellectually that drug use and parenting are incompatible. But not all. Anyone who thinks he can indulge his own dependencies and rear drug-free children is fooling himself. One of the most pitiable sights I've seen was a *60 Minutes* television report about a California couple that had prodded their then thirteen-year-old daughter to smoke marijuana with them. She did so, she said, to feel accepted. Not by her peers, as is often the case, but by her mother and father!

My position on this matter is uncompromising: Parents shouldn't use *any* drugs. If you are a user, stop immediately, for your kid's sake as well as your own. If your spouse is a user, demand he or she get professional help. Sometimes, if a person hasn't been completely subverted by drugs, as I was, the insistence of a loved one and the obligations of parenthood can impel him to clean up his act.

No abuse applies to legal and prescription drugs as well. Whenever you must use any medication, explain why to your child. In our home the only over-the-counter drug we regularly stock is vitamins, but one day my boys wanted to know about the pills I took every morning.

Using terms they would understand, I replied, "Well, because I like to exercise, I burn off naturally produced chemicals that keep me healthy. Vitamins restore those natural substances, which is why they are called a food supplement." I went on to emphasize that I never ingest pills to alter my mood or consciousness—to "feel good."

I recommend strongly that parents dispose of all drugs that either have expired or are used infrequently. A medicine chest resembling a pharmaceutical Fort Knox plants in kids' minds that "in this house we rely on drugs." It also represents a potential danger. Young, impressionable children may innocently imitate their parents by swallowing pills, sometimes in lethal dosages. On one occasion, Adam, our eight-year-old, downed the contents of a Tylenol bottle and had to be rushed to the hospital to have his stomach pumped. The next day we discarded all medications except those that were absolutely essential.

In addition, my wife and I deliberately do not purchase flavored children's remedies or those manufactured to look like TV cartoon characters. Kids begin regarding them as candy and enjoy taking them. Of course I realize that sweet syrups and chewable tablets ease the task of dispensing medicine; I also know too well what it can be like trying to get a head-swiveling, lip-locked child to swallow something he considers "icky" (adjective courtesy of five-year-old Max, our youngest). But you *want* your child to grimace each time you uncap the bottle. You *want* him to associate drugs with something distasteful and unpleasant. In this instance, bitter is better.

Another reason for disposing of pills and capsules is that for some youngsters their parents' bathroom cabinet represents a convenient drug source. In there they are apt to find some of the U.S.'s twenty billion legal psychoactive drug doses. Shortly after I discovered pot I began pilfering prescribed barbiturates from my father. These were the pill-mad 1960s, and his medicine chest was a veritable treasure chest for a teenager looking to get high: Next to the Burma Shave were Valiums, Percodans, Seconals. I would deftly empty each capsule, replacing the powder with flour, then return it to its bottle. My father was never the wiser and a good deal less sedated than his doctor had intended.

Next: Can parents smoke cigarettes? That depends on how committed they are to bringing up a drug-free child. Tobacco, a gateway drug, is the first dependency-inducing substance tried by most youths. As noted earlier and covered in detail in chapter 3, one of the myriad reasons kids turn to drugs is to feel more grown up, and cigarette smoking is especially identified with acting adultlike. Children whose mothers and fathers use tobacco are high risks to become smokers themselves, prompting the question: Could you live with the knowledge that you were indirectly responsible for your youngster's first step down the pathway of drugs? I couldn't. I'd been an occasional smoker for years but quit the day I found our oldest son, Seth, then just two, sucking on a cigarette he'd pulled out of a pack accidentally left within his reach. For me there was no greater incentive for breaking the habit.

Why else shouldn't you smoke? I don't think I have to list the hazards of tobacco, first substantiated by the Advisory Committee to the Surgeon General of the U.S. Public Health Service in its landmark 1964 report, *Smoking and Health*. According to the American Cancer Society, nearly 80% of all lung cancer is found among cigarette smokers, who represent less than 33% of the U.S. adult population. If that isn't enough to persuade you to stop, consider the health risks posed to your kids.

A cigarette's sidestream smoke is drawn into the lungs of those living in the same residence as the smoker, turning them into what are called "passive smokers." Sidestream smoke is undiluted, containing greater percentages of tar, nicotine, and noxious gases than exhaled smoke, and the American Cancer Society reports that newborn-to-one-year-old children in households where one or both parents smoke have double the rate of bronchitis or pneumonia as those in tobaccoless households.

In short, no parent should smoke. If you do, establish immediately a pact with your kids whereby you promise to give up cigarettes and they vow abstention from tobacco, alcohol, and drugs. Declare clean, healthy living a family project. To help you quit, the American Cancer Society publishes a free seven-day plan full of daily instructions and activities.

No drugs. No tobacco. Aren't there any vices for parents? I know what you're probably thinking right about here: *He's going to tell us not to drink either.* The truth is, none of us should drink alcohol. But its use is so pervasive in our culture, most Americans would be averse to giving up their beer at the ball game or glass of Chablis with dinner. And if I espouse a no-liquor rule, you're liable to slam this book closed and use it for a coaster.

It goes without saying that parents should drink sensibly, because their child's sobriety depends on it: The National Council on Alcoholism states, "The best predictor of the drinking habits of adolescents is the attitude and behavior of their parents with regard to alcohol use." For example, children of alcoholics have a four-times-greater risk of developing alcoholism than children of nonalcoholics. Today there are 6.6 million children of alcoholics in the U.S.

How do you drink in moderation and still convey to your child a responsible attitude toward alcohol? I can relate from experience that it isn't easy to answer the question "Mommy, why do you drink?" Adam ingenuously asked that of my wife not long ago, just as she had a glass of wine raised to her lips.

25

At the time, Maria was stuck for an answer and looked to me for support. Big help I was. We stammered a bit, mumbled some flimsy justification, and changed the subject as quickly as possible. We blew it.

We've since learned that honesty works best and today reply to the same query this way:

"Why do I drink a glass of beer or wine on occasion? Because I enjoy the taste."

Here you rely on your parental tightrope-walking prowess: not over-elaborating liquor's pleasurable effects so that you make it sound too appealing, but at the same time not denying some people enjoy alcohol's mood-altering properties. Because should your child ever drink beer, for instance, and discover it doesn't leave him foaming at the mouth as you had claimed, your credibility as an authority on the subject would be shattered.

The next step is to admit what you're doing is wrong: "Drinking really isn't good for anybody," you say. "In fact, a lot of people think that *any* drinking is really dumb. But I'm an adult, and after careful consideration I've decided I will drink a little every now and then because I enjoy it."

And if he counters with, "Then why can't I drink?"

"Because you are not an adult, and it's against the law. When you are of legal age, the choice will be yours. I'm sure you'll be wiser than me, and not drink alcohol at all."

Be sure to stress additionally:

"Like anything, alcohol can be a very bad thing if you overdo it. Eating one candy bar isn't unhealthy, but if you were to eat a whole bagful, you'd get very sick. I never drink so much that it interferes with my ability to make sound decisions or harms me physically."

If he tries applying that logic to tobacco or drug use, spell out the differences for him:

"There is no moderation with cigarettes and drugs because they are poisons. If you were to drink from a bottle of arsenic, it wouldn't matter if you took a sip or downed it all, you'd fall ill. Even if you didn't get sick immediately, in time the poison would do damage to your physical and mental health."

Rehearse these and other responses so that when the question is put to you—and it will be, inevitably—you can reply calmly, rationally, and without seeming like a hypocrite. You will have converted a potentially detrimental situation into a constructive one.

Your stand on alcohol is communicated not only through your personal drinking practices but through the manner in which you regard those who drink to excess. It is confusing to kids when they are commanded not to drink because it's an undesirable habit, yet then overhear an adult exclaim approvingly, "Boy, can he hold his liquor!" As if it's a commendable achievement.

Refrain from making such remarks, even if intended lightheartedly, around your child. Instead, discredit the notion that drunks are the life of the party. Tell him that, on the contrary, inebriates are loud and obnoxious people who others avoid, not flock around. Describe graphically the unpleasant side effects of drunkenness, including the head-throbbing hangover, the traditional kneeling position before the porcelain altar, and don't omit the twenty-six thousand yearly deaths from alcohol-impaired drivers. Those are the images of intoxication you want stored in his memory.

A related point: When you entertain at home, avoid inviting those who habitually drink too much. As a kid, whenever my parents threw a party I crouched at the top of the stairs and peered through the banister at the adults carrying on as if at a Roman Bacchanalia. The impression it left was that drunks were the least inhibited, the most boisterous, and seemed to have the most fun. It made getting loaded look very inviting.

Nondrinking parents should not presume their sobriety absolves them from broaching the subject with their young ones. The National Council on Alcoholism contends that children from homes where both parents are abstainers and where alcohol is never discussed are as susceptible to alcoholism as those whose parents drink. In either case, unhealthy patterns have been established.

Mothers and fathers have much to teach their children about tobacco, alcohol, and drugs. But your most eloquent statement on the subject is expressed through your actions.

MEDIA MESSAGES

Where else do children receive positive reinforcement about drugs and their place in our lives?

From the media.

Kids are inundated daily with prodrug propaganda that is sometimes subliminal but always quite premeditated. From an early age they are conditioned to believe by way of television commercials and print advertisements that for every pain there is a chemical cure. Suffering from insomnia? Take a sleeping pill. Feeling sluggish? Take a pseudo-amphetamine comprised of caffeine. My initial drug education came by way of 1950s TV spots: Speedy Alka-Seltzer promising relief for those who overindulged; animated sledgehammers pounding away at the human skull to demonstrate how Anacin purportedly remedied headache pain.

It is stated by the National Council on Alcoholism that the average child sees alcohol consumed on TV seventy-five thousand times before he is of legal drinking age. Former Federal Communications Commission head Nicholas Johnson once claimed that it was used 24 times more than coffee and 120 times more than milk. Kids not only receive a distorted picture of drinking's prevalence in our society, they receive almost uniformly positive images of alcohol: how it allegedly enhances sociability (back-slapping buddies tying one on in a bar) and magnifies sex appeal (starry-eyed lovers gazing at each other over a bottle of white wine). Signals are frequently crossed, such as when a certain actor's ardent antidrug public-service announcement is followed a short time later by a spot for a wine cooler, with him as the pitchman.

How do these portrayals impact on children? A 1987 poll conducted by the *Weekly Reader* ascertained that TV and movies had the most profound influence in making drugs and alcohol seem appealing to fourth- through sixth-graders. And in a Bureau of Alcohol, Tobacco and Firearms study, adolescents and young adults heavily exposed to TV and print-media alcohol ads were found to be more than twice as likely to perceive drinking as attractive, acceptable, and rewarding as those less exposed.

When I worked in the White House, First Lady Nancy Reagan and I met with representatives from the entertainment industry. Mrs. Reagan, herself a former actress, urged them to reexamine the cues given by many TV programs and motion pictures about alcohol and drugs, and to depict with greater realism the repercussions of abuse. National Institute on Drug Abuse director Dr. Charles Shuster has made similar efforts to enlighten those in New York and Hollywood, and believes we will see more responsible programming and films in the near future.

But in the meantime, what can a parent intent on antidrug education do when the electronic box is switched on seven hours and five minutes a day in the average household, threatening to undermine his honest efforts?

The answer is to casually monitor kids' viewing habits. That is not to say censor; such a reactionary response will only incite them to sneak over to their best friend's house and turn on the tube to see what's making Mom and Dad so upset. Or they'll wait until you are out of the house and get out the remote control.

As reckless as you may find the values promoted by a particular program, let it serve as a catalyst for discussion. Explain your objections to your child and draw him out by soliciting his opinions. For example, Seth and I were watching a sports report the day it was announced that New York Mets pitching star Dwight Gooden had admitted to cocaine use and would miss part of the baseball season to undergo rehabilitation. "Hey, Seth, what do you think of that?" I asked him, making apparent my disapproval. "Here's a young, talented guy earning a million-plus dollars a year, and he nearly blows it all to get high."

"I think it's stupid," Seth replied. "Why would someone do such a dumb thing?" That led to a brief dialogue about drugs' bewitching spell.

"People who do cocaine never know if they're going to be able to quit," I explained, pointing at the screen. "It produces what is called dependency." I gave a brief discourse understandable to a ten-year-old. Seth nodded that he understood, and we returned our attention to highlights of the Chicago Bulls game.

Abruptly switching off the set or sitting there red faced, ignoring the issue, doesn't teach a child anything. Your teenager is watching a cable-TV movie where the plot entails a drunk successfully piloting his car down a highway? Remark how fortunate the character was; that more than half of all highway deaths are alcohol related. "I know you're too smart to ever get in a car with someone who's blasted." Five seconds, and you've rendered loving advice without launching into an interminable antialcohol lecture.

Not all programming relating to alcohol and drugs is to be condemned. Dr. Lloyd Johnston of the University of Michigan Institute for Social Research credits news coverage of the recent crack epidemic with helping to stem the tide of abuse. Many documentaries about drugs and alcohol are produced specifically for kids and are broadcast during after-school hours. Whenever possible, view them with your child. Get as much feedback from him as you can, enabling you to gauge the extent, if any, of his personal involvement with alcohol or drugs. Should your fourteen-year-old say with a shrug, "Yeah, Mom, I know what crack is; those little white pellets that look like soap," you should know to be on alert. Does his familiarity come from drug-prevention classes at school or from firsthand experience with his peers?

Supervising television and home-video viewing is relatively easy, since it takes place in your own home. But how do you monitor the films your child sees, since few self-respecting teenagers would ever be seen with their parents at the local cinema?

Asking other parents about movies their kids have attended and periodically perusing newspaper reviews are ways to stay informed. Both are probably more accurate barometers than the motion-picture industry's vague ratings system. Plenty of PG-rated films for kids under seventeen may not be sexually explicit but substitute drug innuendo and scenes of inebriation for nudity. Parental guidance is not only suggested in such cases, it is essential.

Is it a nuisance to scrutinize your child's viewing habits so vigilantly? Without a doubt. Can it make a difference? Without a doubt. Perhaps we can't prohibit kids from every watching a movie that sanctions drinking or drugging, but we can strive to help them learn something from the experience. Seize those opportunities for discussion and education whenever you can.

Of all mediums, rock music has come under fire as being the most nefarious.

Rock & roll was my generation's voice, and remains one today, a voice to which parents have always seemed to object. Throughout its life span rock music has been criticized, from Elvis to the Beatles to Sting. But its days as a clarion call to social revolution are gone, and the music has melded into the American mainstream. It is now largely TV background noise designed to sell everything from cars to beer. A California State University at Fullerton survey showed that for the overwhelming majority of kids, rock's principal attractions are its melodies, rhythms, and high decibel levels, not its sentiment.

Keep in mind that many contemporary artists extol positive values such as individualism, compassion for the world's less fortunate, concern over the environment, and uniting for peace. Few advocate, much less propagate, abuse of chemicals, if for no other reason that it is bad business: No radio airplay slices deeply into potential sales. And like any other business, the record industry is ruled by the bottom line. However, the main motive behind the decrease in prodrug songs and the emergence of the commendable "Rock Against Drugs" TV ad campaign has nothing to do with dollars and cents: A new generation of acts has seen too many gifted stars die from substance abuse over the years and is trying to effect a change in its audience's attitudes toward chemical use.

Parents should be aware of and take an interest in the music their children listen to. But the interest should be objective. Young people need an art form and heroes they can call their own. It is one way to establish a self-identity separate from their mothers' and fathers'—even if it's a carbon copy of millions of others kids' self-identities.

When your youngster is out of the house, scan the lyric sheets of some of his albums and drop the needle down on a side. The odds are it is no more rackety than the music with which you grew up. In fact, with adolescents increasingly exhibiting an appreciation of 1960's sounds, it could well be the very same rackety music. If something offends you, express your viewpoint to your child. You may be surprised to learn that he doesn't entirely disagree with you but never would have articulated it himself without your prodding.

DRUGS: AMERICAN AS APPLE PIE

Though the media are culpable for helping to pattern our culture's perspectives on alcohol and drugs, by and large they merely reflect an abiding orientation. Using substances to alleviate physical and emotional ills is as much a part of our nation's heritage as freedom of speech, and although the majority of Americans have historically regarded drug abuse as abhorrent, it is by no means an aberration.

As far back as 1790, the U.S. was wracked by excessive drinking, even among the devout, dogmatic Puritans. Intoxication came to be such a public menace the nascent government passed a federal law rationing a daily quarter pint of brandy, rum, or whiskey to each soldier. Alcohol was not the only drug to be abused. By the mid-1800s pockets of the population had discovered the euphoric high of opium, a narcotic made from dried poppy-plant juice. As word of its mind-altering properties spread—and as doctors prescribed it freely—the number of opium addicts ballooned to an estimated two hundred thousand by the late 1870s. Forty years later a *New York Times* report claimed America was home to 1.5 million drug users, probably an exaggeration but indicative of a silently spreading plague.

Beginning with the federal Pure Food and Drug Act of 1906, a flurry of antidrug legislation buttressed by stepped-up drug-trafficking controls appeared to quiet this roiling volcano for the next half century. But come the early 1950s there were felt rumblings from within, as authorities noted perceptible increases in marijuana and heroin use. Just one decade later, the deceptive calm was broken by a violent eruption that sent its ruinous influence raining down upon the American landscape. It hasn't stopped raging since: According to the National Institute on Drug Abuse, in 1962 just 4% of the general population had used some illicit drug; twenty-five years later that figure stood at 37%, or 70.4 million people.

To understand why alcohol and drugs have always been woven into the fabric of U.S. life is to gain insight into why the problem persists today with more serious consequences than ever before. History suggests that the privilege of citizenship in the country with the world's highest standard of living has exacted a toll, and that perhaps we have been remiss in failing to examine critically the ramifications of our frantic quest for progress.

It is no coincidence that the first outbreak of drug abuse to cause national concern occurred at the height of the nineteenth-century Industrial Revolution—a period in American history that parallels greatly our own times.

Still tending to the wounds inflicted by the Civil War, the country forged ahead in industry, science, and therapeutics. Overnight, it seemed, a once stable agricultural and commercial society was converted to a modern, industrial one. Cities grew noisier and more congested. Labor became more specialized and demanding. An increasingly mobile, transient populace left behind extended and supportive families. The cumulative effect was more complicated, stressful lives.

Rapid advances in technology were accompanied by shifting values and social movements, with blacks granted the right to vote by the Fifteenth Amendment, and suffragettes gaining momentum. The world and its demands expanded so abruptly, some citizens weren't able to bear up against the strain. Complaints of insomnia and nervousness abounded.

America had just celebrated its centennial and looked excitedly toward the future. Embracing the past and tradition would only disrupt its full-speed-ahead course. So great was the national spirit of progress that some addicts insisted they used drugs to improve their productivity at work, as if it were their patriotic duty.

"The terrible demands, especially in this country, made on modern brains by our feverish competitive life constitute hourly temptations to some form of sweet, deadly sedative." The writer was Fitzhugh Ludlow, author of the confessional *The Hasheesh Eater,* in the August 1867 issue of *Harper's Monthly* magazine. A century later, the National Commission on Marihuana and Drug Abuse sounded a similar warning: "More and more people are using drugs as if they were the only possible solution to the vicissitudes of life."

The 1960s were to the twentieth century what the 1870s were to the nineteenth century, a decade of unprecedented technological and social reform. America was led by a vibrant young president who spoke optimistically of a New Frontier. But as had been learned one hundred years earlier, with new frontiers came new challenges not all were prepared to meet. The times, as troubadour Bob Dylan sang, were a-changin'—again. Now there was the Space Race. The Nuclear Arms Race. Not to mention the Rat Race.

Drug abuse among the young turned rampant, symptomatic of their rejecting elders' values and disdaining authority. "We need our drugs," the counterculture, as it was called, seemed to say, "to live in your world." Former Harvard psychologist Timothy Leary and other champions of the hallucinogen LSD sang the praises of chemically induced mind expansion, a chorus picked up by a profusion of disaffected teenagers. Illicit drugs also became the condiment to a new, freer sexual morality (or was it the other way around?) that had been set off like Fourth of July firecrackers with the 1960 introduction of the birth-control pill.

The most popular illicit drug was marijuana. That it was a plant that could be cultivated in one's garden or in a college dorm window made it especially appealing to young people subscribing to a professed back-to-nature movement. But there was another, more insidious form of abuse infiltrating American homes: the misuse of licit drugs. Whereas in the nineteenth century thousands unwittingly became addicted to doctor-prescribed opium, in the mid–twentieth century it was to overprescribed tranquilizers. One Beverly Hills shrink, in fact, recommended in all seriousness that sedative-dispensing vending machines be placed on street corners.

What irony, that some parents saw no correlation between their dependence on sedatives—or alcohol—and their children's reliance on marijuana. After all, they were taking medicine, not dope. Such hypocrisy did not go unnoticed by the burgeoning underground, as exampled by the Rolling Stones' 1966 hit song "Mother's Little Helper," a wry observation on pill popping among harried housewives.

Before long, however, the counterculture's utopian ideals withered like flower petals, particularly where drugs were concerned. The substance-related deaths of pop-culture icons Brian Jones, Jimi Hendrix, Janis Joplin, and Jim Morrison presented undeniable evidence that so-called hard drugs were dangerous. But the jury was still out on marijuana, exalted as a harmless giggle or damned as a stepping stone to heroin. The 1973 National Commission on Marihuana and Drug Abuse took a surprisingly lenient stance on grass, focusing instead on what it forecast correctly as the scourge of the next decade: cocaine.

Coke use among high-school seniors more than doubled between 1975 and 1985, by which time nearly one in five had tried it. The level dipped slightly in 1986 and more so in 1987 but is still particularly distressing, notes University of Michigan Institute for Social Research project director Dr. Lloyd Johnston, bearing in mind the media's extensive coverage of the risks run by users.

Another drug that has increased in popularity is alcohol, from 85% in 1975 to 86% in 1987.

On the positive side, since 1980 all other drug use is down—in some instances significantly. Utilizing the 1987 University of Michigan National High-School Seniors Survey, the National Institute on Drug Abuse issued the following data:

- Marijuana, the prevalence of which hit an all-time high in 1979, when 51% of high-school seniors claimed to have smoked it that year, dropped to 36% in 1987, the lowest figure since the survey's 1975 inception.
- Hallucinogens went from a high of 12% in 1979 to a low of 7% in 1987.
- Barbiturates: from a high of 11% in 1975 to a low of 4% in 1987.
- Tranquilizers: from a high of 11% in 1975 and 1977 to a low of 6% in 1987.
- Methaqualone (Quaaludes): from a high of 8% in 1981 to a low of 2% in 1987.
- Stimulants: from a high of 20% in 1982 to a low of 12% in 1987.
- PCP: from a high of 7% in 1979 to a low of 1% in 1987.
- Opiates other than heroin: from a high of 6% from 1975 to 1981 and in 1985, to a low of 5% from 1982 through 1987, with the exception of 1985.
- Amyl and butyl nitrite: from a high of 7% in 1979 to a low of 3% in 1987.

Those figures are conservative, given the number of high-school drop-outs not included in the survey, and are still far too high. Although they indicate adolescent drug abuse topped off around the end of the 1970s, in 1987 levels of heroin use remained the same as the year before, while use of other opiates, LSD, and alcohol crept back up.

Even with the benefit of two decades of substance-abuse knowledge, as we approach the 1990s antidrug messages are still offset by a pervasive societal glorification of drinking and drugging. We've examined how it manifests itself in the home and in the media. Another factor is that abusers are often sports heroes, entertainers, political figures, and well-known public personalities that kids look up to, respect, and want to emulate. Today, instead of bucking the establishment, it seems as if most children endeavor to join it. But, sadly, from their vantage point drugs are an integral part of our entrenched social order. Cocaine, for example, is a symbol of success, traded openly on the sidewalks of Wall Street. In our day, parents worried about the negative influence of mangy, long-haired rock & rollers; today the negative influences are just as likely to be conservatively suit-tie-and-suspendered young professionals.

From too many unprincipled role models, youngsters absorb the following misnomer: *Drugs help you excel.* College basketball coach Lefty Dreisell states publicly that cocaine stimulated several of his players to perform better. I nearly hit the roof when I saw that on the news. Where was his sense of civic responsibility? Then you have famous football New York Giants linebacker Lawrence Taylor's smug refusal to act repentant when his cocaine habit was made public, even though doing so would have benefited thousands of kids who revere him. Youngsters come to believe drugs will help them hurdle or escape the stresses in their lives. And they are considerable.

THE PRESSURES OF GROWING UP

Inexplicably, childhood memories seem to become selective and overly romanticized once we reach adulthood. Many parents are out of touch with their kids' world and feelings because their own adolescence has become blurred in their memories, like faded old photographs.

When mothers and fathers are distanced from their child's reality, they tend to consign his comparatively trivial problems—not qualifying for a club, being teased at school, romantic rejection—to secondary status. Many are so caught up in a realm of mounting bills and sundry pressures that their child's anxiety over a harsh teacher doesn't seem as important as Dad's anxiety over his mulish boss. But it is every bit as real to the youngster, who is facing problems for the first time. Compounding his anguish is the fear of not knowing how to handle them, for he isn't equipped with the coping mechanisms that adults gradually cultivate through experience and hard knocks.

There is an old saying you hear frequently from formerly drug-dependent persons: "Never forget where you came from." It's good advice for parents, too. Remember—*really* remember—what it was like being a kid: the way your emotions seesawed up and down; the insecurities; and how during those times when you were encumbered by youthful difficulties you wanted Mom and Dad to regard your emotions seriously. My mother and father, as dearly as I love them, didn't always do that for me. Now that I'm a father, it seems every time I look at my sons I see myself at their age.

An example:

I was busy at work one day, when I received a phone call from Adam's school. My wife, Maria, was out and could not be reached, and he was in the nurse's office, complaining of not feeling well. I picked him up, drove him home, put him to bed, and in removing his pants noticed the seam had split open from the crotch to the backside.

I had to smile. "Adam, you're not sick at all, are you, buddy?"

He timidly shook his head no. He'd been embarrassed about his underwear showing and afraid the other kids would laugh at him. If I didn't pause for a moment and recall from my own youth how mortifying a split pair of pants could be to someone his age, I might have punished my son for telling a lie. Though I did press home the point that he should always be truthful, I showed him how to tie a jacket or sweater around his waist in the event of a future emergency. "You know why I know to do this? Because it happened to me when I was your age."

"Really, Dad?" Adam asked wide-eyed, though I'm not sure if he found it harder to fathom that I'd once endured the chagrin of a ripped pair of pants or that I'd once been his age. Will employing such empathy pay off in the future? I trust so.

Sensitivity, empathy—precious commodities for any parent because today's kids need so much of both. Each generation likes to believe its growing-up years were the most insufferable, but I doubt too many adults would trade places with 1980s youngsters. Although they have the benefit of support systems we didn't, beginning at an early age and over the course of a short stretch of time, kids now are confronted with having to make crucial choices: about whether or not to drink, take drugs, engage in sex. Rates of alcoholism, drug abuse, pregnancy, and suicide among youths are appallingly high because many are not yet emotionally ready for such big decisions, are unable to comprehend the implications of their actions, and have yet to develop a sense of self and the fortitude to resist peer pressure and temptation. It is understandable some children feel completely overwhelmed, like moving targets in a shooting gallery. Unfortunately, where youthful drug use is concerned, *too much, too soon* is an all-too-familiar refrain.

Your kid will need guidance in order to successfully navigate the turbulent waters of childhood and adolescence. But you cannot offer adequate direction without first studying the prevailing winds and currents. Don't be the type of parent who responds to a troubled child, "We didn't have these problems in my day." The mother or father who says that is utterly correct; they almost assuredly did not. "Things were different when I was your age." They were, radically different. Remember it. Instead of belittling or disregarding a child's anxiety, admit how much harder you're going to have to work to help him cope with something you may have never experienced yourself. Those who sincerely believe life was better and values healthier years ago are perhaps right. But we can never go back in time.

To better appreciate the many reasons kids seek refuge in chemicals, let us examine some of the accelerated strains they face. First, there are those endemic to children of all generations:

- not seeming to be viewed for what you are but for what you may become;
- not having opinions and feelings always taken seriously by adults;
- anxiety over a changing body, developing sexuality, the future;
- searching for self-identity while at the same time wanting to conform to peers;
- feeling caught between adolescence and adulthood, desiring both security and independence.

If the latter seems paradoxical, the lives of today's youngsters are full of contradictions. The threat of sexually transmitted diseases such as acquired immune deficiency syndrome has closed the book on the chapter titled "The Sexual Revolution." Yet teenagers are titillated constantly by a preponderance of sexual imagery in everything from jeans commercials to rock videos (for which writhing, scantily clad female bodies seem to be as requisite as mousse in the performers' hair). In one breath, sex, sex, sex. In the next, a public-service message: Sex can kill you. Raging hormones only exacerbate youngsters' confusion, which extends to matters other than sexual.

Like the San Andreas Fault, society has shifted yet again, back to the more conservative, materialistic ideals that predominated in the late 1950s and early 1960s. Mothers and fathers who used to wear long hair, beads, and leather vests now power-lunch, keep their hair cropped short, and, generalizing here, preach values antithetical to what many of them believed while growing up. *What is going on?* many kids ask themselves. *How am I supposed to act? What am I supposed to be?*

Their yearning for some stability is further shaken by the national divorce rate, which climbed nearly 60% between 1970 and 1981, according to the U.S. National Center for Health Statistics. Though since then it has declined to 4.8%, more than four in ten children have experienced parental divorce, 7% of all households with children under eighteen are headed by single mothers with children eighteen or younger, and slightly more than 1% by single fathers.

Another trend is that of double-income families (60% of mothers with children eighteen or younger are presently in the work force) and their seven million latchkey kids. Teachers surveyed by Louis Harris and Associates cited students being left on their own after school as the number one cause of difficulty in class. That kids are not receiving sufficient supervision at home would seem to be supported by the findings of a survey claiming the average parent spends just *fourteen and a half minutes* a day interacting with his child.

Other factors that can lead to childhood insecurities:

- increased mobility, with some parents taking out-of-town jobs, or families moving and leaving behind the support of other relatives;
- more parents caught up in the tempestuousness of their own lives, questioning their values while their youngster is trying to formulate his;
- teenagerhood lasting longer than ever before. With half of all high-school students going on to college and half the U.S. college graduates continuing their education in postgraduate school, financial security, family responsibilities, and the self-identity often derived from one's occupation are delayed until later in life. Because our culture caters

largely to the affluent Baby Boomer generation's needs, more than ever teenagers seem to be suspended in a state of limbo;
• society no longer imposing such clear-cut limits and guidelines for youthful behavior.

Kids' anxieties are not confined solely to microcosms of school and peer groups, especially once they become more aware of the world around them. They are as affected by sociopolitical issues as were members of our generation: chilled by the Cold War; watching our starry-eyed idealism get shot down by the bullets that took the lives of John and Robert Kennedy and Martin Luther King; and having a bright future overshadowed by atomic clouds and the mushrooming conflict in Vietnam. Unfortunately, today's world is little better, beset by terrorism, economic uncertainty, and that same specter of nuclear annihilation. Global events—and tragedies—are broadcast into our homes with more immediacy and greater impact than ever before. They also seem more random and more likely to affect the innocent.

In a poll of forty thousand adolescents, nuclear war was boys' number one fear; for girls, number two. Some teenagers feel they are growing up in a world for which the sands of time are rapidly running out, and when I talk to young people I often detect the same fatalism that existed among many of my peers. It's as if history were repeating itself, creating a climate ripe for reckless behavior. After all, the gravity of our modern crises is so enormous as to make individuals feel insignificant, powerless. That futility can provide a ready rationalization for substance abuse: "What's the difference? We're all going to get blown to Kingdom Come anyway."

I'm not trying to generalize that all kids are wringing their hands over the fate of the planet, but it is a genuine concern of many. A wise parent speaks to these fears of children, who, not always being able to articulate their feelings, often repress them.

A wise parent also pays attention to signs of depression, which strikes 6% to 7% of all adolescents—a slightly higher rate than for adults. With some kids, substance abuse prefaces the condition; with others, the condition leads to substance abuse. Additionally, it can be caused by a chemical imbalance in the brain and by genetics.

Essentially, depression is a reaction to a loss (or perceived loss) of someone, of something, of one's sense of well-being. Several common causes of adolescent depression, listed in ascending order of severity, are:

- family's moving;
- poor communications with parents;
- family's money problems;
- beginning or end of school year;
- mother's pregnancy;
- parental separation, divorce, or remarriage;
- death of a parent.

Even preteenage youngsters can be afflicted. One survey referred to in a 1987 *Newsweek* cover story on depression put the number at approximately four hundred thousand seven-to-twelve-year-olds. It is documented that infants, too, have exhibited depression symptoms.

However, the signals are not always obvious to adults, whose depression is usually *involutional;* that is, they cry, withdraw, suffer from fatigue, appetite loss, and so forth. But the depression of youths, who tend to mask their emotions, is often *reactive:* they engage in self-destructive behavior such as drug and/or alcohol abuse, sexual promiscuity, and delinquency. Parents should look out for some of the following indicators that a child is suffering from depression:

- Psychosomatic illnesses: ulcers, migraine headaches, colds, colitis, endocrine-gland disorders, insomnia, and dramatic weight loss or gain. *Psychosomatic* is derived from the Greek words *psyche,* for "mind," and *soma,* for "body," but such maladies are by no means figments of the imagination. They are quite real, brought about by displaced emotional stress. Kids are particularly prone to psychosomatic ailments, which may be cries for help; it is generally easier for them to admit to physical pains than to emotional anguish, for fear of being labeled "crazy."
- Mood changes: profound sadness, dejection, listlessness, boredom, despair, apathy.
- Thought-pattern changes: impaired concentration, memory lapses, low self-esteem, extreme anxiety, guilt, self-criticism.
- Behavioral changes: alienation from others, hyperactivity, rebelliousness, partaking in potentially hazardous pursuits such as substance abuse.

Ultimately a child's depression may manifest itself through poor academic performance, truancy, antagonistic or disruptive classroom conduct, recurrent accidents, and suicidal behavior, the latter denoted by a macabre preoccupation with death. Based on studies conducted by Richard H. Schwartz, M.D., medical advisor to the Straight substance-abuse program in Springfield, Virginia, drug-abusing youngsters are approximately ten times more likely to attempt suicide than non–drug users.

Most kids' depression fades away in a matter of days. Lingering melancholia may be symptomatic of substance abuse, or it may point to an emotional disorder requiring professional treatment. Again, because children sometimes cannot—or will not—express themselves clearly, parents need to watch them attentively in order to determine whether or not a problem exists. Always keep in mind that with troubled youngsters, things are often not what they seem.

At times throughout this chapter I've probably sounded like an overzealous kid advocate. I am. I'm not asking you to feel sorry for your child, merely to empathize. Not that parents aren't deserving of a little sympathy too. None of us is born a parent; we all have to make mistakes sometimes to learn the proper way of handling certain situations. However, where drugs and alcohol are concerned, mistakes can be critical and corrections can come too late.

KEY POINTS

● A youngster's attitudes about substances are often shaped by those of his parents, expressed verbally and, more profoundly, through their actions. So before you can hope to impress upon your child the dangers of drugs, examine carefully—and honestly—your own attitudes and addictions.

● Be cognizant of the subliminal message you transmit to your child. When you reach for a bottle of beer, a headache remedy, even a container of ice cream, is it because you want to or *need* to? Eliminate "I need" from your vocabulary.

● Children are more likely to use drugs if their parents smoke cigarettes, abuse alcohol or are alcoholics, take illicit drugs, use *any* substance to help master stress, or impart an ambivalent or positive attitude toward drugs.

● Discard all medications except those absolutely essential. Besides presenting a potential threat to younger children, sometimes parents' medicine cabinets serve as convenient drug sources for teenagers.

● Avoid if you can purchasing pleasantly flavored children's medicines. Kids can unwittingly come to the conclusion that all medicine is candy and begin to enjoy taking it. Never allow drugs to be associated with pleasure.

● Parental drug use is absolutely forbidden.

● Parents should not smoke cigarettes: Children whose mothers and fathers use tobacco are high risks to become smokers themselves.

● Parents can consume alcohol, but in moderation. If your child asks why you imbibe, reply, "Because I enjoy the taste, but I never drink to alter my mood." If he asks why he can't drink: "Because at your age it's physically harmful, and it's illegal."

● Your stand on alcohol is communicated not only through your personal drinking practices but through the manner in which you regard people who drink to excess. Refrain from expressing even lighthearted approval of those who know how "to hold" their liquor.

● Monitor prodrug messages your child may receive from television, films, and music. Never censor, but if something offends you, by all means discuss it with him. Turn it into a learning experience.

● Though a youngster's problem may sometimes strike parents as trivial, remember that he is confronting crises for the first time and is not equipped with the same coping mechanisms as adults. Never forget where you came from: Remember—*really* remember—what it was like being a kid and never dismiss his troubles as "childish."

● Depression may lead to substance abuse for some youngsters; for others, substance abuse may magnify existing emotional problems. However, kids do not always exhibit the signs we tend to associate with depression. Parents should heed indicators such as psychosomatic illnesses, and changes in mood, thought patterns, and behavior.

RECOMMENDED RESOURCES

If you or your spouse needs professional treatment for getting off alcohol or drugs, contact the following organizations for referrals to rehabilitation centers in your area:

Cocaine Hotline
Provided by Fair Oaks Hospital
19 Prospect Street
Summit, NJ 07901
(800) COC-AINE

National Institute on Drug Abuse
Drug-Referral Helpline
5600 Fishers Lane
Rockville, MD 20857
(800) 662-HELP

Therapeutic Communities of America
54 West 40th Street
New York, NY 10018
(212) 354-6000

National Clearinghouse for Drug and
Alcohol Information
P.O. Box 2345
Rockville, MD 20852
(301) 468-2600

The Clearinghouse makes available an approximately three-hundred-page *National Directory of Drug Abuse and Alcoholism Treatment and Prevention Programs*. Its most recent edition was published in 1984 and as of this writing was no longer in stock. However, most public libraries' reference sections should have a copy.

For referrals to accredited hospital inpatient and outpatient programs only, contact:

Joint Commission on Accreditation of
Hospitals (JCAH)
875 North Michigan Avenue
Chicago, IL 60611
(312) 642-6061

Other sources: In the Yellow Pages, look under "Alcohol Abuse and Addiction Information and Treatment" and "Drug Abuse and Addiction Information and Treatment" for local rehabilitation centers; look under "Crisis Inter-

vention Service" for referrals. In the White Pages, look under "Alcoholism" and "Drug Abuse" in the Community Services Numbers for referrals.

Personally recommended treatment programs, many of which admit adults, are in Appendix A. Also contained therein are the address and telephone number of your state's alcohol- and drug-abuse agency, which can refer you to professional help.

If your problem is not severe enough to warrant professional treatment, but you need the support of a self-help group, or fellowship, contact the following organizations' headquarters, to be referred to the chapter nearest you:

Alcoholics Anonymous
P.O. Box 459
Grand Central Station
New York, NY 10163
(212) 686-1100

Cocaine Anonymous
World Services, Inc.
P.O. Box 1367
Culver City, CA 90232
(213) 559-5833

Drugs Anonymous
World Services
P.O. Box 473
Ansonia Station, NY 10023
(212) 874-0700

Narcotics Anonymous
World Service Office, Inc.
P.O. Box 9999
Van Nuys, CA 91409
(818) 780-3951

Other sources: In the Yellow Pages, look under "Alcoholism Information and Treatment Centers" and "Drug Abuse and Addiction Information and Treatment"; look alphabetically in the White Pages.

For referrals to self-help organizations of all types, contact:

National Self-Help Clearinghouse
33 West 42nd Street
Room 620N
New York, NY 10036
(212) 840-1259

For a free guide to giving up tobacco, contact:

American Cancer Society
90 Park Avenue
New York, NY 10016
(212) 599-8200

Local branches are listed under A in the White Pages.

If your child suffers from depression or an emotional disorder requiring treatment, contact the following organizations for referrals to professionals in your area. Explain your problem, what type of therapy you are seeking, and if cost is a factor:

American Association for Marriage and
   Family Therapy (AAMFT)
1717 K Street N.W.
Suite 407
Washington, D.C. 20006
(202) 429-1825

American Psychiatric Association
   (APA)
1400 K Street N.W.
Washington, D.C. 20005
(202) 682-6000

American Psychological Association
(APA)
1200 17th Street N.W.
Washington, D.C. 20036
(202) 955-7600

Family Service America (FSA)
11700 West Lake Park Drive
Park Place
Milwaukee, WI 53224
(414) 359-2111

National Association of Social Workers
(NASW)
7981 Eastern Avenue
Silver Spring, MD 20910
(301) 565-0333

Other sources: For additional referrals (including low-cost therapy) as well as information about fees and therapists' credentials, contact your state's mental health office or administration, the number of which is in the State Government Offices and/or Community Services Numbers listings of the White Pages.

Chapter Three

Causes and Effects

Nearly twenty-five years have passed since that day on the basketball court, when curiosity and the desire for acceptance moved me to smoke my first joint. Today there's a new generation of kids, dressed in tight jeans instead of baggy pants with cuffs, Whitney Houston on the radio in lieu of Connie Francis. Despite an undeniably faster-paced, more complex world, they begin experimenting with drugs for essentially the same reasons.

Kids are always going to have insecurities, do things against their better judgment to fit in with others, get into trouble because they are bored. After all, self-doubt, peer pressure, and monotony are as synonymous with growing up as acne, sweaty palms, and junk food. But insecurity doesn't have to be so overwhelming that youngsters succumb reflexively every time they're among youngsters getting high, and boredom can be countered with activities to supplant alcohol and drugs. This chapter examines the classic causes of substance abuse and how parents' appropriate guidance can have a positive, lasting effect on their children, and make them less inclined to try drugs.

Though some abuse problems are attributable to genetics, by and large youthful drug and alcohol use is a symptom of confusion, unhappiness, loneliness, and alienation. Rehabilitation programs' first priority is to wean kids off substances so that the real work can begin: identifying and treating the underlying emotional, behavioral, or social problems that led to chemical use.

Substance-abusing youngsters often fit familiar patterns. Generally they

- are isolated and alienated from family and friends;
- place little or no value on personal achievement;
- perform poorly academically and show scant interest in school;
- have difficulty expressing their thoughts and feelings;
- feel little personal or social responsibility;
- are unable to cope with stress and frustration;
- are extremely vulnerable to peer pressure;
- are anxious or depressed;
- complain often of boredom;
- are unable to deal with authority;
- lack confidence in their sexuality;
- seem incapable of balancing work and play;
- have high expectations but little self-discipline.

There are numerous theories as to why young people use substances. According to 2,533 ninth-graders and 2,759 eleventh-graders surveyed in California, some of their reasons are:

- to get away from problems:
  grade nine, 51.3%; grade eleven, 52.6%;
- to experiment:
  grade nine, 48.5%; grade eleven, 50.1%;
- because their friends use:
  grade nine, 49.4%; grade eleven, 50.3%;
- drugs and alcohol make them feel good:
  grade nine, 49.2%; grade eleven, 55.2%;
- they have nothing else to do:
  grade nine, 20.5%; grade eleven, 26.8%.

As interesting as the kids' answers may be, there is a fundamental flaw in asking chemical dependents why they do what they do: People drink and take drugs to deny their true feelings. If you had asked me why I needed to stick a needle in my arm, I would have replied defensively, "Because it makes me feel powerful," when in reality heroin kept my own weaknesses and feelings of inadequacy at bay.

That is why we've recruited for their testimony nine drug "experts": young men and women between the ages of eighteen and thirty-three who are currently in treatment for addictions that began when they were in their early teens. Three of the males are white (Anthony, twenty-nine; Ira, thirty-three; and Michael, twenty-seven), two are black (Darrell and David, both twenty-one), and two are Hispanic (Paul, twenty-one, and Carl, eighteen); one of the women is white (Elyse, twenty-one) and one is black (Helen, twenty-one). Though no details of their stories have been changed, each has been assigned a pseudonym.

Each has been clean for a period ranging from several months to nearly two years, which is why their perspectives are so invaluable. Only when a person is unshackled from drugs does he have the courage to peer into a mirror and see his true reflection. It is another primary objective of rehabilitation to progressively break down an abuser's ego until he is forced to confront his frailties and begin understanding how and why he came to rely on drugs or alcohol.

Whenever I listen to drug-dependent kids pour out tales about how and why they got started, I'm always struck by how they seem to echo one another's stories—and my own. The most oft-repeated reason is:

REASONS: PEER PRESSURE, SEEKING ACCEPTANCE

"Where I grew up, a lot of kids were involved in negative activities: drinking, drugs, stealing cars. I wanted to be a part of it, 'cause if you weren't, they'd call you 'punk,' say you were a sucker. I didn't want to be like that, a square. I was fifteen years old, kind of shy, and I wanted to get involved with girls and everything, you know? I didn't want anybody to laugh at me, to look at me differently. So I chose to become part of them by smoking reefer [marijuana] and, within a year, by snorting cocaine.

"I tell you, fighting off the peer pressure was very, very hard."

—Darrell

A child's desire to be accepted by his peers is perhaps the strongest motivating factor in his life. The growing years may be dominated by the question "Who am I?", but, ironically, the answer often comes from others his age.

Add to that another paradox peculiar to youth: the simultaneous yearning for independence from parents, with whom a child's identity has been intertwined, and dependence on peer approval. Young people want to be individuals, but not so individual that they risk ostracism. In the end many youngsters merely transfer their conformity from one authority (parents) to another (the peer group) and comply with standards set by equals instead of by parents. When the *Weekly Reader* asked kids why they smoked marijuana, the majority of fourth- through sixth-graders replied, "To fit in with others."

Sometimes children seem to exist in a vacuum. Because they have yet to perfect their communication skills—or are simply too self-conscious to unload on their friends—many go through their youth thinking their problems are unique; for example, that they are the only ones to feel anxious over a gangly body. With few peers to validate their feelings, they are often left isolated, confused, and vulnerable.

I became involved with drugs at a time in my life when I didn't have a whole lot to grab on to. My parents, though well meaning, were more concerned with providing creature comforts than emotional support. I wanted to belong but wasn't sure what I had to offer. That all changed once I fell in with the group of kids that used drugs.

Imagine that your child's social circle is comprised of different clubs. To join the Jocks Club you have to be an exceptional athlete. Membership to the Mensa Club requires a high I.Q. The Drug Club has the lowest standards of all—you only have to drink, smoke a joint, and so on—and for many kids lacking confidence or an identity, it provides a common denominator for acceptance, without any other requisites.

You don't need a talent other than an aptitude for procuring drugs. You don't have to be a stimulating conversationalist, as getting high becomes *the* invariable topic and communal focus. My friends and I spent hours together not even taking drugs but just talking about them—seeing who had the best war story to tell about nearly getting busted or having a horrific acid trip.

With drug use comes an identity, which, though it may be negative— "bad boy" or "bad girl"—is a mark of distinction that some kids wear proudly. Michael, a former heroin addict who now counsels drug-dependent clients, is tall and redheaded, with handsomely chiseled features. Growing up, he says, "It sometimes seems like you have to be either good or bad; as if there is no in-between stage."

"And when you're in between, you're lost," adds Ira, a slightly built and restless man with dark, curly hair. After years of doing pot, cocaine, and other drugs, he enrolled in New York City's Daytop Village, one of the country's oldest rehabilitation programs. Keenly intelligent, at age thirty-three he is just now completing college and reassembling his life. When he was just seven, he was placed on tranquilizers for hyperactivity, which made him a target for ridicule from his peers. However, once his classmates discovered marijuana and other illicit drugs, "I began smoking with them, to conform."

Peer pressure conjures the image of a hapless child surrounded by others twisting his arm to take a drink, to smoke a joint, to shoplift. But it is usually subtler and insidious—words needn't even be spoken—and can occur at a startlingly early age. One in three fourth-graders polled by the *Weekly Reader* reported feeling pressured by others to drink, and the figures increased steadily as the kids got older:

- fifth grade: 39% reporting pressure to drink;
- sixth grade: 46%
- seventh grade: 61%;
- eighth grade: 68%;
- ninth through twelfth grade: 75%.

WHAT YOU CAN DO

Build Up His Self-Confidence and Self-Esteem

Kids with a positive self-image stand up better against peer pressure. They have been raised to believe they can say no to drugs and still be accepted by those in their group. And if saying no leads to their expulsion from the group, they are more equipped to handle the rejection. How do you know if your child has low self-esteem? To you, he or she is a precious being whose talents and attributes are obvious. No wonder that parents often have difficulty reading the sometimes contrary clues, which are often evident even at an early age:

- a need to be the center of attention; or an unreasonable fear of participating in activities, of answering and asking questions;
- a fear of new people and places;
- an arrogant, know-it-all attitude; a refusal to admit when wrong;
- intolerance of and indifference toward others;
- selfishness;
- a lack of friends; or too much concern that others like him.

Already I see indications that our eight-year-old, Adam, lacks self-esteem: the way he wants to belong so badly, the way he *has* to dress exactly like his friends, in loud Hawaiian print shirts, surfer's jams, and dark sunglasses. (And we live in Illinois; go figure it.) Probably I'm concerned because I see a lot of my young self in him. Though Adam is bright and a good athlete, he has a tendency to be hard on himself, and he discourages easily.

So my wife and I work with our son, praising him when he does something well. When he does not succeed as well as he would like, we reassure him that we love him and are always proud of him. Children need to hear that. I'm not saying to lavish your youngster with unrealistic praise, which will only set him up for a traumatic fall. Correct and criticize him when appropriate, but make it a point to pat him on the back too. Let him know he is a valued addition to any group on the basis of his personality, talents, and character alone. And if he is expected to drink or to use drugs in order to be part of a certain clique, tell him, "You've got too much going for you"—and specify some of his attributes—"to let yourself be dragged down by kids who need that stuff. Drug abuse is *dumb*, and you're too smart."

Siblings can be enlisted to provide additional support. We had a situation where Seth, our oldest, constantly teased Adam. "You stink," he'd taunt him. "I can beat you at anything."

One day I took Seth aside. "You're the big guy around here. Rather than putting Adam down, how about helping me and your mom make him feel better about himself? Why don't you try building him up?"

Our little talk served a double purpose: Besides making Seth realize how cruel he was being to his younger brother, he'd been given some adult responsibility—helping us to encourage Adam. Kids thrive on being treated like grown-ups, and although some of the teasing continued, Seth responded by acting as Adam's personal self-confidence coach, giving him pep talks before his Little League games and school exams.

Encourage All Positive Interests

Ask a child with poor self-esteem to describe his strengths, and the response may be a mournful, "I'm no good at anything." Sadly, he honestly feels that way about himself.

But then, how much has he been allowed to experience? Many children are endowed with natural gifts not always cultivated by our educational system. Their only proving grounds often seem to be academics, athletics, and physical attractiveness. The latter qualifier alone can be enough to ensure or deny popularity, until youngsters mature and learn to appreciate other people's less visible but more substantial qualities.

It is up to parents to promote all interests, no matter how "trivial" they may seem. A child constantly banging his silverware in time to music might be a budding Ringo Starr, and although you may prefer he cultivate an interest in biology (it's quieter), his musical ability is a means to make him feel better about himself. Special. In time, perhaps he and several friends form a band, in which he learns the importance of responsibility, punctuality, and mutual cooperation. There is something to be gained from any new experience.

The alternative to extracurricular interests is lack of interest, which commonly leads to trouble.

Respect Their Individuality

Teach your child to be proud of who he is. How many parents reprove their child, "No one else dresses like that," "No one else does that," then wonder why he has such a deep-seated desire to fall in line with others? *Then* they reprimand, "Do you have to do something just because everyone else does it?" (followed by the immortal "If so-and-so jumped off a bridge, would you?").

You must respect your youngster's personality and let him be himself. If you have more than one child, nurture each one's unique character. It is enough of a struggle for kids to attain individuality among their peers, much less have to battle for it at home. You couldn't hope to find more polar opposites than Adam and Seth. The eight-year-old is a punker, with a spiky haircut and fashionably offbeat clothes, while the ten-year-old is so conservative he won't even wear jeans. Maria and I approve of their distinctly different personalities and how they choose to express them. Our hope is that in the future they won't need to act out in search of their self-identities, and that they will take pride in their individualism. Not just where hairstyles are concerned, but possibly their decision not to drink or take drugs.

Though children should be helped to explore their potential, they should not be pushed against their will. When I say respect kids for who they are, I include those facets of their personalities that might secretly disappoint you. For example, an introverted youngster should not be thrust into social situations that make him squirm uncomfortably. Work with him little by little to improve his skills in relating to others. Sometimes children (and adults) who feel ill at ease in social settings rely on alcohol or drugs to overcome their skittishness, as was true for Paul, a street-smart youth with olive skin and inquisitive brown eyes. As a teenager, he was an extremely self-conscious stutterer. "I used to be petrified to open my mouth in public," he says without a trace of a speech impediment, "but when I was stoned I didn't care if people laughed at me."

Not all introverted children are simply shy; as with Paul, there may be related physical problems that should be examined. We had some concerns over Max, our youngest, who was incommunicative when he was three years old. Medical tests confirmed that he had a slight hearing loss, which has since been corrected and has made a world of difference in his interaction with others.

Monitor and Guide Their Friendships

Like the moon's pull on the tides, the crowd with which an adolescent associates can exert a tremendous power. This is particularly true of a kid with low self-esteem, who will often gravitate toward those possessing qualities he believes he lacks, or who will make no demands on others. Paying close attention to your child's companions, therefore, can tell you a great deal about his feelings of self-worth. For that reason it is important you get to know them.

With preschoolers, school-agers, and preteens this is relatively effortless, since kids tend to congregate in group members' homes. But there is usually one or two households in which youngsters feel especially comfortable. There practically isn't a day when I come home from work and don't find other children scurrying about the house. I welcome it (sometimes reluctantly, I admit) because it affords me the opportunity to observe my kids at play, to see how they relate to others.

Other children's conduct is often indicative of the values they are taught at home. Before we allow our boys to spend too much time at a youngster's home, we try to get to know the family. Does their kid come home to an empty house after school? Is there little or no adult supervision? As a concerned father, I have every right to know these things before I permit my child to play there. If you don't socialize with the parents, ask your youngster, "When you were playing at Johnny's today, was either his mom or his dad there?" If not, suggest that he and Johnny make your home their recreation center. Does this make you paranoid? Overprotective? Considering the considerable effort you put into raising your child properly, such concern is entirely appropriate. Especially since kids who don't receive, or feel they don't receive, direction and protection at home fit the profile of a high-risk candidate for alcohol and drug abuse.

Presiding over teenagers and their friends is a thornier problem because once they get wheels—be it two or four—they disappear. Moreover, as they graduate to larger secondary schools that often combine students from several elementary schools, their circle of friends broadens to include nonneighborhood kids, whose parents you don't know. Without sounding accusatory, tell your teen you would like to meet his new companions; extend invitations to dinner. And when you are introduced to his acquaintances, talk to them. Try evaluating the extent of parental guidance received at home. Conversing with your youngster's friends may yield a dividend: As they enter adolescence many children become increasingly reticent around their mothers and fathers, whose influence is gradually superseded by that of their kids' peer groups. If your child's pals feel relaxed opening up to you, he just might too.

Should you suspect a youngster exerts a dangerously negative influence over your kid, ask one of your other offspring about his reputation at school. Too, if there is another couple with whom you can speak confidentially, discuss his behavior with them. It's always advantageous for the parents of each child in a group to informally monitor activities and to contact one another if they suspect alcohol or drug use. Ideally, parents should commit to allowing the group in their home only if at least one adult can be present. When mothers and fathers work together, sharing information, acting as chaperones at parties and imposing uniform curfews, their chances of spotting problems early on are heightened substantially.

If you determine that a certain child's behavior does indeed present a threat to your kid's well-being, you have every right to forbid your child to see that friend. Before you do so, however, make sure your conclusion is well founded. You don't want to jeopardize your youngster's trust in you by haphazardly indicting every long-haired, denim-jacketed teen as a drug abuser. Neither good kids nor bad kids always conform to the stereotypical image. And one character flaw does not necessarily dictate that you terminate the friendship. Analyze it. Does the child in question have other, positive traits that your son or daughter can benefit from? What degree of influence does he wield over your kid?

Reflect on your own adult friendships and how complex they are. Surely you know someone who has a problem—not necessarily with substance abuse. Though it may disturb you, perhaps you maintain the relationship because his attributes outweigh his shortcomings. So long as you have confidence in your child's resolve not to use drugs, you can allow him to remain friends with an occasional drug or alcohol user. Perhaps he can even learn an important lesson in friendship by trying to persuade the person to stop.

Assessing the seriousness of another child's substance dependency takes on greater importance if your youngster's teenage friends drive. Forbidding him to see a companion—or even a steady date—might initially strike you as overly harsh. Consider, then, how you would feel to be startled awake by a late-night telephone call informing you that your child had been seriously injured in a drunken-driving accident; or that he'd been jailed along with his intoxicated buddies; or that he'd been killed.

When insisting a friendship be discontinued—at least until it can be proved satisfactorily that the friend in question has received ample help for his substance dependency—be sure to clarify for your youngster

- the reasons behind your action;
- why you have good cause to believe "Eddie" drinks or takes drugs;
- that this is in no way a punishment, though it may seem like it.

"Eddie appears to have some problems," you say sympathetically. "I see you putting a lot into this relationship and getting very little in return." Be compassionate toward the troubled child, for condemning him ("That kid is no good") may only drive your youngster back to his friend out of loyalty. As always, conclude by telling him you love him and are concerned about his welfare.

When my family lived in Washington, D.C., there was one kid, "Ted," whose parents were neglectful. We learned from our son Seth that they were rarely home, and it was obvious from Ted's hyperaggressiveness and destructiveness that he was seldom disciplined. He acted out constantly in search of attention: stealing, throwing rocks at windows. One night after dinner I went up to Seth's room and explained calmly, "Your mother and I feel Ted could be a bad influence on you, and we'd rather you spent your time with your other friends, whom we like very much." I expected an argument, but when I asked Seth his feelings about what I'd just said, he shrugged and admitted he'd been disturbed by this other boy's behavior for some time.

"I didn't really want to play with him anymore anyway," he said. And that was the end of it. Instead of assuming an adversarial position and placing your child on the defensive, talk over matters rationally. Underline your concern for *him*.

In chapter 4 we give instruction on the refusal skills children should be taught to prime them for effectively turning down offers of drugs and alcohol. If your youngster complains that peer pressure is still unbearable, suggest he leave that circle of friends. But don't wash your hands of his predicament, thinking it is settled. For if he has difficulty making new friends, he may retreat to the comfort and companionship afforded by the old group. Or he might move on to an even less desirable clique. Work with him to find ways of forming new friendships and never pretend that such a drastic step is easy. Offer your support and optimism, and build up his self-esteem: "It may be rough for you at first, even lonely, but in time you'll have a new set of friends that truly appeciates you for the fine person you are."

Naturally it is impossible to get to know every youngster your child comes in contact with. We have a playground in our community that is packed with as many as one hundred kids at a time, and, needless to say, I recognize a mere handful of the faces. But when children are raised properly and are taught the meaning of true friendship, even they know to avoid troublemakers, just as Seth grew increasingly uneasy in the company of his delinquent playmate Ted.

Besides keeping watch over his friends, help direct your child toward quality friendships. "If Jennifer insists you drink or smoke pot against your will just because she does, that's not being a good friend. A true friend respects others' decisions." Teach by example; discuss with your youngster your own relationships and what makes them work.

When kids bring their pals home, they are to abide by the household rules. Your sixteen-year-old daughter's best girlfriend is allowed to smoke cigarettes? Not in your home. Period. And you know to keep an eye on her, for children who use tobacco frequently advance to other dependency-producing drugs.

With families relocating more often—and I know that well, having shifted my wife and kids from Houston to Washington to Chicago within three years—the task of monitoring a child's friends takes on additional importance, since environment can factor vitally into whether or not a child abuses substances. David, a heavyset black youth who speaks calmly and deliberately, recalls that when he lived in Florida with his grandmother, "I was doing real good, going to school, not hanging out. I had good friends there." But a move to a Brooklyn, New York, ghetto notorious for pervasive drug abuse placed him among a different, criminal element.

"There, all the kids smoked marijuana and stuff. At first I resisted, but then they started putting me down, saying things to me like, 'You're soft, man.' " Being the new kid on the block can be trying enough, as a youngster strives for acceptance while adapting to what may be alien customs. As David saw it, smoking grass was the only way for him to fit in. But soon his use escalated to cocaine and crack, and his life fell apart. "Surrounded by all those negative kids," he says ruefully, "it was like I didn't have a chance, you know?"

Should you be contemplating a move to a new area, research community standards as thoroughly as you would mortgage rates. Drive around town during the day and at night. Are there clusters of kids loitering on street corners, or do there seem to be organized activities in parks and playgrounds, with adult supervision? What is offered to youngsters culturally? Are there nearby libraries, movie theaters, museums, and sports and entertainment venues? Inquire at the town or county government headquarters about available youth programs.

Visit the police department and ask questions about the prevalence of drug abuse. How committed are they to cracking down on drug offenders? Do they work closely with the school district? Additionally, make an appointment with the superintendent, principal, or some other school administrator and query him about drug-prevention classes and drug awareness among teachers. Does the district employ a substance-abuse counselor? These are things to learn *before* you move, not after.

REASONS: BOREDOM, HOPELESSNESS

"Boredom played a big part in my drinking and doing drugs. Like, when I was a teenager, I'd be sitting home watching TV, feeling empty and bored. I'd get up, leave the house, and go score some coke, figuring that was going to give me the excitement I wanted.

"Even now, having been in treatment for over a year, I still get afraid whenever I'm feeling bored. I start pacing the floors. I *hate* being bored."

—Anthony

Protests of boredom sometimes seem compulsory for any card-carrying teenager. Place him in a room with a wide-screen TV, a joystick controller, a shelf full of magazines, record albums, and *Police Academy* videos, and still there is the interminable whine, "I'm b-o-r-e-d!"

Today's youngsters have more free time on their hands than did previous generations, and for some getting high conveniently fills what seems like an infinite void. It becomes an activity in itself. And if substance abuse progresses beyond occasional use, it can become an absolute life-style. For me merely getting stoned wasn't satisfying enough. Immediately afterward I was scheming to get more drugs, because I longed for the excitement of scheming to get more drugs. The rituals of preparing the drugs. Even the paranoia.

WHAT YOU CAN DO

Provide and Promote Alternatives to Drugs

We have to give our children something better than drugs, something that makes them feel as good and monopolizes their spare time. Let sports, the arts, academic pursuits, pets, volunteer work, gardening, book reading—the list is endless—become their drug.

Kids should be exposed to as many interests as possible as early as possible. Young children, still so attached to their parents, are naturally inquisitive and generally receptive to activities you suggest. And even those you don't suggest. Like many former drug users, I'm a physical fitness enthusiast, probably because of all those years I abused my body. Racketball is my particular passion, and once my sons saw me play at our neighborhood health club, they wanted to learn the game.

However, I'm sure that once they reach their teens, most recreational ideas I suggest will be dismissed with an exasperated, "Racketball? That's wimpy." Or whatever the popular colloquialism of the 1990s is destined to be.

Certainly do not allow TV to become their drug substitute. It has been theorized by some child psychologists that junior couch potatoes are more apt to transfer their dependency from television to substances. Like drugs, TV viewing is passive, demanding little intellectual interaction. What's more, many programs offer oversimplified, unrealistic solutions to problems. If your youngster is spending more than one and a half hours a day (two hours for teenagers) in front of the set, it's time to steer him toward a pastime.

I suggest a combination of structured and unstructured activities. Time has to be allotted for daydreaming, for kids to explore their boundless imaginations and to amuse themselves. Haven't you ever purchased an expensive toy only to find your toddler is much more engrossed by the box it came in? To him it's an impregnable fort or an enchanted castle. The upshot for youngsters who are whirled through a maze of piano lessons, football practice, and so on is that once structured time is over, boredom sets in again.

At our house, we've found a good rule of thumb is limiting each child to two activities per season. Throughout the year Seth is involved in football, basketball, and baseball; Adam in ice hockey, karate, and soccer; and Max in ice skating. It doesn't leave Maria and me much time, but . . . welcome to the service.

Recommendations

Physical exercise of any kind yields a multitude of benefits. Because it stimulates the brain's production of endorphins—a morphinelike substance that alleviates pain and fear, producing a natural high of sorts— kids discover early on there are alternatives to chemically induced pleasurable sensations. Through exercise children also learn important lessons about the gratification derived from self-discipline, from setting and achieving a goal.

Feeling physically fit enhances one's self-image, particularly for kids in the midst of adolescence and its attendant anxiety over their physique (and their complexion, which can be improved through exercise). Building muscles builds self-confidence as well as health consciousness, so that when children are taught how substances destroy young bodies, they are more likely to avoid them.

Finally, exercise is a family activity. Our health club recently began holding aerobics classes for youngsters. On days when the kids are off from school, my wife, who is an aerobics instructor, takes them with her. She teaches her class, they exercise or play, constantly supervised, and through watching Maria, our sons receive further reinforcement about the effort required to meet objectives.

Drug-free youth groups such as Just Say No clubs, of which there are some fifteen thousand nationally, offer a variety of educational, recreational, and services activities in an atmosphere that promotes sobriety.

First Lady Nancy Reagan provided the inspiration for the clubs while speaking at an Oakland, California, grade school in July 1984, and today remains the Just Say No Foundation's honorary chairman and strongest advocate. When a youngster asked her, "What should I do if someone wants me to try drugs?" she replied, "Just say no." It became such a rallying cry among a number of youngsters, they established a club in which members encouraged one another to say no to drugs while having fun and making new friends.

For children from seven to fourteen, Just Say No clubs have sprung up in a wide range of communities. They meet in schools, houses of worship, and community centers, and each is led by an adult volunteer plus one or more teens.

The fundamental idea behind the clubs is to employ peer-pressure reversal, making drugs unacceptable. Uncool. Simplistic though it may sound, Just Say No works on several levels: teaching children how to say no; exposing them to positive adult and teen role models; and providing structured extracurricular activities and opportunities for developing new skills, which in turn enhances self-esteem. Other youth groups, such as Project LEAD, Students Against Driving Drunk, and Youth to Youth, are guided by similar principles.

Constructive home entertainment should be made available. If compatible with your family budget, I highly recommend purchasing a computer. We bought a relatively inexpensive model and can barely get our five-year-old away from it. The video games he plays on it are educational as well as recreational, requiring interaction—unlike the probable alternative, TV. Plus, on inclement days it serves as a hub for our kids and their friends, keeping them in the house and within sight.

Part-time employment for teenagers whose academic records are satisfactory. Besides teaching dependability and the value of a dollar, it heightens self-esteem and puts cash in their pockets. And youngsters with their own money to spend on recreation are for the most part less bored than those without.

There are countless other alternatives to drugs, and becoming involved can make a difference for your child. "Without a doubt," says Ira, who regrets that his parents discouraged an interest in music. "The more positive outlets a person has, the less chance he'll gravitate toward negative outlets. If there is something to occupy his mind other than drugs, that's one less reason to get high."

Some youngsters gripe about more than just transient, "I-don't-have-anything-to-do-today" boredom. Theirs is a hopelessness about bettering their lives and about their future. They believe their fate is sealed and that nothing will change: from the acne splotching their foreheads to their lack of popularity in school.

Feelings of aimlessness are bound to be magnified by our competitive society and erratic economy, which has more parents asking their children at a younger age, "What are you going to do with your life?" Many don't have a clue, and the less internal direction they have, the more likely they are to drift into the treacherous currents of substance abuse. Without pressuring their youngsters, parents must assist them in mapping out long-range goals, beginning when they are in junior high school.

School career-guidance programs have improved enormously over the years, but for more personalized attention I suggest professional career counseling. These centers, listed in the Yellow Pages under "Career and Vocational Counseling," incorporate interviews and a battery of tests to match a child's aptitude and personality with corresponding occupations that he probably never dreamed existed. The experience can prove both enlightening and heartening.

Most career-counseling programs entail several visits, cost approximately $250, and maintain libraries of current information pertaining to each field's salaries, scholastic and/or apprenticeship requirements, future prospects, and so forth. Another, usually free-of-charge resource is your state or county youth board, many of which provide vocational counseling and job placement. Its number is in the State or County Government Office listings of the White Pages.

Yet another way to expose your child to different vocations he might find appealing is to utilize the work experiences of adults you know. Your son or daughter has expressed an interest in aerospace engineering? Surely if you check with friends, family, and neighbors you can find a professional delighted to spend some time explaining his line of work to an inquisitive youngster.

REASON: TO FEEL LIKE AN ADULT

"I'm the baby of my family and the only daughter. I've always looked young for my age, and my parents were overly protective. With three older brothers, all pretty straight, it was like living with five bossy parents.

"I think the reason I started to smoke pot and angel dust was that for once I was controlling my life. It was *my* decision to take drugs, and I felt pretty grown up about it. And more than anything else, I wanted to feel grown up."

—*Elyse*

Kids associate growing up with independence, power, self-determination and as such yearn for adulthood; not necessarily its responsibilities, mind you, but its freedoms, or what they perceive to be its freedoms. At age three they wish they were six so that they could cross the street on their own. Whey they are fifteen and still riding bicycles to school, they look on enviously as older teenagers pull their cars into the parking lot.

Unfortunately, many kids also associate growing up with smoking, drinking, and drugging. To youngsters who must wait several years before they can legally drive a car or vote, substances are tempting symbols of instant "adulthood." A substantial number of children polled by the *Weekly Reader* about why they think their peers take drugs responded, "to feel older."

Furthermore, ingesting chemicals represents control, a most cherished asset at a time when Mother Nature seems to play nasty tricks on your body and you feel the yoke of parents, teachers, and other authority figures, including those your own age.

WHAT YOU CAN DO

Help Your Child Feel Grown Up in Ways Other Than with Drugs

Youngsters should be assigned household chores at age four or five, or as soon as they can grasp the meaning of accountability.

Our family runs on a token-reward system similar to that used in therapeutic-community drug rehabilitation: Each boy has a small domestic job to do. If he completes it acceptably, we praise him and reward him with more responsibility—just like a grown-up, my wife and I explain. Compensations are constructive, such as extra time on the computer rather than a candy bar.

We do not simply delegate tasks, which keeps kids trapped in children's roles; we work alongside them. And in families with more than one youngster, older siblings reinforce for their brothers and sisters the idea that obligation is a privilege that comes with age. Once Adam saw Seth helping us around the house, he wanted to know when it would be his turn. And after young Max watched Adam handle a broom, pretty soon he was wielding it without having to be asked. Which leads me to a brief word of caution.

If you're envisioning weekends of lounging in the hammock, contentedly sipping iced tea while the offspring enthusiastically mow the lawn and paint the porch, forget it. Although my kids' eagerness to help is heartwarming, their execution can be heartbreaking. Max may be keen on sweeping the kitchen, but were he to perform his chore unsupervised, we'd undoubtedly have to replace our china every other week. If you want efficiency, do the job yourself, but to impart such a valuable lesson is certainly worth the added effort.

Permit youngsters to make informed decisions about matters that affect them—then allow them to abide by the outcome of those decisions. With preteens and school-agers, start simply: Instead of purchasing their entire school-year wardrobe for them, occasionally give them a selection of clothes from which to choose. When at a restaurant, suggest several items from the menu but let them ultimately place the order. Have them accompany you to the grocery store and hand them a list of items to find. One time, when Seth was just learning to read, he joined me on a supermarket trip. Asked to get a loaf of bread from the baked-goods aisle, he returned with both the bread and a warning. It seems that a decorative cake box stocked next to the bread was emblazoned with "since 1897."

"Mom would never buy food that old, Dad," Seth said innocently. He mistook it for the expiration date.

Besides allowing children to feel more grown up, these random opportunities help to develop their decision-forming skills, which is so important: Kids sometimes say yes to drugs because they are inexperienced at making choices and abiding by their own judgment. Even a foolhardy decision can be beneficial, teaching children they must live with the adverse consequences. They learn to consider more carefully the next time, especially if you impress the moral upon them verbally as well.

Teach your youngster responsibility to others. My kids understand that the Barun family is a team whose members are answerable to and dependent on one another. If one person doesn't pull his weight by not performing his chores, to use one example, the whole team suffers because more work is created for everybody else.

Children have to learn that personal choices impact on others, not just on them. It is a lesson you can help instill by occasionally permitting each youngster to decide on an issue that affects the whole family, such as where to travel on a weekend outing. Kids who are encouraged to always consider the feelings of other people may be more likely to reflect, *How will this affect my family? What would my parents think if they found out?* when being prevailed upon to commit wrongdoing. Because their parents have tutored them that drugs are wrong, they are internally motivated to say no; indulging would make them feel bad inside and uncomfortable with themselves.

REASON: TO ESCAPE PROBLEMS

"There are five basic feelings: hurt, pain, anger, fear, and pleasure. Using drugs was a way for me to feel the pleasure but to avoid the other four."

—*Ira*

As the history examined in chapter 2 should have made abundantly clear, depending on substances to help mitigate the stresses of daily living is nothing new. In the California survey of drug and alcohol use among junior- and senior-high-school students, "escaping problems" was the reason most given by ninth-graders and the second-most for eleventh-graders.

WHAT YOU CAN DO

We have to teach our children that hardships are as much a part of life as good fortune. Becoming an adult entails accepting that truth, not running away from it. Unfortunately, the only way a youngster can learn to hurdle obstacles is if his parents let him risk stumbling and falling.

Now, I know there is nothing more painful than to watch your child hurt. Nevertheless, kids whose well-meaning but misdirected parents constantly shelter them from life's stark realities become emotionally immunized from coping. And their bodies never learn how to respond to stress. When the protective shield is finally lifted, stressful situations send them into a tailspin they may feel can be corrected only with alcohol or drugs.

Children should be assured, however, that when a burden seems too great they always have your absolute support; and if they are uneasy discussing certain problems with you, that there are many resources available to them. In the Community Services Numbers section of the White Pages and the "Crisis Intervention Service" listings of the Yellow Pages are the telephone numbers of national and local hotlines. Write them down on a piece of paper and post it conspicuously in your child's room. Urge him to call the trained volunteers at these hotlines whenever he is troubled and wants to confide in someone other than you. Explain that hotline personnel not only dispense valuable advice, they're good listeners. And they care.

Ultimately, youngsters must be taught that drugs and alcohol offer only temporary respite from pain and problems—never solutions—and that trying to handle difficulties by getting high is like fanning the flames of a fire, as Carl, who was badly strung out on crack, can attest:

"I used to get into these tremendous fights with my father, and I'd be so upset and angry I sought escape through drugs." An extremely articulate, good-looking teenager with wiry, jet black hair, he says that smoking crack "made me feel like I had no problems at all. But when I came down, everything seemed to intensify, and I felt like crap. Which only made me want to get high all over again."

REASON: REBELLION

"A good friend of mine came from a very wealthy family. Father was a lawyer, mother bought and sold antiques. Beautiful home, the whole bit. But they were pretty neglectful of him, and to my friend they were a couple of shallow, materialistic phonies. Smoking pot and eventually shooting up dope became his way of rebelling. He was essentially saying to them, 'I don't want to be like you,' in the most extreme way possible, by destroying himself.

"He overdosed a few days after his nineteenth birthday."

—Ira

Adolescent rebellion is a necessary part of the maturation process kids undergo. It's healthy—for them, that is, not necessarily for you. If you are the parent of a teenager, you probably feel at times as if the two of you are on a perpetual collision course. But try not to take their spurning of society's (and your) values and conventions personally. They are partly testing you and partly testing themselves, rolling out their newly discovered analytical abilities like heavy artillery at every given opportunity.

You may notice that suddenly your teenager is more reclusive; he's positively mortified to be seen with you in public. Such ostensible rejection is bound to hurt and make you wonder, *Why this sudden detachment?*

For one thing, adolescents may subconsciously alienate themselves from their parents to help ease separation and their eventual leaving of the nest. Also, dismissing their parents' ideals enables them to discover themselves and their own standards. For virtually all of their lives they have been seen largely as reflections of their mothers and fathers: "There goes Mary's daughter." Some kids, however, are so desperate to be seen for themselves, they reject their parents' values completely. This is called *oppositional behavior*, where they evolve into the very antithesis of Mom and Dad. So if the parents are seen as "good," the child will become "bad."

For some hostile children, hurting themselves by using drugs and alcohol is a subliminal way of wounding their parents, who have invested so much in them.

WHAT YOU CAN DO

Learn to Let Go

Beyond question, the hardest part of parenthood isn't birthing or raising, it's letting go. Unfortunately, every parent must come to grips with the fact that his or her job—helping children to grow and to be independent—sows the seeds of its own obsolescence.

It is natural to want to retain that job indefinitely; after all, for some people motherhood or fatherhood defines their very existence. Further, they feel that to control their youngsters' lives is to control their own, and who can blame them? Kids who accept our values and beliefs are surely easier to handle than those who does not.

Parents have a choice: They can resist their teenagers' separation and risk estrangement. Or they can gradually loosen the reins so that their children don't need to declare their independence self-destructively. Whether or not parents bestow their blessing, youngsters will quest after their own sovereignty.

Letting go should not be confused with abandonment. Does it mean that you are losing them? Yes, to themselves. You will always remain their parent, though the dynamics of the relationship will change; you become less disciplinarian and more confidant—and friend. Possibly you will grow even closer. In families with a great deal of parent-child friction, reconciliation often occurs after the child leaves the home.

Believe it or not, my wife and I look forward to our kids growing up. Watching them mature is a gas. Certainly our philosophy is that once they leave home for college and career, they will sink or swim on their own. We'll advise them and assist them in any way we can, but we firmly will pass on to them that we cannot live their lives for them.

REASON: DRUGS MAKE KIDS FEEL GOOD

"Why did I get stoned? Because pot and crack made me feel better than I did when I wasn't stoned. I wasn't bored anymore. Life was . . . *fun*."

—*Paul*

NOT "WHAT YOU CAN DO" BUT "WHAT *CAN* YOU DO?"

In this instance there are no behavior-modification techniques to exercise, only vigorous antidrug education, which forms the basis of chapter 4. Parents have to impart to their children that any time a person uses drugs, he pays for his pleasure: through unpleasant side effects, destroyed brain cells, a loss of ambition. Some drug abusers pay with their lives.

We cannot deny that drugs *may* promise temporary euphoria. But we must explain to our kids there are many other ways to feel good than by getting stoned. Then we must walk them down some of those avenues of natural self-gratification: the physical high of exercise, the creative high gained from goal achievement, and the satisfying high enjoyed when helping others. Show your child by example how to enjoy life through accomplishments, through loving and being loved. Drugs kill; but partaking in fulfilling pursuits helps people to live.

Make Home a Haven

"I never felt comfortable in my house. Besides the fact that I didn't get along with my father, he and my mother were always fighting. They'd scream at each other, and I'd sit in my room with my fists clenched. It was like being a prisoner in a jail cell.

"To get out of there, I'd do anything: 'Mom, I'm going to the store!' And I'd be gone for a couple of hours. I just didn't like being there, you know? I hated it."

—*Carl*

A University of Michigan Institute for Social Research study of high-school seniors concluded that those who spent little time at home were more likely to be daily drug users, pointing up how important it is that home be a haven for kids; a place where they can seek sanctuary after a day on the battlefield that is school, not a place from which to escape.

I was a teenager who always snuck out of the house at night. When my parents got wise and installed a lock on my door, I'd slip out the window to be with my drug-using friends. On those occasions when I did stay home, sitting with my mother and father at the dinner table, I was usually in a drug-induced stupor, giggling a lot for no apparent reason. I would steal off into my own world because I didn't feel comfortable in theirs. I didn't think that my problems were important to them; that they would be listened to, much less understood. The lack of communication in our home eventually drove me to look for it elsewhere, and I became a high-risk kid.

At the beginning of this chapter we sketched a composite of the high-risk child inclined to abuse drugs and/or alcohol. These youngsters often come from families that also fit a certain profile. Do any of the following characteristics apply to yours?

In families that contribute to youthful substance abuse,

- affection is rarely expressed;
- parents are neglectful or abusive;
- parents are too lenient or too strict;
- parents are separated or divorced;
- parents and/or siblings use tobacco, alcohol, or drugs;
- parents are dependent on the child, burdening him with their own responsibilities;
- rules are not enforced or clearly defined;
- drug use is not discouraged or is not discussed;
- economic pressures arise frequently; either there is too little or *too much* money.

In "low-risk" families,

- children receive love from both parents;
- parents consistently provide support and advice;
- parents firmly disapprove of drug use and do not smoke, drink to excess, or use drugs themselves;
- control and discipline are emphasized;
- family members communicate with one another.

Control and Discipline

Starting in the late 1950s, it seemed, too many parents abdicated their duties as disciplinarians, undeniably a factor in the high rates of youthful chemical use, pregnancy, and suicide that followed. Kids not only need restraints, they privately welcome them because today's adolescent world can be so confusing. Though on the surface they may appear to be the envy of their friends, children whose parents do not set limits sometimes confuse overpermissiveness with unconcern. So they resort to attention-provoking misbehavior: promiscuity, substance abuse, delinquency.

Children also look to parents for the stability so fleeting in their ever-changing lives, which is why both mother's and father's discipline should be consistent. Kids are easily confused by contradictory regulations. And, because they often take the path of least resistance, youngsters will tend to play the more lenient parent against the stricter one. Maintaining a united front, therefore, is essential.

Discuss with your spouse where lines will be drawn on all issues, from allotted TV time, to dating, to use of bicycle or car. Because kids' memory banks have a convenient habit of short-circuiting when confronted with a transgression ("You never told me I couldn't do that! You did? When?"), I suggest drawing up a Family Contract outlining a youngster's household responsibilities, privileges, curfew, and so forth. An example might be:

Family Contract

I, _____(child's name), pledge to abide by the following rules:

1. No use of alcohol or drugs, ever.
2. No tobacco use.
3. Performing the following chores: taking out the garbage and cleaning the cat box once a week.
4. A daily one-and-a-half-hour maximum of TV time.
5. A weekday curfew of 10 p.m. and, on weekends, of 12 a.m.

6. Mom and Dad promise to provide transportation to recreational activities three times per week.

Date effective: ———

Signed:

_____
(Child's name)

_____
(Parent's name)

_____
(Parent's name)

Keep a copy for yourselves and affix the other to the refrigerator or to a bulletin board in his room. In families of two or more children, naturally older siblings enjoy more freedoms than their younger brothers and sisters. But they also share more obligations. Make it clear you are not showing favoritism and that contracts will be reevaluated periodically; the more responsibility demonstrated, the greater the number of privileges.

Have a family discussion about the contract in which you stress that your imposing standards is in no way punishment. Explain that "It's not as if we couldn't function without a contract, but in order for our family to run smoothly, everyone should know what is expected of him. This is as much for your benefit as it is for ours."

The penalties for misbehavior must be made perfectly clear. Needless to say, they should never be physical: Kids learn from punishment's inevitability, not its severity. When guidelines are broken, certain privileges are either rescinded or reduced until the child proves deserving of them again. It is important to follow through, for although you want to be reasonable, you don't want to be manipulable. You don't have to be a tyrant to instill discipline, but you do have to command your youngster's respect.

Rules should not be so rigid or impractical that infractions are inevitable. Unless you want your son's or daughter's childhood to be a raging war, learn to pick your battles and know when to let things slide. Determine your priorities. What is *really* important? That your thirteen-year-old girl drinks beer because she "likes the taste"? Yes. That she dresses like Madonna? No. Unless she brings home a Sean Penn act-alike as a prospective bridegroom.

When disciplining children, establish that their behavior is the source of your displeasure, not they. Sometimes in fits of pique, such as when you discover a pool of pancake syrup on your tax return, you may snap, "What are you, stupid?" Though it can be difficult in the heat of the moment, try to catch yourself, for you can't assume kids will make the leap of faith and understand what has you so angry.

Finally, discipline in accordance with the misconduct's seriousness. To chastise as severely for socks left in a bathroom as for cigarettes found in a jacket pocket turns all reprimands into so much white noise. And unlike the white noise of your youngster's latest heavy-metal heroes, yours he will tune out.

Communication

To some parents *communication* means getting your point across to your child effectively. That's only half of it, the transmission. You also have to learn to be a good listener, or receiver. And the only way to do that is by taking the time to listen to your kid.

I don't mean that you schedule family rap sessions. Between school and extracurricular activities, a young person's life is so structured, "Family Hour" becomes just another tedious demand. And who's to say if parent or youngster will be in an effusive mood at that designated time? You have to be flexible and spontaneous, responsive to those moments when he is anxious to talk. A qualifier: as flexible and spontaneous as possible. There are nights when I come home from work late, feeling exhausted, and simply cannot summon the energy to converse with my kids. When that happens I ask them if they can wait until the next day, "so Dad can give you his undivided attention." And I make good on my promise.

I find that children tend to be most talkative at informal settings such as breakfast or dinner. It's great listening to them speak excitedly about events that happened in school, and it's fun to help them with a problem. Not that children will always volunteer information. Sometimes you have to draw them out by asking questions. I'll ask Adam what he did in school that day, he'll reply, "Nuthin'," and leave it at that. I don't. "You mean to

71

tell me," I'll counter, "you sat in school for eight hours, and nothing at all happened?" It's usually enough to prompt a laugh and, frequently, conversation.

Other subtle methods of getting them to open up are: touching them and making eye contact; never interrupting, even if you detect a fallacy in their story and wish to address it; helping them communicate by occasionally supplying words or clarifying thoughts, which are repeated back to them ("What you're saying is . . ."). Surefire ways of making them clam right up are to correct their grammar while they're trying to convey something that is important to them, and ridiculing their ideas.

Mealtime doesn't have to be dominated exclusively by kid-talk about school and Little League. Particularly if you have teenagers, invite them into your discussions about the larger issues that affect all family members. Solicit their opinions. Kids enjoy feeling that their input is valued, which helps to shore up their self-confidence and to make them feel more like adults. Who knows, *you* might learn something.

If your family's communication skills are poor—no one seems to hear what's being said; statements and viewpoints are habitually obscured—role-playing sessions can be a helpful technique for reducing static on the line. In role playing, a child portrays a parent, the parent his child, and together they reenact a typical discussion. Each party's interpretation of the other can truly be eye-opening and articulate truths that would otherwise be left unsaid. Seeing how our children see us, and we them, can lead to better understanding and the realization that what we thought was so clearly communicated was not.

Families where relations seem irreparably strained may need the objective perspective of a family counselor or therapist. I recommend counseling when

● the rapport between parents and children disintegrates;
● parents feel unqualified to discuss certain issues with authority, either because of lack of knowledge or past experiences that would make them appear hypocritical;
● problems seem irresolvable.

Counseling may not spawn immediate solutions to family conflicts, but trained therapists are often skilled at identifying problems, having experienced them with other families. They are also expert communicators who can improve family members' abilities to articulate their feelings and to listen. The different classes of therapists include

- psychiatrists, who must hold an M.D. degree, a state license, and three years' supervised residency. They are the only therapists permitted by law to prescribe medication and are specially trained to treat mental, emotional, and behavioral disorders;
- psychoanalysts, who are required to be M.D.'s, Ph.D's, M.S.W.'s (Master of Social Work), or social workers claiming additional years of study;
- psychologists, who have to be licensed or certified in most states. They must have attended college, four years of graduate school, and one year of supervised psychology training. Many but not all are Ph.D's.
- Social workers, who are to have completed college, two years of graduate school, and either an M.S.W. or D.S.W. (Doctor of Social Work) degree. In most states it is required they be certified;
- Lay therapists, such as family and marriage counselors; for whom no training is required.

To locate a family therapist, contact any of the following organizations, the addresses and telephone numbers of which are listed at the end of this chapter and in Appendix A: American Association for Marriage and Family Therapy, American Psychiatric Association, American Psychological Association, Family Service America, and National Association of Social Workers. Explain your problem to these associations' personnel, who can put you in touch with professionals in your area.

As for cost, it varies greatly, with many therapists charging on a sliding scale based on ability to pay; for low-cost therapy, inquire at your state's mental health office, which can additionally furnish information about fees and therapists' credentials. Family counseling is often covered by private health plans, but rarely by Medicaid.

Sessions are generally conducted once or twice weekly, then tapered off. If, once in therapy, you are not satisfied with the progress being made or are simply uncomfortable with the therapist, don't hesitate in finding a new one.

Today's parenting is more demanding than ever, and sometimes it may seem impossible to make the necessary time deposits without becoming overdrawn. The only answer to that dilemma is, if you can't spend quantities of time, spend quality. Let your children accompany you to the office one day, encourage them to keep you company while you're working around the house, take them with you to the auto-repair shop to wait for the exhaust system to be replaced. *Quality time* isn't just those hours spent on children's activities. Often, kids just want to be with their mothers and fathers, even when they are doing "Mom things" and "Dad things," as my sons call them.

If you are away from home on business frequently, as I am four days per week, phone them, even if just for a minute. Inquire about their day, explain to them what you are doing and why you have to be away from them. It bothers me to have to leave my kids so much, and I tell them that. I let them know how much I miss them and love them.

Therein lies the key: that children feel secure in their parents' love. You've no doubt seen cars sporting the bumper sticker "More hugs than drugs"? It's not just a clever slogan; doing so can truly make a difference.

KEY POINTS

- Reasons for substance abuse: peer pressure, seeking acceptance.

Preventative measures: Build up a child's self-confidence and self-esteem, encourage all positive interests, respect his individuality, monitor and guide his friendships.

- Reasons for substance abuse: boredom, hopelessness.

Preventative measures: Provide and promote alternatives to drugs, such as physical exercise, drug-free youth groups, a part-time job for adolescents. However, children should be limited to two structured activities per season, for they need time to daydream and to explore their imaginations.

Kids should have access to constructive home entertainment such as a home computer. They should not have access to television for more than one and a half hours daily; two hours for teenagers.

- Reason for substance abuse: to feel like an adult.

Preventative measures: Help your child feel grown up in ways other than with drugs. Assign him household chores, permit him to make certain personal decisions, teach him responsibility to others.

- Reason for substance abuse: to escape problems.

Preventative measures: Inform your children that when burdened by problems they feel uneasy discussing with you, there are resources at their disposal. Provide them with the telephone numbers of national and local crisis-intervention hotlines.

74

- Reason for substance abuse: rebellion.

Preventative measures: Learn to let go. Gradually loosen the reins so that your children won't feel the need to declare their independence self-destructively.

- Reason for substance abuse: drugs make kids feel good.

Preventative measures: Impart to your kids that drug users often pay dearly for their pleasure. Introduce them to avenues of natural self-gratification.

Discuss with your spouse where lines will be drawn on allotted TV time, dating, use of bicycle or car. Then draw up a Family Contract outlining each youngster's household responsibilities, privileges, curfew, and so forth. Guidelines should not be so rigid or impractical that infractions are inevitable.

Techniques for improving communication with your child: Draw him out by asking questions; touching him and making eye contact; never interrupting, even if you detect a fallacy in his story and wish to address it; helping him communicate by occasionally supplying words or clarifying thoughts, which you repeat back to him ("What you're saying is . . ."). Surefire ways of making a youngster clam right up are to correct his grammar while he's trying to convey something that is important to him, and ridiculing his ideas.

If you can't spend quantities of time with your kids, spend quality. Let them accompany you to the office or keep you company while you're working around the house; take them with you on errands.

RECOMMENDED RESOURCES

For children's drug-free clubs and organizations, contact:

The Just Say No Foundation
1777 North California Boulevard
Suite 200
Walnut Creek, CA 94596
(800) 258-2766; in California,
(415) 939-6666

Project LEAD (Leadership, Experience
and Development)
Quest International
6655 Sharon Woods Boulevard
Columbus, OH 43229
(800) 446-2800

Students Against Driving Drunk
  (SADD)
P.O. Box 800
Marlboro, MA 01752
(617) 481-3568

Youth to Youth
700 Bryden Road
Columbus, OH 43215
(614) 224-4506

Other sources: Many county youth boards sponsor free recreational and cultural programs for kids. They are listed in the Community Services Numbers of the White Pages.

If your child feels temporarily distressed by problems but is uneasy discussing them with you, have him contact:

National Adolescent Suicide Hotline
(800) 621-4000

Other sources: For local hotlines, look in the Community Services Numbers of the White Pages or under "Crisis Intervention Service" in the Yellow Pages.

If your family needs counseling to improve communications and relations, contact the following organizations for referrals to professionals in your area. Explain your problem, what type of therapy you are seeking, and if cost is a factor:

American Association for Marriage and
  Family Therapy
1717 K Street N.W.
Suite 407
Washington, D.C. 20006
(202) 429-1825

American Psychiatric Association
1400 K Street N.W.
Washington, D.C. 20005
(202) 682-6000

American Psychological Association
1200 17th Street N.W.
Washington, D.C. 20036
(202) 955-7600

Family Service America
11700 West Lake Park Drive
Park Place
Milwaukee, WI 53224
(414) 359-2111

Minnesota Institute on Black
Chemical Abuse
2616 Nicolet Avenue South
Minneapolis, MN 55408
(612) 871-7878

National Association of Social Workers
7981 Eastern Avenue
Silver Spring, MD 20910
(301) 565-0333

Other sources: For additional referrals (including low-cost therapy) as well as information regarding fees and therapists' credentials, contact your state's mental health office or administration, the number of which is in the State Government Offices and/or Community Services Numbers listings of the White Pages.

Chapter Four

Teaching Your Child about Drugs

Not simply about drugs but *against* drugs is how you should educate your child. *Anti*drug education. Just as you tell him firmly from an early age that touching a hot stove will burn his fingers, you alert him repeatedly that drugs are harmful and can kill him. By the time he is offered his first hit on a joint, he will have been conditioned to associate them with danger.

Unfortunately, too many kids receive their drug education outside the home. The survey of California eleventh-graders revealed that only 29% were taught about substances by their parents, while 66% learned from friends; 59% from school classes, and—as often happens when parents fail to touch on the subject—38% from personal drug experience.

It is unfair to suggest that parents avoid educating their children out of neglect. Some believe, wrongly, that if they discuss drugs they somehow condone their use. The same with drinking. And sex. However, it is only when given the facts that young people can make informed, sensible decisions.

Another reason many parents leave drug education up to the schools—or simply leave it alone—is that they don't feel expert enough on the subject. But something so crucial to a youngster's welfare should never be entrusted entirely to anyone else, regardless of his or her qualifications. Who else has a more profound influence over your kid or a greater interest in him than you? Nobody. And if you take the time to properly educate yourself, no one else is more fit to teach him.

Despite the pervasiveness of youthful alcohol and drug use, parents and school drug-prevention programs do have a distinct advantage: Time is on their side. Because children are so impressionable, the chances of molding their values about drugs and alcohol are excellent. However, you have to move quickly, before other, dubious information sources such as prodrug peers and media propaganda negatively influence your kids.

PARENTS AND DRUG EDUCATION

How Early Do You Start?

As early as possible: at five years, even four. Time may be on your side, but there is still none to lose, as the typical child now tries alcohol at age twelve, and drugs at age thirteen. According to the National Institute on Drug Abuse, the current average grade level of first use, per substance— although the age of onset may vary dramatically depending on locale—is

- seventh to eight grades for inhalants;
- ninth grade for tobacco, alcohol, marijuana, stimulants, sedatives, barbiturates, and methaqualone;
- tenth grade for tranquilizers and heroin;
- eleventh grade for amyl and butyl nitrite, LSD and other hallucinogens, PCP, and opium;
- twelfth grade for cocaine.

From these statistics we can safely say that chemical use has infiltrated our grade schools.

It may be difficult for you to accept the urgency of informing a four- or five-year-old about drugs. What is the world coming to, anyway? You look at his innocent face, and it seems almost cruel to introduce him to such a potential evil. Will you be able to do it? Could he possibly understand?

There is no question that you must do it. And we know now that even preschoolers are able to grasp basic concepts about drugs. When my son Adam was just five years old, I asked him if he knew what peer pressure was. "Sure," he replied, "that's when another kid tries to get you to do something you shouldn't. It's a bad thing." He'd learned it from a children's cassette tape. Hopefully, when Adam does one day experience real-life peer pressure to try drugs, he will be able to identify the situation, reflect on the antidrug values gleaned at home, and reject the offer—or, at the very least, review it critically.

Though it may not be possible for all parents reading this book, children should ideally be taught about drugs before they reach adolescence. Think back to your own teen years, and to how invincible you felt: Your body was strong and sinewy, and you were just beginning to test your wings, intellectually, physically, emotionally, sexually. In this state of mind, lectures about drugs' long-term risks tend to have a limited effect, especially on extremely present-oriented youngsters. High-school graduation seems eons away; who can be bothered to think about a potential health problem that may not manifest itself for years? When I was a teenager, I heard all the warnings but was too stoned to pay heed. Addiction? That didn't apply to me; at the time, I was only smoking pot. And death? The word wasn't even in my vocabulary. I was just coming alive.

Before you can educate your kids about drugs, you must educate yourself using accurate material; a conservative criterion for any book or pamphlet is that it be no more than five years old. There is no surer way of alienating a child and tainting your credibility than to spout hyperbolic misinformation, particularly when talking to a teenager who may already have some drug experience.

Another reason up-to-date data are so essential is that new studies on substances' effects frequently contradict well-established ones. A case in point is marijuana, which has been the subject of over seven thousand studies since 1965.

As recently as several years ago it was believed by many in the medical and mental health fields that marijuana was relatively safe—the least pernicious of drugs. But the American Medical Association now states emphatically, "There is no doubt at all that marijuana is a dangerous drug, with great potential for serious harm to young Americans." More than 90% of marijuana research has concluded that it is far from innocuous.

The results of a study conducted by the University of Houston and the University of Miami Medical Center, made public in August 1987, provided the first documentation of long-term adverse consequences. Thirteen years earlier, forty-one chronic pot smokers and forty-one nonsmokers were tested. At the time, no striking disparities were found medically or psychologically between the two groups.

But when examined again in 1986, startling differences in the same two groups' thought processes were discovered, with habitual users observed to have far more lapses in concentration and more learning difficulties. They gravitated toward physical work rather than mental work and also tended to be more socially isolated. Marijuana, maintains anthropologist Bryan Page, one of the researchers, may reduce "human potential." The evidence uncovered by the study was everything my generation refused to believe twenty years ago.

Furthermore, the *Cannabis sativa* that my generation smoked went the way of love beads and Day-Glo posters. Today's crop is as much as five to twenty times stronger, containing up to ten times the content of THC, pot's main psychoactive, or mind-altering, chemical. Materials on marijuana published before the mid-1980s, therefore, might as well be discussing a completely different drug.

In addition to containing misinformation, pre-mid-1980s publications may also contain either obvious or subtle prodrug slants. Put back on the shelf any book or pamphlet that promotes "responsible" or "controlled" use, as well as the philosophy that there is no such thing as a "bad" drug, merely improper use.

RELIABLE DRUG-INFORMATION SOURCES

Chapter 5 of this book contains drug information culled from a wide variety of sources, many of which distribute literature. These include organizations dedicated to spreading educational material to parents, such as:

- Committes of Correspondence (also publishes material helpful to screen drug abuse information for accuracy)
- Families in Action National Drug Information Center
- National Clearinghouse for Alcohol and Drug Information (NCADI)
- Parents' Association to Neutralize Drug and Alcohol Abuse (PANDAA)
- National Council on Alcoholism
- National Federation of Parents for Drug-Free Youth (NFP)
- National Parents' Resource Institute for Drug Education

All publish quality pamphlets and data sheets, and I find most of these to be accurate, current, and informative.

In addition, print information can be requested from each state's agency on alcohol and drug abuse; from self-help organizations such as Alcoholics Anonymous, Drugs Anonymous, Cocaine Anonymous, Families Anonymous, Al-Anon, and Alateen; and from virtually all of the drug- and alcohol-rehabilitation programs recommended in Appendix A. The National Institute on Drug Abuse even sponsors a free-loan collection of drug-education films and videocassettes.

The purpose of educating yourself is not only to impress upon your child the dangers of abuse but to help you discern the signs of a problem. I strongly recommend familiarizing yourself with drug paraphernalia. If you cannot identify vials, bongs, cocaine kits, and roach clips, go to a smoke shop (what used to be called a head shop) and take a good look. Just try not to be too disturbed by the sales clerk's amused or bewildered expression.

Once you've assembled all your materials, review them with your spouse so that the two of you can be consistent in your stand against drugs and equally acquainted with the facts. If you are separated or divorced, this is especially important, since kids from one-parent homes have a higher incidence of alcohol and drug abuse. Because relations are often strained between the ex-partners, they sometimes fail to confer on behavioral standards for their children.

No matter how awkward or painful, however, it is essential they cooperate when it comes to discipline and setting limits. My first wife and I were estranged for a full decade, but eventually I was able to rebuild the bonds of trust between us. Today we share a warm friendship as well as frequent discussions about how to handle teen-related matters such as alcohol and drugs with our seventeen-year-old daughter. It is in a child's best interest that the absent parent consistently support the at-home parent's antidrug position. In some instances—and I've found this to be true—the absent parent may be endowed with greater influence, probably by virtue of not being the primary disciplinarian.

THE BOTTOM LINE: NO DRUGS ARE ALLOWED

Regardless of your youngster's age, your posture on substances is stated unequivocally: He is to touch no tobacco, no alcohol, no drugs. Given the extent of substance abuse among the younger population, you would think that position would be universal among today's parents. Yet in a California survey of eleventh-grade students, one in ten claimed his parents either favored or were neutral to adolescent pot smoking, while one in four declared his parents held similarly casual attitudes about alcohol.

Tobacco, alcohol, and marijuana are commonly referred to as gateway drugs, and in that order are the ones with which youths typically start. When California ninth- and eleventh-graders were asked to name the substance that produced their first high, 38% and 53%, respectively, reported alcohol; 14% and 15%, respectively, marijuana or hashish. (Tobacco was not included in this survey.) Amphetamines, psychedelics, and other drugs comprised a relative minority: 0.3%, 0.2%, and 1%, respectively, for ninth-graders, and 0.3%, 0.4%, and 0.8%, respectively, for eleventh-graders.

Of course not all gateway drug users advance to cocaine, LSD, heroin, and so forth, but consider the following:

Tobacco and other drugs: On the authority of former White House drug chief Dr. Robert L. DuPont, Jr., twelve-to-seventeen-year-old cigarette smokers are twice as likely as nonsmokers to drink alcohol, nine times as likely to ingest depressants and stimulants, ten times as likely to smoke marijuana, and fourteen times as likely to use cocaine, heroin, and hallucinogens.

Alcohol and other drugs: According to figures issued by the National Council on Alcoholism, as many as half of all heavier youthful drinkers also smoke marijuana regularly, at least once a week.

Marijuana and other drugs: A nationwide survey of more than five thousand students revealed that 26% of those who used marijuana also experimented with cocaine, hallucinogens, and opiates, as opposed to just 1% of nondrug users. And another national poll found that 93% of all cocaine users smoked marijuana first.

In effect, no one becomes dependent on or addicted to *a* drug. Substances that are part of the same classification—alcohol and sedatives, for example, which are both depressants—act similarly on the body. A person hooked on liquor, therefore, is more susceptible to becoming codependent on sedatives, and vice versa.

The stock argument against the "stepping-stone" theory is that one joint won't turn a child into a dope fiend. If there were no variables to this equation—one joint and one kid equals zero problem—perhaps. But there are variables, such as kids' natural curiosity. Once he tries marijuana, for instance, and suffers no ill effects—at least not that he is aware of—he is liable to engage in more frequent pot smoking, as well as eventually experiment with other substances. Furthermore, any drug use, no matter how "minor," casts him into a corruptive peer subculture.

Inevitably, someone within that clique of kids is going to flirt with other, more dangerous substances, either out of inquisitiveness or as a way to enhance his stature with his friends. It is interesting that some children get high as a way to escape the pressures of academic, athletic, and social competition, and yet the drug world is not without its own competitiveness: Who has the purest cocaine? How close to the edge are you willing to stray? Whenever my friends and I reached a certain plateau in our chemical use, one of us always scouted the mind-altering thrills that lay ahead.

Every group of youngsters usually includes at least one such person. If use is limited essentially to grass, he saunters in to a party holding some cocaine. And even if they didn't premeditate to snort the drug, other kids end up inhaling it anyway—simply because *it was there.* When I first became involved with drugs, I hardly ever sought them out on my own. I didn't have to. There was always someone more worldly than I, to act as a mentor of sorts. "You think amphetamine's high is intense? Wait'll you try this."

A rationalization maintained by some mothers and fathers is, "I'd rather have my child drink or smoke pot at home, supervised, than out on the street."

Admittedly, if we're speaking of legal-age youngsters and alcohol, that position has some merit: Better he be passed out on the living room sofa than driving home drunk from a bar. But giving tacit approval to illegal substance use (drugs *and* alcohol for minors) in the home is unsuitable. Parents who do so are condoning criminal behavior, destroying any foundation for future discipline, and practically inviting their kid to reel out of control.

It is a flawed philosophy that, though practical sounding, does not work. The same is true with the unfounded belief that if drugs and alcohol are no longer taboo, youngsters soon tire of them. That strategy usually backfires, since virtually all substances create psychological or physical dependency. Not long after I began using heroin, I grew bored to death of it, deriving no pleasure from the drug whatsoever. But I couldn't put down the syringe, because my body demanded daily doses.

Monotony as an antidote to drug use? Sometimes it's quite the opposite: For example, my weariness of marijuana's recurrent paranoia and lethargy led to a maddening fling with stimulants such as amphetamines and cocaine.

Then there are parents who wink at youthful drug and alcohol use "in moderation." How does one measure *moderation?* Is it one beer or a six-pack? Anytime a person abuses substances he enters a high-stakes crap-shoot, since there is no way to foretell how a chemical will interact with his body and psyche. A tab of LSD that seems to produce a pleasurable mind excursion for one person can send another on a terrifyingly turbulent flight. Cocaine may straightjacket one person into dependency within several months, yet take twice that long to entrap someone else. You just never know. Therefore, allowing a child to drink, to use marijuana—even to smoke cigarettes—is like rolling the dice and praying Lady Luck is on your side.

Use of *any* substance should be forbidden and so stipulated in the Family Contract. Say to your child:

"Smoking cigarettes is not permitted because it is unhealthy and can leave you breathless, literally. It can turn you old before your time, and it can kill you.

"You are not allowed to use alcohol until you reach legal drinking age. Besides the fact that it can wreck your mind and body, and kill you, it is against the law.

"We will not tolerate any drug use. In addition to being plain stupid, it too is illegal and can kill you.

"I'm telling you this because I care about you and love you."

Impose these restrictions as early as possible, and though you generally loosen the reins as your kids grow into adulthood, never moderate your antidrug policy.

If your child counters that so-and-so's parents let him smoke or drink, reply, "Perhaps his parents aren't aware of the dangers. I am, and I'm going to share them with you, for your protection. I will also let your friend's parents know how I disapprove."

WHAT TO SAY AND HOW TO SAY IT

First of all, never lecture. Lectures turn children off—just as they did when you were a kid. And lectures are associated with punishment. Make

85

it very clear that you are neither taking them to task nor accusing them of using drugs.

You don't have to formally announce, "Let's sit down and talk about drugs," which will cause a youngster's eyes to glaze over quicker than any illicit substance could. There are countless opportunities to broach the subject casually, such as when watching TV together, listening to the radio, or reading. Most drug discussions with my sons occur in the car, at the supermarket, or in restaurants.

Don't affect the oratorical zeal of a fire-and-brimstone preacher. Let the most persuasive evidence you have work for you—the facts. And never employ unnatural language: incomprehensible psychoanalytic terms and, especially, your kid's colloquialisms, which most parents don't latch on to until years after they're passé anyway. Having their own vernacular is one way adolescents assert identity and independence from Mom and Dad. Adults incorporating "dude" and "rad" into their speech will only foster resentment, not to mention snickers.

Children expect and want their parents to act like parents—as well as their friends. I tell Seth, Adam, and Max that it's my duty as their dad to explain the dangers of drugs and alcohol to them "because one day you may have to deal with that danger; let's say that a kid tries getting you to drink or smoke something you shouldn't. I'm going to help you understand what drugs and alcohol are, the pressures you may face to try them, and how to face down those pressures."

If you have children of diverse ages, I suggest working with them individually and adapting your language accordingly. Because these are such complex issues, it's always better to overexplain than to underexplain; whether your child is a preschooler or a teenager, you can never take for granted he understands. For five-year-old Max I simplify everything to its most basic. For example, when he's under the weather and has to take an aspirin:

"Max, do you know what this tablet is?"

He'll shake his head no.

"This is an aspirin. We take it when we're sick to make our bodies well. But *only* when we're sick." I never say that we take aspirin "to feel better."

"Do you understand?"

The odds are he'll continue shaking his head no. So I'll repeat what I said, adding, "We don't like taking medicine, or drugs, but sometimes we have to."

DISCUSSING DRUGS WITH PRETEENS AND TEENS

Using photos and illustrations from books, educational films, and videocassettes, show your youngster what the different drugs look like. Should he one day have pellets of crack thrust at him, for example, he'll be able to recognize them, and a warning light will flash in his head—*This stuff is bad for me*—because of the information gathered from you.

Be careful not to overwhelm him with too much information, however, as kids have rather short attention spans. Boil down to its essence what you have to say. It is not necessary that he know marijuana contains 426 chemicals, only that it causes memory loss, stunts psychological growth, and erodes ambition. In short, it is no good for him.

Another precaution: Overemphasizing substances' pleasurable effects may only stimulate his curiosity. Yet you cannot fail to acknowledge that some people do derive enjoyment from alcohol and drugs. *If they didn't at all*, a child with any common sense might wonder, *then why do so many people use them, as my parents keep telling me?* To maintain an accurate balance, accentuate the negative. For instance, tell him how a person who buys drugs from a dealer—or from a friend who bought from a friend who bought from a dealer—never knows what he is putting into his system. It could contain laxative or rat poison. It could make him very sick or even kill him.

Realistically elucidating what can happen to people who use drugs is chilling enough that you don't need to resort to scare tactics. Such an approach was popular years ago among professional drug educators, who habitually distorted the facts. Unfortunately, it frequently boomeranged when kids learned through other sources that the picture exhibited to them was a fraud.

For instance, I'd always heard that marijuana turned users into raving lunatics, a perception widely advanced by the infamous 1936 antimarijuana film *Reefer Madness*. In it, potheads were portrayed as quivering, wild-eyed candidates for rubber rooms. When I smoked grass and nothing seemed to happen—certainly no signs of insanity—I dismissed all the information I'd received as sheer propaganda, even that which was deadly accurate. To young people of the sixties and seventies, *Reefer Madness* wound up as nothing more than a campy cult flick to view while stoned and to titter at.

Explain the effects in general terms, to create an impression. When

Adam, who is eight, asked me what cocaine was, I put it this way: "It's a white powder that comes from the coca plant. . . ." Taking down a book from our home library, I showed him what it looks like and summed up its origins in a sentence: that it was developed for medicinal purposes, "to ease pain," but that some people began using it for fun because they thought it made all their problems go away.

In another book containing an illustration of the human body, I pointed out the central nervous system. "When I do this to you"—and I pinched him on his big toe—"the pain you feel isn't really in your toe, it occurs in your brain. It travels there along a network of nerves"—again indicating the illustration—"which are like tiny wires connecting your brain to the rest of your body.

"Now, if I were to squeeze the big toe of a person on cocaine, he wouldn't feel the pain as much because his brain never got the message. The drug blocked it from traveling along the wire and into the brain. Do you understand so far?"

Detailing the adverse physical and psychological consequences of drugs is important—kids should know how substance use can harm them—but even more meaningful is addressing the reasons people drink and ingest chemicals. A parent's number one priority is to help shape his child's attitude about drugs, not necessarily to turn him into a walking medical encyclopedia.

Continuing our discussion about cocaine, I said to Adam, "Some people use drugs so that they don't have to feel pain. I don't mean physical pain, but the kind you feel inside when you're unhappy or upset." And I asked my son if he remembered how awful he felt after being teased by some older neighborhood boys. Always try employing examples they can see, such as an illustration; one they can feel, like my toe-squeezing demonstration; an emotion they have experienced—in general, something applicable to their lives, something comprehensible to them.

"Unfortunately, we can't always avoid feeling pain. Sometimes, in fact, it's even good for us. Pain may feel bad, but it is not necessarily a bad thing.

"What is bad is that when people take a drug to get rid of their unhappiness, the drug wears off and the pain comes back. Only now it feels worse because the person has never bothered to fix the problem. So he takes more of the drug. Eventually, he no longer knows how to feel good, to smile, to have fun without it.

"And if he uses cocaine enough times, it begins to gnaw away at his body like mice eating cheese. The drug doesn't even make him feel better, but by then he can't stop using it."

The entire discussion should take no more than five minutes, as kids can only retain so much. A few days later, a week later, whenever, you bring it up again.

"Say, Adam? Remember the other day when you asked me about cocaine and what it does?" And I'll review briefly what we had talked about before advancing his understanding some more. "I remembered another effect of the drug. Cocaine is very expensive. Now, there are fathers—just like me—who use the drug all the time. They can't quit. And they spend so much money on cocaine that one day maybe someone comes and takes away the family car because the payments haven't been made on it; or maybe they and their family have to move out of their home because they can't afford to live there anymore. Sounds pretty frightening, doesn't it?"

Make the issue seem tangible. Remember that to most kids under thirteen *drug abuse* is still an abstract concept. Relatively few have experimented with chemicals, and only a minority have been negatively affected by them—or know anyone who has. Whenever the media, so saturated with drug-related news, reports on a celebrity's substance-abuse problem, I call it to my sons' attention ("Know what I just saw on TV?"; "Know what I read yesterday?"). They see how tragedies triggered by drugs and alcohol befall *real* people, many of whom they are aware of or idolize. For thousands of kids, including my avid sports-fan son Seth, the cocaine-connected deaths of two young men, college basketball star Len Bias and NFL footballer Don Rogers, powerfully brought home the ugly reality of drug abuse.

In addition, many rock musicians whose images are regularly beamed into your home by way of music-video channels have openly admitted to serious drug and alcohol addictions, including such well-known names as Keith Richards, Ozzy Osbourne, Eric Clapton, and David Crosby. Point out to your child that none of these stars advocates taking drugs or looks back fondly on his days as an abuser. Without exception, they say that drugs nearly ruined their lives and almost put them in their graves. These popular figures' public disclosures can impact greatly on kids.

Another valuable technique is to relate any personal experiences you've had with substances. Don't worry, it won't make them think, *Since Mom and Dad once did it, it's okay for me too.* If anything it seems to establish credibility with them—especially those convinced their parents think grass is something that needs mowing every weekend. For instance, in discussing the risks associated with alcohol abuse, I told my sons a true story about a childhood buddy of mine, Kenny. When my friends and I were seventeen we snuck into a bar and drank ourselves into a stupor. Kenny, who was a bit of a wise guy to begin with, picked a fight with another intoxicated kid, went outside, got punched, and was so drunk that he lost his balance and struck his head on the pavement. He died the next day. Just like that.

"We all wanted to drink to be cool," I told my kids. "But it didn't feel real cool when Kenny died. And none of us felt real cool a few days later at his funeral."

Naturally I am not proud of my past, but admitting the mistakes I made as a young man impresses upon my sons how substance dependency can afflict anyone, even so-called respectable people. Like their dad. "But why did you take drugs?" Seth wanted to know.

"At the time, I needed to get high because I didn't like myself enough to face the world without drugs, and I lacked the courage to confront my problems. I was miserable all of the time. Now my life is good because I'm older, wiser, and don't use drugs anymore. That's why we're having this talk, so that I can help you guys to stay out of the trouble I got into."

One evening I said to them soberly, "You know, if I hadn't gotten off drugs, you guys might not have had me as a father." And Adam replied brightly, "Well, Dad, just look at it this way: If we hadn't gotten you, we would have gotten someone else."

OTHER APPROACHES

Ask questions of youngsters rather than fire off fact after fact as if giving a board-meeting presentation. You're watching TV with your child; a news report comes on about a young bicyclist killed by an intoxicated motorist; ask him how severe a penalty he thinks the drunk driver should suffer. "It's bad enough," you say, "that people who drink or use drugs slowly kill themselves, but as you can see, they endanger others' lives as well. You'll be receiving your driver's license next year, and I know that you're too smart to ever get behind the wheel drunk." Notice how the last remark is delivered as a compliment of his common sense, not as an accusation: "You better not be so stupid, or I'll never loan you the car."

If you initiate a conversation about drugs, and your youngster cuts you off with, "Oh, I know about that stuff already," counter with, "Really? Tell me about it. Maybe you can teach *me* something." Then go ahead and launch into the subject anyway. "It's not going to hurt you to hear it again. Maybe you don't know everything about drugs; *I* don't know everything. But I don't need to know every little detail to understand that drugs are bad for you."

Take your teenager to an open meeting at a nearby drug- or alcohol-rehabilitation program. Most clinics, as part of their community relations, have nights where parents and children can listen to residents in treatment volunteer their stories. The benefit is incalculable, as adolescents hear young men and women their own age describe lives ravaged by substance abuse. You'll benefit from the visit too, expanding your insights into teenagers and what drives them to alcohol and drugs.

To learn where and when such meetings are held, contact your state agency on alcohol and drug abuse, the address and telephone number of which are in Appendix A. It can refer you to several programs in your area. Call and inquire about their open-house policies.

Inform children not only about the physical dangers of drugs and alcohol but the legal ramifications as well. They should know the penalties for possession, trafficking, driving while intoxicated, and vehicular manslaughter. How sobering for a fifteen-year-old to learn that a first-time offender caught with a small amount of cocaine could be imprisoned for two to ten years in Oklahoma, two to fifteen in Georgia, and four to eight in Colorado. Or that in New York the mandatory *minimum* sentence for selling two ounces of cocaine is fifteen years to life; in Pennsylvania, between five and ten years; and in Massachusetts, between three and fifteen years. Or that first-time drunk-driving offenders are subject to heavy fines, license suspension, or jail terms.

DON'T SIMPLY TELL THEM TO SAY NO, TEACH THEM HOW

Kids sometimes capitulate to peer pressure to drink and to drug because no one ever taught them how to say no. Parents must provide them with those refusal skills and coach them until spurning offers of chemicals becomes a reflex action.

In other words, advice to "just say no" is not nearly enough preparation. Though a great beginning to teaching antidrug awareness, those three words constitute an effective motto but not a thorough manner of turning someone down. Because when a child just says no, the person proffering the joint or the bottle usually responds, "No? Why not?" Drug and alcohol users are always looking to recruit others as a way for them to reconcile the fact that handling substances is wrong. They can be more insistent than solicitors at airports, so if a child hasn't been taught a rejoinder, or if his no is tentative, all too often his resistance is worn down, and he ultimately says yes.

It's hard for kids to decline getting high, because the offers generally come from their friends, not from anonymous drug pushers in dark shades and cream-colored Cadillacs. California seventh-, ninth-, and eleventh-graders, asked to list in order where most students get their drugs, responded "school," "parties," "friends outside school," then "dealers." Only 7% of the seventh-graders, 14% of the ninth-graders, and 21% of the eleventh-graders said dealers were their primary drug source. And who are the dealers? Very often their friends' older siblings.

One-third of the surveyed eleventh-graders claimed they usually used drugs at social gatherings, where the sharing of a joint can take on as much symbolism as the ancient Indian peace pipe—a sort of sacrament. To say no, therefore, can brand a kid not just an outcast but a veritable heretic. As Carl, a New York City teenager, found out, turning down a friend can be tantamount to an insult.

"I lived on the same block for eight years, and all my friends got into drugs," he says. "One of my best friends offered me angel dust once, and I said no thanks. He got so upset, it placed our friendship in jeopardy. So I gave in. I just couldn't say no to a friend."

Adds Elyse: "Sometimes I'd stop getting high for a month or so, but then my friends would come over, light up a joint, do some dust, and say to me, 'Aw, c'mon, that's not like you, to not get high. We know you better than that.' They'd just keep working on me until finally I couldn't stand it anymore."

When tutoring your child to say no, explain that you understand how difficult it can be. Comfort him with an anecdote from your own experience about resisting peer pressure. Tell him, "I can't pretend that not going with the flow is simple; it's not. But it *is* worth it. You won't always have to live with those other kids, but you will have to live with yourself."

WAYS TO SAY NO

Saying no doesn't have to be accompanied by self-righteousness. So long as your kid can decline graciously, it doesn't matter if he converts a soul to his antidrug position.

The Just Say No clubs use a three-step refusal technique:

Step One: Figure out if what your friend wants to do is okay.

Other children don't always state explicitly, "Hey, wanna smoke pot?" Such invitations are often couched in suggestions such as, "Hey, wanna hang out with us in the woods?" Help your child to identify situations that are likely to lead to trouble: friends' propositions to loiter in out-of-the-way areas or abandoned buildings; attending parties in the homes of strangers; or fraternizing with older crowds. Whenever he finds himself in that type of circumstance he should ask, "What will we do there?" and "Are we allowed to be there?"

And he should ask himself, "Do my parents allow me to go there?", "What would they think?", and "Is doing this going to make me feel bad inside?"

Step Two: If it is wrong, say no.

Once your child deduces that what his peers propose is wrong for him, a firm but friendly "No thanks" should be his immediate response, followed by:

Step Three: Turn around the peer pressure and suggest other things to do instead.

"No thanks. I'm going to the movies. Want to come along?"

I don't advocate that kids be encouraged to lie; for example, pretending to drink along with friends at a party by putting orange juice and ice in a glass and christening it a screwdriver. They should learn to feel pride in having the courage of their convictions and that it's *cool* to stand up for what you believe in. However, one saying-no technique other kids will usually accept, nodding in sympathy, is: "My parents would ground me for the rest of my life." If it helps your child to stand his ground, let him go ahead and make you the villains.

Some other recommendations include:

- Say no repeatedly. "Wanna drink?" "No thanks." "C'mon!" "No thanks." "Not even a sip?" "Nope."
- Allude to the dangerous side effects. "No. I know drugs are bad for me. I'm not interested."

- Change the subject. "No thanks. By the way, are you going to Janice's party Saturday night?"
- Return the challenge. "What's wrong? Scared to do it by yourself?"
- Use reverse peer pressure. "Drugs are boring. I can't believe you need to do that stuff."
- Base an excuse on an activity. "I can't drink; I'm in training for football," or, "I can't go with you; I have a dance recital coming up and have to practice."
- Simply give the person the cold shoulder; ignore him.
- If in a situation where drugs or alcohol are being used, hang around with nonusers.
- And if the pressure seems too threatening, walk away.

Refusals can be handled affably, with good humor. Help develop your child's ability to say no confidently by role-playing pressure-filled situations with him. In role playing, you—or better yet, a sibling—portray someone cajoling him to drink or drug. Simulate a confrontation your youngster is likely to face. Repeat role playing until his responses seem natural and self-assured.

Another scenario to role-play is, What to do with a driver who is intoxicated. According to a Gallup poll, one-third of all teenagers admit they have been in a car with a driver their age who was impaired by alcohol or drugs.

A child should know that he can call home at any time and receive a ride home if he is marooned with a driver who is drunk—or if he is intoxicated himself. Draw up an informal contract, whereby he pledges to phone for advice or transportation, and parents promise to pick him up or pay for a taxi at any hour, from any place. Additionally, parents give their word not to discuss the issue until the following day. However, in implementing such an agreement, state explicitly that it is not to be interpreted as consent to get blasted. Drinking—or hanging out with others who are drinking—is still unacceptable.

But with alcohol-related auto accidents the number one killer of fifteen-to-twenty-four-year-olds, it is a sensible agreement. It may be in a kid's best interest to pay the price for drinking or using drugs—and he will, through your stricter discipline—but not when it costs him his life.

SCHOOLS AND DRUG EDUCATION

For every couple that depends on the school system to educate their child about drugs, there is another that believes only they should provide any form of moral guidance. Kids benefit most, however, when both parents *and* trained instructors support one another in a double-barreled prevention program.

The one-on-one sessions you have with your youngster at home are indispensable, but so is a classroom setting in which he learns about drugs in the company of his peers. Not only is school where kids spend half their waking hours, it is a marketplace for drug deals and use: According to a survey conducted by the national Cocaine Hotline, 57% of the teenage respondents bought drugs there. And a poll of 1986 high-school students revealed that 33% smoked marijuana and 60% took amphetamines while on school grounds.

Like most drug-treatment professionals, I am an ardent advocate of in-school drug-prevention curriculums. Yet to date there is little foundation for optimism regarding their influence on students. In 1980 the National Institute on Drug Abuse commissioned a study of 127 drug-ed courses and found only "minor effects" on youthful attitudes—drug habits. But to place its conclusion into perspective, most programs back then would have received an F grade.

Where did early drug ed go wrong? For one thing, it was introduced to young people far too late, usually in high school. By then an overwhelming majority of them had drank alcohol and nearly half had tried marijuana. Because their outlook on drugs had already been molded, warnings about abuse's hazards frequently sailed in one ear and out the other.

Plus, many teachers' credentials were suspect. They were often health instructors with a limited command of the subject matter or a delivery verging on hysterical. Either way, students invested little faith in the source and the information. Other problems, based on a report by the *Journal of School Health,* included

- emphasizing drug knowledge but not drug attitudes;
- failing to address the reality that drugs can make people feel good—something already known by many adolescents and an omission that further crippled educators' credibility;
- failing to show children that the decision-making principles and skills learned in class could be applied in real life;

95

- the lack of a system for rating program methods and effectiveness—a perennial shortcoming.

(If your child's school is currently casting about for a quality drug-ed course, refer to Appendix C, which lists several carefully assessed and highly recommended by Just Say No Foundation president William T. Adams.)

Responding to the woeful state of in-school drug prevention, Congress voted in September 1986 to spend $150 million on instructional programs, while Secretary of Education William J. Bennett proposed guidelines to rid schools of drugs. Parents can receive a free copy of the U.S. Department of Education's informative eighty-page booklet *What Works: Schools Without Drugs* by calling (800) 624-0100. Anticipate four to six weeks for delivery.

The heart of Bennett's antidrug strategy is to expand education beyond the classroom, involving parents, teachers, police, and students. National Institute on Drug Abuse director Dr. Charles Shuster concurs, saying, "A drug-abuse curriculum in school isn't going to have much impact if kids go home to a different set of values, if teachers' attitudes about drugs are inappropriate, or if police do not crack down adequately on drug traffickers." It takes joint action.

From the "Schools Without Drugs: The Challenge" campaign, and incorporating my own thoughts, the steps below make up an ideal school policy and program for administrators to follow.

Research the Problem

- Conduct anonymous surveys of students and teachers in order to gauge the extent of the problem.

- Mail copies of the survey, including a clearly worded assessment of the problem, to community members.

- Have school personnel indicate where on campus drugs and alcohol are routinely purchased and used.

Develop a Policy

- The policy is simple: No drug use, possession, or sale is tolerated on school grounds at any time, including after class and on weekends. Sometimes kids seem to regard Friday-night dances and Saturday-afternoon football games as oases from prosecution for drugging and drinking. This rule applies to faculty members as well.

● Notify in writing all students, parents, and teachers about the policy. The memo clarifies what constitutes a drug offense, defines illegal substances and paraphernalia, and outlines the school's jurisdiction. Under the Comprehensive Crime Control Act of 1984, drug sales within one thousand feet of school property constitute a federal crime punishable by up to double the sentence that would otherwise apply.

Also describe the procedures for handling violations, including legal issues, confidentiality, due process, search and seizure, notification of parents when a child is suspected of use or is caught with substances, and notification of the police.

Though this probably will not endear me to the American Civil Liberties Union, in schools where drug use is known to exist, I believe in random locker searches. They are legal, stated a 1985 Supreme Court decision, if officials have reasonable grounds to suspect that a student's locker contains an illegal substance.

The secretary of education recommends that first-time violators' parents be called in to meet with school officials and to sign a contract acknowledging their child's drug problem. The youngster, meanwhile, agrees not to use drugs and to participate in a counseling or rehabilitation program. More severe measures, depending on the seriousness of the infraction, include suspension, in-school suspension, assignment to an alternative school, or Saturday detention with close supervision and rigorous academic assignments. Additionally, the child may be reported to the police.

Repeat offenders are subject to expulsion, legal action, and referral to treatment.

● Before instituting the policy, enlist legal counsel to ensure that it complies with federal, state, and local laws, and obtain appropriate insurance coverage for protection against lawsuits filed in response to disciplinary actions.

Enforce the Policy

● Based on the problem's magnitude, increase school security. If drug use is rampant, guards bar nonstudents from school grounds and patrol for trafficking. Request police assistance if necessary.

Implement a Curriculum

● Start antidrug education in kindergarten and continue through twelfth grade. Encourage teachers other than health instructors to touch on the subject when relevant, such as in the aftermath of a student drug bust or overdose.

● Further contributing to a more multidimensional program, occasionally bring in local physicians, psychiatrists, drug counselors, ex-abusers, and police as speakers and arrange field trips to drug-rehabilitation facilities and police stations.

● To help coordinate home and school education, distribute drug literature to parents, or hold adult evening-hour classes.

● Hire trained drug counselors, preferably one for each school in the district. If financially infeasible, one counselor should rotate among the different levels. An alternative is to train one or more members of the guidance-counseling staff.

● Instruct teachers on the signs of abuse so that they can report instances of children asleep at their desks or exhibiting other obvious drug-induced behaviors.

● Enlist student volunteers for teaching drug awareness to younger kids. All participants benefit, as the older youngsters take part in a creative program that helps to build their self-esteem. As an example, at Riverside High School in El Paso, Texas, students conceive and produce slide-show presentations for the lower grades. Antidrug education doesn't just have to be for kids, it can be *by* kids.

● Coordinate the school with the county youth board, which generally sponsors a variety of free programs. These include recreational and cultural activities, job placement, and counseling. Unfortunately, children and parents are frequently unaware of the resources available to them. The school should obtain literature from the youth board to distribute to its students, and teachers should encourage kids to utilize the services.

● Coordinate the school with the local business community to help provide summer and after-school jobs for students.

Once a policy on curriculum, penalties, and enforcement is implemented, parents and teachers meet periodically to evaluate its effectiveness.

To that end, the school maintains records of verified drug use and sales over a period of time.

Schools such as Phoenix's Greenway Middle School and Annapolis, Maryland's Anne Arundel County School adopted similarly tough pro-education and antidrug policies. Drug offenses declined by 90% and 60%, respectively, over the course of six years. Other institutions have reported to the U.S. Department of Education similarly positive results, as well as significant improvements in scholastic performance.

Of course, few of these recommendations for quality drug-prevention programs come without a price tag attached. Yes, your school taxes are likely to increase. But isn't a future generation of more productive, drug-free young adults worth it? Especially when you consider how communities victimized by drug abuse are taxed in other ways, such as through increased crime rates, vandalism, and so on.

PARENTS CAN—AND SHOULD—GET INVOLVED

In areas where school boards have proved unresponsive to youthful drug abuse, concerned mothers and fathers have mobilized to form parents groups. Surmounting bureaucratic inertia, however, is just one purpose of these organizations, founded on the premise that in numbers there is strength. They began springing up in the mid-1970s, and since then thousands of parents have pooled ideas and energy to bring about local, even national, change.

For example, Mothers Against Drunk Driving (MADD)—started in 1980 by Candy Lightner, whose thirteen-year-old daughter Cari was killed by a drink driver—has campaigned aggressively and successfully for passage of tougher drunk-driving laws. The National Federation of Parents for Drug-Free Youth, established that same year as a parents network with the assistance and support of Nancy Reagan as honorary chairman, has done an outstanding job of spreading drug awareness. Today there are more than seven thousand parents groups nationwide having to do with drug abuse among American youth.

I am certainly a proponent of parents groups but must stress that joining them in no way takes the place of time spent with one's child, for ultimately the crusade against drugs will be won at home. Groups are essential in helping parents share experiences, feelings, and ideas with others.

Parents groups usually consist of between four and twelve adults, and meet once a month in houses of worship, schools, or other facilities generally receptive to accommodating these kinds of fellowships. Members can also take turns holding meetings in their homes. It goes without saying that no alcohol is to be served.

Some of the constructive goals of parents groups include

- sharing drug-education materials;
- working together to coordinate curfews and party rules;
- pressuring schools to institute drug-prevention programs adhering to the standards set by the secretary of education, and supporting administrators who are firmly antidrug;
- petitioning local government to develop and promote more youth programs;
- pressuring bars into stopping the practice of serving alcohol to under-age children;
- if necessary, urging police to more actively patrol public parks and other areas where drug abuse and sales occur regularly.

Groups do not have to be affiliated with any existing, national organization, nor do they have to be formal. The meetings I have with my neighbors are conducted casually in backyards or at kids' scheduled activities, where we compare notes on our youngsters' behavior, discussing not only drugs but other child-related problems as well.

WILL TODAY'S EDUCATION ENSURE A DRUG-FREE TOMORROW?

Though dedicated educators have been laboring for years to improve drug-prevention programs, *quality* drug prevention is still in its infancy, so it is hard to say. However, new studies have turned up encouraging signs. Of California eleventh-grade students requested to evaluate recently completed drug-ed courses, less than 3% responded negatively, and 41% responded positively. As for what impact the programs had on them and on ninth-graders, their self-reports showed that after having participated in the programs, they were more likely to

- avoid alcohol or reduce consumption:
  grade nine, 37%, grade eleven, 37%;

- avoid other drug use or reduce consumption:
  grade nine, 29%, grade eleven, 33%;
- resist pressure from others to drink or use drugs:
  grade nine, 32%; grade eleven, 35%;
- avoid driving under the influence:
  grade nine, 28%; grade eleven, 41%.

Only 8% of the ninth-graders and 6% of the eleventh-graders claimed that drug education had no influence on their behavior, while 32% and 31%, respectively, said they had already decided not to use drugs or alcohol.

One way to estimate the effect today's drug prevention will have on tomorrow's young adults is to look at the correlation between the increased awareness of marijuana's dangers and the downward trend in use.

In 1975, 43% of high-school seniors believed regular marijuana smoking posed a great health risk; 6% were daily users. Eleven years later, the figures were 71% and 4%. The same relationship holds true for those who thought even occasional use posed a great risk: Between 1979 and 1986, recognition of the dangers rose from 14% to 25%, while occasional use dropped from 51% to 39%. Of course, some of those marijuana smokers probably gave up grass in favor of harder substances such as cocaine.

But, on an optimistic note, look at the responses of fourth- through twelfth-grade students asked by the *Weekly Reader* to outline their own effective strategy for stemming drug abuse:

- Teach us the facts about substances, in school and at home.
- Have television broadcast more programs about drugs' and alcohol's dangers.
- Parents: Discuss our problems with us.

I'll go along with that. After all, who knows more about what they need than the children themselves?

KEY POINTS

- Because the average age of first use is currently twelve for alcohol and thirteen for drugs, begin antidrug education as early as possible: at five years, even four.

• Marijuana is an example of a drug once thought to be safe by segments of the medical and psychological communities. Today we know better. Hence the importance of obtaining only current material from which to learn. Conservatively speaking, avoid books and pamphlets that are more than five years old.

• Do you know what vials, bongs, cocaine kits, and roach clips look like? If not, go to a smoke shop and familiarize yourself with these and other drug paraphernalia.

• Tobacco, alcohol, and marijuana are gateway drugs—those with which youths typically start. Studies have shown that all can contribute to further drug use, indirectly or otherwise.

• Mistakes parents make:

1. "I'd rather have my child drink or smoke pot at home, supervised, than out on the street."
2. "If drugs and alcohol are no longer taboo, youngsters soon tire of them."
3. "Drugs and alcohol are acceptable in moderation."

These flawed philosophies frequently backfire. No drug use should be permissible. Enter that stipulation in your Family Contract.

• What to say, how to say it:

1. Never lecture. Lectures are associated with punishment.
2. Don't formally announce, "Let's sit down and talk about drugs." There are countless opportunities to broach the subject casually: watching TV with the kids, listening to the radio, or reading newspapers and magazines.
3. Don't affect the oratorical zeal of a fire-and-brimstome preacher. Let the facts work for you. And speak naturally, employing no incomprehensible psychoanalytic terms and, especially, no kid colloquialisms.
4. If you have children of diverse ages, work with them individually, adapting your language accordingly. Because these are such complex issues, it's always better to overexplain than to underexplain.
5. Incorporate photos, illustrations, films, and videocassettes into your home drug-education program.
6. Don't overwhelm kids with too much information. Explain drugs' effects in general terms, to create an impression.

7. Don't just fire off fact after fact. Ask youngsters questions; get them to open up.
8. Inform children not only about the physical dangers of drugs and alcohol but about the legal ramifications as well.

● Make the issue seem tangible. Remember that to most kids under thirteen, *substance abuse* is still an abstract concept. Call to their attention print articles and TV news reports about lives negatively affected by alcohol or drugs. Let them see that these problems befall real people.

● Take your teenager to an open meeting at a nearby drug- or alcohol-rehabilitation program. Most clinics, as part of their community relations, have nights where parents and children can listen to residents in treatment volunteer their stories.

● Ways of saying no to substances:

1. Say no repeatedly.
2. Allude to the dangerous side effects.
3. Change the subject.
4. Return the challenge.
5. Suggest something else to do.
6. Base an excuse on another activity.
7. Use reverse peer pressure.
8. Give the person the cold shoulder.
9. If in a situation where drugs or alcohol are being used, hang around with other nonusers.
10. And if the pressure seems too threatening, walk away.

● Make a contract with your child, whereby you pledge to pick him up or pay for a taxi home if he is marooned with a drunk driver or is too inebriated to operate a vehicle.

RECOMMENDED RESOURCES

For print materials and videotapes on drugs and alcohol (most of which are free), contact:

Families in Action
National Drug Information Center
3845 North Druid Hills Road
Suite 300
Decatur, GA 30033
(404) 325-5799

Just Say No Club Members' Handbook
The Just Say No Foundation
1777 North California Boulevard
Suite 200
Walnut Creek, CA 94596
(800) 258-2766; in California,
   (415) 939-6666

National Clearinghouse for Alcohol
   and Drug Information
P.O. Box 2345
Rockville, MD 20852
(301) 468-2600

National Council on Alcoholism
12 West 21st Street
Seventh Floor
New York, NY 10010
(212) 206-6770

National Council on Alcoholism
1511 K Street N.W.
Washington, DC 20005
(202) 737-8122

National Federation of Parents for
   Drug-Free Youth
8730 Georgia Avenue
Suite 200
Silver Spring, MD 20910
(301) 585-5437
(800) 554-KIDS

National Parents' Resource Institute for
   Drug Education
100 Edgewood Avenue
Suite 1002
Atlanta, GA 30303
(800) 241-7946

Parents' Association to Neutralize Drug
   and Alcohol Abuse
P.O. Box 314
Annandale, VA 22003
(703) 750-9285

What Works: Schools Without Drugs
   (Handbook)
U.S. Department of Education
400 Maryland Avenue S.W.
Washington, D.C. 20202
(800) 624-0100

For free films and videocassettes:

National Institute on Drug Abuse
Free-Loan Collection
U.S. Department of Health and
Human Services
Public Health Service
Alcohol, Drug Abuse and Mental
Health Administration
Rockville, MD 20857

Order through:
Modern Talking Picture Service
Scheduling Center
5000 Park Street North
St. Petersburg, FL 33709
(813) 541-5763

Other sources: Virtually all drug-re-habilitation programs and self-help groups will supply parents with free print information on drugs.

For answers to your questions about alcohol, drugs, and their abuse, contact the following drug-information hotlines:

Cocaine Hotline
(800) COC-AINE

National Federation of Parents for
Drug-Free Youth
(800) 554-KIDS

National Institute on Drug Abuse
Drug-Referral Helpline
(800) 662-HELP

National Parents' Resource Institute for
Drug Education
Drug Information Line
(800) 241-7946

Parents' Association to Neutralize Drug
and Alcohol Abuse
The Listening Ear
(703) 750-9285

Recommended In-School Drug-Prevention Programs:

Alcohol/Drug Program
Archdiocese of Louisville
Office of Catholic Schools
1516 Hepburn Avenue
Louisville, KY 40204
(502) 585-4158

DARE (Drug Abuse Resistance
Education)
Los Angeles Police Department
P.O. Box 30158
Los Angeles, CA 90030
(213) 485-4856

Hampton Intervention and Prevention
Project (HIPP)
Alternatives, Inc.
1520 Aberdeen Road
No. 102
Hampton, VA 23666
(804) 838-2330

"Here's Looking at You, 2000"
(multimedia presentation)
Comprehensive Health Education
Foundation
20832 Pacific Highway South
Seattle, WA 98198
(206) 824-2907

Project Star (Students Taught
Awareness and Resistance)
The Kauffman Foundation and
Marion Laboratories, Inc.
9233 Ward Parkway
Kansas City, MO 64114
(816) 363-8604

Pros for Kids
1710 South Amphlett
Suite 300
San Mateo, CA 94403
(415) 571-6726

REACH America (Responsible
Educated Adolescents Can Help
America {Stop Drugs!})
National Federation of Parents for
Drug-Free Youth
8730 Georgia Avenue
Suite 200
Silver Spring, MD 20910
(301) 585-5437
(800) 554-KIDS

"Say No" to Drugs and Alcohol
City of Tempe, Arizona
1801 East Jen Tilly Lane
Suite C-4
Tempe, AZ 85281
(602) 731-8278

Talking With Your Kids About Alcohol
Talking With Your Students About
Alcohol
Prevention Research Institute, Inc.
629 North Broadway
Suite 210
Lexington, KY 40508
(606) 254-9489

Other sources: For the addresses and
numbers of other in-school substance-
abuse prevention programs, contact the
National Association of State Alcohol
and Drug Abuse Directors (NASA-
DAD), 444 North Capitol Street N.W.,
Suite 520, Washington, DC 20001,
(202) 783-6868.

For free information on how to form or join one of the approximately seven thousand parents support/drug-education groups, contact:

Committees of Correspondence
57 Conant Street
Room 113
Danvers, MA 01923
(617) 774-2641

Families in Action
National Drug Information Center
3845 North Druid Hills Road
Suite 300
Decatur, GA 30033
(404) 325-5799

Informed Networks, Inc.
200 Ramsay Road
Deerfield, IL 60015
(312) 945-5021

Mothers Against Drunk Driving
669 Airport Freeway
Suite 310
Hurst, Texas 76053
(817) 268-MADD

National Clearinghouse for Alcohol
    and Drug Information
P.O. Box 2345
Rockville, MD 20852
(301) 468-2600

National Federation of Parents for
    Drug-Free Youth
8730 Georgia Avenue
Suite 200
Silver Spring, MD 20910
(301) 585-5437
(800) 554-KIDS

National Institute on Drug Abuse
Drug-Referral Helpline
5600 Fishers Lane
Rockville, MD 20857
(800) 662-HELP

National Self-Help Clearinghouse
33 West 42nd Street
Room 620N
New York, NY 10036
(212) 840-1259

Parents' Resource Institute for Drug
    Education (PRIDE)
100 Edgewood Avenue
Suite 1002
Atlanta, GA 30303
(800) 241-7946

Other sources: Contact your state's alcohol and drug abuse agency, the address and telephone number of which are contained in Appendix A.

Intervention

Chapter Five

Where There Is Smoke
There Is Fire:
Identifying Problems

This chapter belongs equally in the **Prevention** and **Intervention** sections. Learning about drugs and their effects prepares you not only to educate your child but to recognize a crisis while it is still a spark and hasn't yet blazed out of control. Unfortunately, it takes most parents *one year* before realizing their youngster has a drug problem, according to the National Parents' Resource Institute for Drug Education.

Substance abusers can do a remarkable job of keeping their habits secret. Only 29% and 46% of 160,000 thirteen-to-eighteen-year-olds surveyed for the book *The Private Life of the American Teenager* said their parents knew they smoked pot and drank alcohol, respectively. For example, by the time Anthony's parents confronted him about his drug problem, he'd been addicted to alcohol, cocaine, and heroin for years. "They didn't have the foggiest idea," he says in a raspy voice. "I was working, saving money, bought a new car. Naturally I was stealing money at my job, but as far as my folks could tell, their son was straight and doing just fine." Should they have noticed the telltale signs? Anthony smiles ruefully. "Of course they should have. I left clues all over the place."

Most drug users do, though not all evidence is as glaring as a smoking gun. Or, for that matter, a smoking joint. You have to be on the lookout for more inconspicuous tip-offs.

PHYSICAL CLUES OF ABUSE

Hard proof such as hidden liquor bottles, drugs, and drug paraphernalia is certainly the most blatant indicator of substance dependency. Therefore, if you have good cause to suspect your youngster of drinking or drugging, don't delay in searching his room. Now, I'm sure the thought of rummaging through a child's belongings goes against most parents' nature. But please note the qualifier: *good cause.* Sometimes kids' privacy has to be violated. Their welfare is at stake. Besides, by disobeying the Family Contract's no-drugs rule, they have forfeited their right to unconditional privacy.

Here is what you look for:

- packets of rolling papers, for smoking marijuana;
- roach clips (also called alligator clips), used for clamping the tiny end of a marijuana butt, or roach, so that it can be puffed without burning one's fingers;
- water pipes, or bongs, which are usually glass and range in size from several inches to over a foot. They are constructed in three sections— pipe, bowl, and water chamber—and are used for smoking hashish, hash oil, and freebase cocaine. Other, more conventional-looking pipes are made of wood, metal, plastic, and paper, with tiny brass screens for filtering out ashes and small particles;
- syringes, for injecting narcotics, cocaine, amphetamines, and barbiturates;
- small spoons, sometimes made of silver or gold, for sniffing powders such as cocaine.

Not all paraphernalia is so exotic. Some are everyday household items, such as

- plastic bags, Baggies, Zip-loc pouches, glassine envelopes, aluminum foil strips, small bottles, boxes, and vials, all used to store, or "stash" marijuana, pills, tablets, capsules, powders, and solutions;
- desktop scales, for weighing marijuana, cocaine, heroin, and other drugs;
- razor blades, used to cut drugs such as cocaine, blocks of hashish, pills, and tablets;
- kitchen spoons and bottle caps burnt black on the bottom, in which narcotics and/or other substances have been cooked over a flame;

- blood-stained pieces of cotton, indicative of intravenous-drug use;
- over-the-counter eye drops for clearing bloodshot eyes;
- containers of rubbing alcohol, used to sterilize needles and to rub on skin abscesses;
- butane lighters and matches, for heating narcotics and other substances; also for lighting pipes, joints, cigarettes.

When children use drugs, you have to be equally cognizant of disappearing medicines and missing or half-empty liquor bottles. Maintain careful inventory. Know how many bottles of liquor you have, marking levels on the back of each with a grease pencil. Count the number of pills in a bottle. Better yet, install locks on both medicine and liquor cabinets.

Tabs should also be kept on the amount of money left in wallets and purses. Drugs are expensive, and a youngster with a habit to support thinks nothing of stealing—especially from his own parents. If he were to get caught, is the user's reasoning, what mother or father would prosecute his or her own flesh and blood?

Another thing to look for is burn holes on clothing and furniture from dropped joints and from marijuana seeds, which "pop" when hot.

Identifying signs of drug and alcohol abuse requires using your nose as well as your eyes. Sniff around, literally, for marijuana's and hashish's sweet aromas; the acrid odor of burnt cooking implements; the pungency of sulfur from spent matches; incense and room deodorizers, for masking smells of alcohol and smoke; and mouthwash on your youngster's breath, for covering up alcohol, pot, and hashish.

BEHAVIORAL CLUES OF ABUSE

In the **Prevention** section we emphasize the importance of minding your child and paying attention to deviations in his behavior. Intervention is no different. Of course, with kids it can be problematic determining if changes such as moodiness, rebelliousness, and withdrawal denote substance abuse or simple adolescent growing pains.

Whenever a youngster of drug-vulnerable age seems to be acting peculiarly—or he just doesn't seem "like himself"—jot down in a notepad your impression and what triggered it. Then date the entry. This way, if the unusual conduct reoccurs you can at least rest assured your imagination is not playing tricks on you. Here are some common hints of trouble for parents to heed:

113

Long periods spent in the bathroom: When I was drug dependent, I practically took up permanent residence there. The clatter of paraphernalia being assembled on the counter could be conveniently drowned out by the splashing of running water and the hum of the exhaust fan, which additionally cleared marijuana smoke. Plus, a locking door ensured relative privacy.

Sudden, unexplained availability of money: Occasionally compute the approximate totals of your child's allowance and, if applicable, salary from a part-time job. Estimate how much cash he should have on hand, or flip through his bankbook if you believe he is engaged in drug use. Extravagant and/or frequent expenditures may be a sign that besides cutting lawns or washing cars for minimum wage he is moonlighting as a drug dealer. According to a survey of teenage users conducted by the national Cocaine Hotline, 42% of the respondents admitted to selling substances, while 62% admitted to buying them—often with their school lunch money.

Secretive behavior: Some withdrawal is normal for adolescents, but drug-using kids spend inordinate amounts of time either locked in their rooms or roaming the streets. They whisper on the telephone, volunteer little information about their whereabouts and daily agenda, or provide *too much* circumstantial information.

Changes in friends and hangouts: Once I started using chemicals, other abusers became the only people to whom I could relate. Straights were squares incapable of understanding me or my need for drugs. And if I couldn't convert them at once to my new religion, I thought, the hell with them. As time went on and my use grew worse, my social circle became even more stratified to include heavy drug users only.

When a child is involved with drugs and the drug crowd, pay attention to new, nameless faces slipping through the front door—often at odd hours for clandestine drug deals. In the past your youngster may have customarily introduced you to his friends, but now he seems reluctant to bring them home. If you ask about them, he is evasive, knowing you would probably disapprove. The few times they do loiter in the front hallway, waiting for your kid, they tend to be standoffish. On the phone, they rarely identify themselves to you.

Mercurial mood changes: Substance users' emotional control has been abandoned to chemicals. They may appear hypersensitive, unusually antagonistic, resentful of all authority, irritable, even violent. When the subject of drugs is brought up, they are often unsuitably defensive and seem to anticipate your questions.

Irresponsibility at home and at school: Drug users neglect household chores and other obligations. They'll forget your wedding anniversary or disappear the day of an important family occasion. They'll lie chronically. A most telling sign of substance abuse is a noticeable decline in academic performance. U.S. Department of Education research shows that marijuana users are twice as likely to average Ds and Fs as nonusers; in another study, it reports, drug-abusing high-school seniors were more than three times as likely to skip school as abstainers.

Kids seriously under the influence will disregard flagrantly all rules, break curfews, clash with school and possibly law-enforcement officials, and drive recklessly. Thirteen percent of teens polled by the Cocaine Hotline had been involved in car accidents.

Preoccupation with drugs: Though he denies ever handling substances himself, a drug-abusing child's conversation and jokes are liberally littered with drug references. T-shirts, wall posters, and car bumper stickers bearing prodrug slogans are also clues to take note of.

Deteriorating health and physical appearance: Typically, dress and hygiene become sloppy, eyes are often bloodshot, droopy lidded, with dilated pupils; skin tone is wan and pallid. Children on drugs may exhibit decreased appetite and considerable weight loss, except for marijuana smokers, who are afflicted with the notorious munchies—a craving for food, particularly sweets—and sometimes put on pounds. Other common medical problems: infections, digestive and respiratory disorders, high susceptibility to flus and lingering colds, plus bumps and bruises incurred in falls.

Loss of ambition: Generally speaking, drug use encourages passivity. As stated by famed researchers Helen C. Jones, and the late Dr. Hardin B. Jones, when taken in large doses or frequently for a long period of time, *all* psychoactive drugs "produce toxic changes in the brain that are detectable on microscopic examination." Hard-core users generally suffer impairments such as long- and/or short-term memory lapses, limited attention span, poor concentration, and slurred, incoherent speech.

The aforementioned behavioral changes may unfold over the course of several months or more than a year, usually advancing in four stages that have been called "experimental," "casual," "progressive," and "terminal." The second and fourth are misnomers, since "casual" implies there is such a thing as a "casual" drug-related problem, and with quality professional drug treatment, few addictions are "terminal."

For our purposes, we'll simply refer to them as stages one through four.

Stage One

Drugs used include:
 tobacco
 alcohol
 marijuana
 inhalants

Behavior and attitude toward drugs:
 Motivated by peer pressure and curiosity, a stage-one child indulges occasionally but never purchases his own substances. Though drugs play no significant role in his life, he learns that moods can be elevated through chemicals. No behavorial changes are evident as of yet, and most experimental users give up drugs altogether.

Stage Two

Drugs used include:
 tobacco
 alcohol
 marijuana
 inhalants
 hashish
 amphetamines
 barbiturates

Behavior and attitude toward drugs:
 A stage-two child gets intoxicated more frequently, usually at weekend social gatherings or during school holidays and summer vacations. His use is not premeditated, and he does not go out of his way to find substances. Because he has yet to suffer any serious physical or psychological effects, he believes he can quit drugs or alcohol at any time; possibly a serious miscalculation. Stage three has already begun.

Stage Three

Drugs used include:
 tobacco
 alcohol
 marijuana
 hashish

amphetamines
barbiturates
cocaine
crack
hallucinogens

Behavior and attitude toward drugs:
Drug *abuse* as opposed to drug *use*. The key difference is that the stage-three child actively seeks to alter his mood believing comfort and pleasure are derivable only through chemicals. His emotions are of extreme highs and lows, with no middle ground. He gets stoned by himself, including during the week, and goes out of his way to procure substances. Most significantly, he has developed tolerance to and psychological dependence on certain drugs.

Grooming and schoolwork decline, friendships change, family relationships sour as he becomes secretive and alienated. Drugs and their attendant culture occupy a great deal of the stage-three kid's time and thoughts. He becomes careless about his habit, perhaps forgetting to conceal substances, paraphernalia. He denies vehemently having a problem.

Stage Four

Drugs used include:
All of the above plus:
heroin and other opiates

Behavior and attitude toward drugs:
A stage-four youngster's condition deteriorates drastically. He is now psychologically and/or physically dependent on substances and desperately needs higher doses just to feel "normal." The bulk of his time is spent getting hold of and using drugs, and he cannot kick his addiction without professional treatment. Friends are exclusively other users, and home life becomes a shambles, marred by constant arguments and running away. A stage-four abuser has usually flunked or dropped out of school; cannot hold a job, so he steals or deals; and is beset by guilt and feelings of worthlessness. He may suffer from blackouts, impaired memory, flashbacks, frequent illness, suicidal thoughts, overdose.

TODAY'S DRUGS OF CHOICE AND THEIR EFFECTS

Drugs act on the body in different ways, with each individual experiencing a unique reaction. You probably know someone who can "hold his liquor" and someone else who is a "one-beer drunk." When educating your child, that is an important point to stress: No one ever knows if he has high or low tolerance to substances until the damage is done.

Tolerance means the point at which the body requires more of a drug to achieve the same high. *Psychological dependence* refers to the state of compulsive use, where drugs are taken to stop from feeling bad mentally. Kids who develop psychological dependence think they cannot manage without chemicals. Should they become *physically dependent*, their bodies can no longer function without drugs and, when deprived of them, plunge addicts into the physiological trauma called withdrawal.

The difference between the latter two is primarily a matter of semantics; either way, alcohol or drugs have become the center of a child's life. Even after suffering adverse physical and emotional consequences, he still craves getting high. The person who can no longer stop himself is an addict.

Even if you have firsthand drug experience, it is imperative to stay informed of the ever-changing drug culture. Like fashion and the arts, substances go in and out of style. To illustrate, since 1980 methaqualone use has dropped dramatically, while cocaine has surged in popularity.

In the 1960s young people searched for an alternative to the culture at large, which was reflected in their enthusiasm for mind-altering hallucinogens such as LSD. In the 1970s mind expansion gave way to mind mollification, through soothing, hypnotic sedatives. In the 1980s the favored drugs reflect our cultural obsession with competition and status-consciousness. Near the top of the chemical hit parade are those drugs that facilitate—or seem to facilitate—performance: stimulants such as coke, which is also a "prestige" drug, viewed as a symbol of success in certain circles; even by some young children.

America's preferred substances in 1987, according to polled high-school seniors were

alcohol: 86%
tobacco (figure not available)
marijuana and hashish: 36%
stimulants: 12% (including amphetamines, methamphetamines, dextroamphetamines, others)

cocaine: 10%, crack: 4%

inhalants: 8% (including amyl and butyl nitrite)

hallucinogens: 7% (including LSD, PCP, mescaline, peyote, psilocybin, others)

opiates other than heroin: 5% (including codeine, meperidine, opium, methadone, others)

sedative-hypnotics: 4% (including barbiturates and methaqualone); tranquilizers: 6%

heroin: 1%

ALCOHOL

Looks like: beer, wine, wine coolers, distilled spirits; comes in cans, bottles and cartons.

Look for: the smell of alcohol or mouthwash on your child's breath; red, yellowish, or glassy eyes; puffy face; cold and clammy skin; slurred speech; intoxicated, disoriented behavior; and hangovers, which are characterized by headache, nausea, extreme sensitivity to light and sound, thirst, and exhaustion.

Related paraphernalia: bottles, cans, and cartons; phony I.D. cards for purchasing liquor.

Method of ingestion: taken orally.

More California ninth- and eleventh-grade students reported their first intoxication came from alcohol than from all illicit drugs combined. Statistically, teenagers imbibe nearly as much as adults, with one in twenty high-school seniors drinking *every day.*

Ironically, adolescent boozing has accelerated over the last two decades, even with so much attention focused on the "drug" problem. Our society tends to view alcohol as somehow separate from other drugs; in fact, some parents are actually relieved to discover their kids are "only" tipping the bottle and not smoking pot or swallowing pills. But alcohol is a drug, a depressant, and causes more deaths among young people than any other substance. You might say that liquor differs from other substances only in that it is legal, cheap, and relatively easy to get—even for minors—thus making it all the more dangerous.

Its active ingredient is ethyl alcohol, or ethanol, produced by fermentation. Remove the water from ethyl alcohol and you wind up with ether, an anesthetic that essentially puts the brain to sleep. To "overdose" on alcohol is to become drunk, which is dependent on body size, the proof (percentage of alcohol), the quantity consumed, how fast it is washed down, the amount of food in the stomach, environment, past drinking experiences, and the drinker's frame of mind.

Immediate Effects

Though alcohol slows down the central nervous system, it is as likely to energize some persons as it is to sedate others. When taken in small amounts—approximately six ounces—it can suppress anxiety, inspire self-confidence, and induce feelings of tranquility. However, as someone drinks more, the initial euphoria is reversed, and depression may ensue. The liver can metabolize only one ounce per sixty minutes, so more than one or two drinks in an hour will generally cause inebriation.

In order, alcohol affects

- the digestive system, especially the liver, which must process 90% of the alcohol, the remainder being disposed of through sweat, breath, and urine;
- the circulatory system. Blood vessels enlarge, generating a warm, flushed feeling, though body temperature in fact lowers;
- the brain, depressing mainly its right hemisphere, which controls thought, recognition of textures and shapes, and space between objects. Speech, memory, and judgment are impaired, vision is blurred, gait and hands become unsteady, reflexes are slowed, and a teenager may behave bizarrely, even violently.

Intoxication can last anywhere from one to twelve hours. Most kids first get drunk on beer and wine, which are every bit as harmful as hard liquor. A twelve-ounce bottle of beer contains the same amount of alcohol as a four-ounce glass of wine and one and a half ounces of eighty-proof whiskey. A newly favored drink is the wine cooler, with an alcohol content of approximately 5%—less than half of most average-priced wines, but enough to get plastered on. Yet in a 1987 *Weekly Reader* survey, only 25% of seventh- through twelfth-graders considered wine coolers to be a drug; and only 21% of fourth- through sixth-graders. Two-thirds of the older kids reported feeling pressure to try the sweet-tasting alcoholic beverages.

Because it is so easy to obtain, many times youngsters combine alcohol with other drugs such as depressants. This produces *synergism*, whereupon each chemical's effects are multiplied. The whole becomes greater than the sum of its parts, increasing the risk that a child will underestimate the physical consequences.

Another typical, and dangerous, combination is booze and pot, the THC content of which can switch off the brain's "vomit control." Normally, when too much alcohol is consumed, the pylorus—a valve that allows the transportation of substances from the stomach to the small intestines—receives orders to close, protecting the rest of the body from this toxin. Essentially, it traps the alcohol in the stomach, which in turn becomes irritated, and vomiting is induced. But when the brain is temporarily unsettled by THC, the message to seal off the passageway is never transmitted to the pylorus, and a person is apt to drink much more than his body can handle safely.

The most hazardous consequences of all befall teenagers who drink and drive. Twenty-five percent of boys fifteen to eighteen, and 11% of girls fifteen to eighteen do so *regularly*, according to an Insurance Institute for Highway Safety study. Alcohol scrambles a young person's ability to track small objects and dilates the pupils, so that the eyes are extremely sensitive to light. The glare from oncoming headlights, therefore, can be blinding. In addition, it impairs retention of recent events, which for many youngsters include driving skills only recently learned.

Even once a child feels "down" from his high psychologically, he is still physically drunk and will continue to be for several hours. Under no circumstances should he operate a vehicle. For example, if a youth weighing between 120 and 139 pounds guzzles three drinks in an evening, he should wait five hours before getting behind the wheel; a teenage girl should hold off even longer.

Traditional remedies to sober up—black coffee, fresh air, exercise, cold showers—have absolutely no effect on the body's ability to absorb the alcohol, the concentration of which decreases about .015% per hour. Without implying that alcohol use is condoned, these are vital facts to convey to teenagers and preteens, that if they should happen to drink or be with an intoxicated driver, to stay out of the car.

Long-term Effects

We all know that alcohol is psychologically and physically addicting and can lead to alcoholism. But according to the Alcohol, Drug Abuse and Mental Health Administration, whereas it takes men ten to twelve years to develop the disease of alcoholism (somewhat less for adult women), teenagers can become addicted within six months because their bodies and minds are less mature.

Notice that I referred to alcoholism as a disease. It was first declared as such in 1957 by the American Medical Association. An alcoholic, as defined by the self-help organization Alcoholics Anonymous, is "a person who is physically addicted to alcohol, with an emotional drive to drink . . . a compulsive drinker." Alcoholism has four stages, and by the time a person reaches the third, Gamma, his craving for drink is physically uncontrollable and his free will destroyed. Signs of alcoholism include

- drinking greater amounts and more often;
- making excuses for drinking to friends and family;
- becoming moody and withdrawn, as well as prone to illness and accidents;
- suffering hallucinations, nervous disorders, and phobias (illogical fears).

Seventy percent of all alcoholics have blackouts, regaining consciousness after a bout with the bottle and remembering nothing of preceding events.

In the fourth stage, Delta, the alcoholic cannot physically abstain from alcohol for even one day without withdrawal symptoms. The most severe, called delirium tremens (DTs), is an awful spectacle to witness, as I did on many occasions while a Cenikor counselor. The withdrawing alcoholic goes into a seizure similar to an epileptic's, writhing on the floor; he also may hallucinate demons and vipers. I remember several patients crying out, "Did you see that? Did you see that?" Sad to say, teenagers' withdrawal is no less excruciating than adults'.

Alcoholism destroys irreplaceable brain cells and often overworks the liver so that fats congest internally. Eventually this may leave scar tissue, a potentially fatal condition of cell devastation known as cirrhosis, one of the top ten killers in the U.S. Teenagers can develop cirrhosis after just fifteen to twenty months of drinking. You might also inform your child that one thousand Americans die each year from alcohol poisoning and that, on the average, alcoholics live twelve to fifteen fewer years than nondrinkers.

TOBACCO

Looks like: cigarettes, cigars, pipe and chewing tobacco, tins of loose tobacco or snuff.

Look for: frequent, dry coughing, especially in the morning, when a smoker's lungs attempt to expel irritants; yellow-stained teeth and, with chronic smokers, fingertips.

Related paraphernalia: matches, butane lighters, rolling papers.

Methods of ingestion: inhaled, taken orally.

Though it was in 1964 that the Advisory Committee to the Surgeon General issued its report about the perils of tobacco, even the early seventeenth-century English King James I described the cigarette habit brought back from the New World as dangerous and "filthy."

According to the Associated Press, about half of all high-school seniors who smoke say they did so daily by the time they were in the ninth grade. They should know that tobacco use kills 350,000 Americans a year and that cigarette smokers have a 70% greater chance of early death than nonsmokers. The habit causes 85% of all lung-cancer deaths, 30% to 40% of heart and blood-vessel disease, and 80% to 90% of deaths from pulmonary disease. Moreover, the National Fire Protection Agency (NFPA) claims that fires started by cigarettes result in an estimated 2,500 deaths per year.

American Cancer Society statistics show that cigarette smoking among teens dropped by approximately one-third between 1974 and 1979, but has since stabilized.

Immediate Effects

Cigarettes contain nicotine, tar, and carbon monoxide. The latter is the same colorless, odorless gas emitted from your car's tailpipe, and it displaces oxygen in the red blood cells. As for the nicotine, a natural alkaloid toxin, it stimulates the brain and the central nervous system. So after he takes a puff, a smoker's blood pressure rises, and his heart beats as much as 40% to 50% faster per minute—even though deprived of the extra oxygen it demands. The tar is comprised of several thousand chemicals, as well as cancer-causing carcinogenic gases such as hydrogen cyanide and nitrogen oxide.

Long-term Effects

Extensive smoking (five cigarettes a day for a year, one cigarette a day for five years, one pack a day for one to two months) leads to psychological and physical dependence. Though filter-tip cigarettes reduce the risk of disease slightly, it is not enough to make them safe. The incidence of lung cancer among filter-tip smokers is lower than those who favor nonfilters yet is still six and a half times greater than that of nonsmokers. Even low-tar/low-nicotine brands do not diminish the hazards substantially, while menthol, found in nine of ten U.S. brands, has absolutely no effect in lessening cigarettes' dangers.

Other forms of tobacco use, such as chewing it and inhaling snuff, also produce addiction, at which point many users are tempted to switch from the smokeless variety to cigarettes. Teenagers have been known to die from mouth and jaw cancers caused by chewing tobacco.

MARIJUANA AND HASHISH

Looks like: a mixture of dried greenish or brownish leaves, stems, twigs, yellowish flowers, and tiny, oval-shaped seeds. Hashish resembles gummy, brown or black bricks, balls, or fingers, while hashish oil is a dense, sticky liquid, its color ranging from black to brown to yellow-red to clear.

Look for: the sweet smell of marijuana or the even sweeter smell of hashish on your child's breath, hair, and clothes; incense, room deodorizers, and mouthwash to cover the smell; nicotinelike, yellowish stains on teeth and fingertips; respiratory problems; bloodshot eyes and bottles of eye drops to cover them; pale complexion; marijuana roaches (butts); seeds and stems.

Related paraphernalia: roach clips, rolling papers, scales, straight-edge razor blades, pipes, small plastic bags, foil-wrapped cakes of hash, matches, and butane lighters.

Methods of ingestion: inhaled into lungs, sprinkled over or baked into foods such as brownies and eaten.

THC, marijuana's main psychoactive ingredient, comes in soft gelatin capsules and is swallowed. However, little pure THC is available; what is sold on the streets are usually other drugs such as PCP.

Hashish can be eaten, which lessens the effect, or smoked in a pipe, while hashish oil can be puffed through a water pipe or added to a marijuana cigarette.

Marijuana (also called pot, grass, weed, reefer, herb, smoke) is derived from the *Cannabis sativa* plant, which has been used in the manufacturing of rope and paper, its oil used as a paint ingredient, and its seed as animal feed. It is one of the oldest mind-altering drugs, with descriptions of its effects appearing in four-thousand-year-old Chinese literature.

The once-pervasive notion that grass is harmless has been junked alongside the free-love idealism of the sexual revolution. We know now that marijuana is a highly complex drug, a mosaic with properties of sedatives, stimulants, tranquilizers, and psychedelics all in one. Plus, it contains 426 chemicals that, when smoked, are converted into 2,000. The primary of these, and the one most responsible for generating the two-to-four-hour high, is Delta-9-tetrahydrocannabinol (THC).

Today's marijuana joint has 5% THC, or about fifty milligrams, as compared to approximately .2% THC in the 1960s. Clearly, it is a much more powerful drug. And some strains, such as Sinsemilla, Colombian, Acapulco Gold, and Thai stick, contain as much as 14%.

Immediate Effects

A marijuana high can be described as euphoric. Within minutes young smokers' inhibitions relax. Some act more sociable, while others become withdrawn, disoriented, and stare off into space. The big claim among users I knew was that grass enhances the senses: music sounds more vibrant; lights burn incandescently; banal conversations seem profound and witty, the participants giggling incessantly. I remember me and my friend Howie munching out on tuna-fish sandwiches in my parents' kitchen, stoned out of our heads and sporadically erupting with laughter. My folks would ask, "What's so funny?" and Howie and I would look at each other, blurt, "Nothing!" and start snickering all over again.

But then there were those times when, for myriad reasons, the circumstances were not conducive to an enjoyable high. Paranoia set in: the feeling that everybody in the room is looking at you disapprovingly, or that narcotics agents are hovering just outside the door.

Grass's physical effects include bloodshot eyes, dry mouth and throat, a drop in body temperature, and the ravenous hunger known as the munchies. Smokers may appear to be relaxed and dreamy, but their hearts beat as much as 50% faster. This contributes to a condition scientists call acute panic anxiety, where kids fear they are losing control and begin to panic for as long as several hours.

Young people who are high do not retain information, time-and-distance perception is altered, and coordination and short-term memory are impaired, making teenage potheads a major highway hazard. National Institute on Drug Abuse research shows that nearly four of five have driven while stoned. Would the same 80% get behind the wheel of a car while intoxicated on alcohol? Probably not. But marijuana users tend to underestimate the degree and duration of its effects. The facts are that after smoking just one joint, a person's reaction time while driving is reduced by 42% for four to six hours; after two joints, by 63%.

Though overdoses are not fatal, those who do use the drug inordinately can fall into a trancelike state. Children also face the danger of unsuspectingly inhaling marijuana laced with harmful chemicals such as phencyclidine (PCP, or angel dust), formaldehyde, and insecticides.

Long-term Effects

Marijuana is not physically addictive but can bring about tolerance and psychological dependence even for occasional smokers, nearly 33% of whom become daily users within three to five years. What with increased calls for drug testing in schools and in the workplace, your youngster should know that it can take the body as long as thirty days to rid itself of THC, which accumulates in the body's fatty tissue such as the liver, ovaries, and testicles.

Not to mention the brain: Habitual use destroys brain cells and does harm to short-term retention. I know for a fact that my own memory has been depleted, and I've heard the same admission from others who used to indulge regularly.

In addition, continued use can lead to what is called amotivational syndrome: lethargy, reduced attention span, neglect of personal appearance, and a general lack of interest in anything but getting high. My memories of smoking grass include one weekend when some friends and I drove to the country in upstate New York. It was fall, the leaves were turning color, the scenery was breathtaking and made you want to frolic outdoors. Unless you happened to be holding some Colombian Red, as we were. For the entire weekend, not one of us ever left the guest house in which we were staying. We didn't move a muscle save to light the next joint. Marijuana dulls the senses, though at the time that was precisely why I smoked it.

Dr. I. R. Rosengard concluded from his study of thirty-seven thousand subjects that heavy use can cause brain atrophy, especially in the cerebrum. Habitual users may be characterized as "burnouts," seeming slow, dim-witted, and forgetful, and to varying degrees undergo personality changes. Marijuana does not cause mental disorders, but it can exacerbate existing psychological problems by bringing them to the surface. The National Federation of Parents for Drug-Free Youth claims that every month over five thousand people seek professional help for problems related to grass use.

In the 1960s a pothead's patented rationalized response to disapproving parents was that marijuana was safer than cigarettes and alcohol. But it has since been substantiated that, quite to the contrary, the drug contains more cancer-causing agents than tobacco smoke. Because the unfiltered smoke is inhaled deeply and held in the lungs as long as possible, it is also more damaging to those organs. The UCLA School of Medicine recently studied 229 marijuana smokers and found that in addition to a prevalence of acute, chronic bronchitis, the large airways and bronchial passages in the subjects' lungs were harmed. Even heavy tobacco users do not sustain such severe physical damage. Researcher Dr. Donald Tashkin concluded that marijuana users may be at "exceptionally high risk" of contracting lung cancer from the deposits of tar and other carcinogens. Smoking five marijuana cigarettes, he contends, is the equivalent of *one hundred twelve* tobacco cigarettes.

Other important, sobering facts to impart to growing youngsters: Marijuana diminishes the body's ability to protect itself from illness by reducing the division of disease-repelling white blood cells. Therefore, a child who smokes regularly is more likely to get sick. Too, there is evidence that boys who use marijuana before puberty may have less-than-normal sexual development as a result of lowered testosterone, the principal male hormone; while in adolescent girls the drug has been shown to disrupt the menstrual cycle and, in some cases, to inhibit ovulation.

Hashish, the dried resin exuded by the cannabis plant, is approximately five to ten times stronger than marijuana. Its one-to-three-hour high produces similar effects but with slightly more euphoria and sometimes encompasses hallucinations. Hashish oil is a crude extract that is boiled in a solvent to filter out the waste. Two to four times more potent than hashish, its THC content is extraordinarily high: up to 60%. Like hashish, the oil can generate hallucinations as well as delusions (irrational beliefs) and paranoia.

COCAINE

Looks like: a snow white or yellowish powder or paste. (Coca paste has caused serious health problems in South America, but its use in this country is limited primarily to South Florida and New York.)

Look for: chronic runny nose and red, irritated nostrils, white powder on nose, skin abscesses and needle marks, long sleeves, chest pains, sore throat and hoarseness, significant weight loss, pallor.

Related paraphernalia: straight-edge razor blades; scales; small mirrors and other smooth, flat surfaces; rolled-up dollar bills and straws for snorting; small spoons and spoon necklaces; ceramic mortar and pestle for crushing rock cocaine; pipes; syringes; glass vials, small plastic bags, foil strips, and "snow seals" of folded white paper containing cocaine; leather-bound paraphernalia and/or freebasing kits; bottles of chemicals such as ether, potassium carbonate, and sodium hydroxide, used for freebasing; matches and butane lighters.

Methods of ingestion: inhaled, injected, swallowed, smoked, introduced anally, dissolved in water and inhaled nasally from an eye dropper.

Cocaine, also called coke, snow, blow, flake, and Big C, is made from the leaves of the South American coca shrub. Its reputation as a glamorous, powerful stimulant predates the Inca Empire, whose inhabitants chewed on the coca leaves they believed to be of divine origin.

The cocaine alkaloid was first isolated from the leaf in 1855 by German chemist Friedrich Gaedcke. For years it was used medicinally as a local anesthetic, and among its early enthusiasts was an Austrian neurologist named Sigmund Freud, who exclaimed that just a small dose "lifted me to the heights in a wonderful fashion." The drug was added to a great number of tonics, elixirs, and salves, which were marketed along with the claim, as in one case, that the ingredient cocaine was a "great antidote for the blues." Indeed.

Before long the alkaloid was the object of so much abuse, nonmedical applications were outlawed in 1914. It is widely regarded as the champagne of drugs, and for many years was primarily an upper-class indulgence. Though coke is still worth three times its weight in gold, prices have de-escalated. The reduced cost factor, plus its availability in purer forms such as crack, and a relative dearth of prescription amphetamines, have all contributed to the cocaine epidemic of the 1980s, in which it has become the fastest-growing drug problem among school-age children.

Cocaine is routinely mixed with hydrochloric acid, then is cut, or adulterated, with agents such as mannitol sucrose, lactose, dextrose, and talc. The cocaine powder available on the streets is usually between 5% and 40% pure. It may be snorted, diluted with water and injected—even introduced anally—and smoked by way of a process called freebasing.

Freebasing converts the powder into a much purer, concentrated form devoid of adulterants. To do so requires using highly flammable solvents that are hazardous in themselves. In 1980 comedian Richard Pryor suffered third-degree burns when the ether with which he was drying the freebase ignited accidentally, engulfing him in flames.

Immediate Effects

When snorted, coke speeds into the bloodstream within three minutes; when injected, thirty seconds; and when freebased, several seconds. It narrows blood vessels, stimulates heart rate, breathing, and blood pressure, and produces an intense high lasting from five to thirty minutes. Users usually rhapsodize the litany of its euphoric effects, as was true of the addicts to whom we spoke: "exhilarating"; "It gave me this overwhelming sexual urge and endurance"; "I felt alert, so together." Kids on coke typically become highly excitable, loquacious, and hyperactive, and mental acuity seems—to them, at least—enhanced.

However, once the initial rapture, or "rush," wears off comes *dysphoria*—the crash, marked by depression, anxiety, irritability, and lack of motivation. I particularly recall feeling despondent and edgy after doing coke. Though its euphoric and anesthetic effects wear off quickly, cocaine can keep users awake for hours and sometimes days. To avoid crashing, they ingest more of the drug so that they never come down, setting in motion a destructive cycle.

Like other substances that do not have to be administered intravenously, cocaine beguiles, instilling in users a false sense of security that they cannot fatally overdose. But since 1981 the number of coke-related mortalities has tripled, caused mainly by cardiac arrest and suffocation from massive brain seizures. The majority of victims injected or freebased the drug, but fatalities have ensued from snorting. A dose of sixty milligrams (approximately two lines) or more is potentially lethal, and deaths are random. Heart palpitations, angina, and arrhythmia are other conditions that can be precipitated by cocaine use.

The crystalline powder is also one of the hardest substances from which to withdraw, and addicts' relapse rate is high. The main reason why, asserts physician David Walsh of the Fairview Treatment Programs in Edina, Minnesota, is that their symptoms often outlast rehabilitation.

Long-term Effects

Cocaine can produce tolerance, and both psychological and physical dependency. According to a Cocaine Hotline study, the average teenager progresses from first use to chronic abuse in just fifteen and a half months, as compared to over four years for adults. Once they begin ingesting it compulsively, it is not unusual for addicts to go on runs, or binges, for a week, sometimes longer. There were times when I stayed wired on coke for three weeks, spending most of my waking hours conspiring with others to get more. To illustrate the extent of the obsession, an experiment was conducted in which monkeys were given choices of food, water, enjoyable activities, and various drugs, including cocaine. All selected the latter, which they continued to inject until they went into convulsions and died. Such extreme cravings were not exhibited with any other substance.

If your child is snorting cocaine, his compulsiveness is likely to manifest itself in eccentric behavior. For example, he may clean his room continually, call the same person on the telephone repeatedly, or return to the store several times because he forgot what he went there for.

The Cocaine Hotline also found that half the confirmed users in its survey suffered from chronic depression, occasional panic attacks, memory loss, and low sexual drive. How ironic, in view of the fact that cocaine is highly touted as a potent aphrodisiac. Other signs that parents should mind are moodiness, absence from school or work, appetite loss, nervous twitches, hyperactivity, insomnia, humorlessness, irritability, poor concentration, paranoia, physical neglect, and teeth grinding. In extreme cases, called cocaine psychosis, children experience hallucinations such as Magnan's sign, imagining "cocaine bugs" are crawling beneath their skin. To stop the uncomfortable itching, they may attempt to extricate them with needles.

Long-term physical symptoms include fatigue, nausea and vomiting, digestive disorders, severe headaches, respiratory infections, cold sweats, persistently dry throat, and perforations of the nose's septum and/or cartilage, requiring surgical reconstruction. As with any drug that is injected, users run the risk of skin abscesses, and hepatitis and AIDS from shared needles.

CRACK

Looks like: light brown or beige pellets, or white rocks that resemble soap chips.

Look for: chest pains, chronic runny nose, chronic hoarseness, black phlegm, singed eyelashes and eyebrows from crack's hot vapors, significant weight loss, pallor.

Related paraphernalia: glass vials, foil pouches, water pipes, pipes.

Method of ingestion: inhaled through a pipe.

Crack (base, baseball, rock, crank) is a freebase variant made by mixing cocaine crystals with baking soda, creating a paste that hardens and is cut into chips. It is then sprinkled on marijuana cigarettes and smoked, or is vaporized and inhaled through a glass pipe. The name *crack* comes from the crackling sound the drug makes when the sodium bicarbonate and other chemicals used to process it are ignited. Two to twenty times purer than cocaine, crack has been called the fast food of drugs because of its cut-rate prices. A single dose, or hit, goes for as little as five to ten dollars, putting it within reach of children.

Immediate Effects

Because crack enters the bloodstream through the lungs and reaches the brain in seconds, its high is more intense than coke's but is of shorter duration. The physical and behavioral effects generated are the same as cocaine's, only multiplied five to ten times. In addition, kids on crack frequently become violent (31%, according to a Cocaine Hotline caller survey) or suicidal (18%). Not only is crack more addictive than coke, psychopharmacologist Arnold Washton of Fair Oaks Hospital in Summit, New Jersey, claims it is the most addictive substance presently known to man.

Long-term Effects

Crack touches off an explosive release of neurotransmitters in the brain, producing an extreme craving for more stimulation. But the craving can never be satisfied, making crack perhaps the most ruinous of all drugs, including heroin. The only thing that will stop the user is a depleted drug supply, lack of money, or physical illness. Anthony was able to keep his dope addiction from his parents for years. But "as soon as I picked up the

131

pipe, there was no hiding it anymore. Everything got crazy, and I just went wild, stealing money right in front of my own mother." Two injections of heroin a day can satisfy a junkie, but a crack addict needs another hit within minutes. Enslavement to a "cheap" drug thus becomes a very expensive habit. Per gram, crack is actually twice as costly as coke. The rapidity with which it unravels lives is frightening.

Darrell, one of the addicts we spoke to, recounts how "once I started smoking crack, everything just turned into chaos. I stopped caring about anything except hitting the pipe. I would stay out for a week straight, stopped going to work, stole from my family; do anything I could to get money for more crack.

"And that wasn't like me. I'd been brought up to treat people—and myself—with respect. But when I smoked crack, those values just went right out the window. If I hadn't been sent to treatment, I would have wound up dead or in jail."

More than any other drug, the horror stories told about crack are true.

OTHER STIMULANTS

(Amphetamines, Methamphetamines, Dextroamphetamines)

Look like: capsules, pills, tablets; methamphetamine comes in pills, yellowish and white crystals, and a waxy rock.

Look for: dilated pupils, glassy eyes, chain-smoking, appetite loss, bad breath, dry hair, gum disease, skin abscesses and needle marks, long sleeves.

Related paraphernalia: vials, small plastic bags, and bottles; syringes; rolled-up dollar bills and straws for snorting; spoons, bottle caps, and other drug-cooking implements; bloody cotton balls; matches and butane lighters.

Methods of ingestion: taken orally, inhaled, and injected by crushing pills or tablets, dissolving them in liquid, and heating them.

Many adolescents first use stimulants to cram late at night for an exam, or to pep themselves up before an athletic event. Amphetamines are part of a drug family that includes methamphetamines and dextroamphetamines, and were first used medically in the 1920s to combat narcolepsy, or sleeping sickness. Fifty years later there existed more than thirty different amphetamine preparations available by prescription under brand names such as Preludin, Appedrine, Desoxyn, and Dexedrine.

As implied by the slang terms *uppers* and *speed*, amphetamines are used to heighten alertness and physical energy. They are also prescribed to help control obesity. Unfortunately, youngsters often obtain their first stimulants from parents' caches of diet pills.

Immediate Effects

The high from uppers lasts from a half hour to two hours, is distinguished by increased heart rate, breathing rate, and blood pressure, and has been described by users as "a whole-body orgasm." Pupils dilate, appetite subsides, and dry mouth, sweating, headaches, blurred vision, dizziness, sleeplessness, and anxiety may be experienced. Excessive doses can produce tremors, coordination loss, fever, chest pains—and fatal strokes or heart failure, especially if the drug is injected.

When a child ingests amphetamines, he feels restless, anxious, excitable, and falsely self-confident. He may chatter incessantly until his jaw aches. I could always tell amphetamine users because they were constantly opening and closing their mouths to mitigate the pain. Under the influence of uppers, a person feels indestructible, as if he could stay awake forever and accomplish great tasks; though he never does.

As with cocaine, amphetamines' high is counteracted by a depressive crash, the avoidance of which can lead to psychological dependence. The crash from methamphetamines is particularly intolerable, like plummeting down a bottomless pit.

Long-term Effects

Amphetamines produce psychological dependence, possibly physical addiction, and tolerance develops quickly. Habitual users get taken on roller coaster rides of euphoric highs and crushing lows, which they sometimes make worse by attempting to cure their upper-generated insomnia with downers. Such a cycle is extremely stressful on the body, but cross-addictions to these two drugs are common among young people.

The child who uses amphetamines regularly deteriorates physically, contracting conditions such as ulcers, skin disorders, malnutrition, and diseases linked to vitamin deficiencies. Excessive doses can result in brain damage as well as amphetamine psychosis—similar to cocaine psychosis, with hallucinations, delusions, and paranoia, but longer lasting. Amphetamines may also instigate violent behavior, and they cause most of the prolonged drug-induced psychotic mental states in the U.S.

Persons who inject the drug run the added risk of skin abscesses, hepatitis, and AIDS, lung or heart disease, and damage to the kidneys and other tissues.

Multiplying the dangers of amphetamines is the preponderance of look-alike and act-alike drugs sold on the street as speed or uppers. Often these relatively weak substances consist of nothing more than 300- to 500-milligram doses of caffeine, ephedrine, and phenylpropanolamine—the equivalent of roughly three to five cups of coffee. However, youngsters who start out on look-alikes may ingest the same amount of real amphetamine without realizing the discrepancy in potency, paving the way for an overdose.

INHALANTS

(Nitrous Oxide, Amyl and Butyl Nitrite, Hydrocarbons, Chlorohydrocarbons)

Look like: clear, yellowish liquid in ampules (amyl nitrite); butyl nitrite is also a liquid but is normally sold in small bottles.

Look for: persistent cough and/or sneezing, irritated eyes, odors of chemicals on your child or his clothing, rashes of the nose or mouth, nosebleeds, fatigue.

Related paraphernalia: handkerchiefs and paper bags reeking of inhalants; aerosol cans; small metal cylinders with an attached balloon or pipe, which are called buzz bombs and are for sniffing nitrous oxide.

Method of ingestion: fumes are inhaled.

Youthful abuse of legal inhalants, sometimes called *gunk*, has become such a public menace that several states have introduced legislation to ban sales to minors of everything from typewriter correction fluid to aerosol paint cans. It is most common among kids between the ages of seven and seventeen. Because the psychoactive vapors come from everyday household items such as airplane glue, gasoline, lighter and cleaning fluids, toluene-based solvents—even a whipped cream can in the refrigerator—it can be a formidable task for parents to keep track of abuse taking place in their very homes. There is little exotic paraphernalia to look for, so behavioral signs may be your only clue.

Immediate Effects

The high from inhalants varies from product to product. Nearly all bring about effects similar to those of anesthetics, including decreased blood pressure, heart rate, and respiratory rate. Two of the most popular types, butyl nitrite (sold as Locker Room, Rush) and amyl nitrite (called snappers, poppers, and illegal since 1979), produce three to five minutes of dizziness, disorientation, and a feeling of weightlessness, after which many kids become drowsy and fall asleep. I never understood the enjoyment derived from the inhalant high. It was slow, draggy, yet you felt as if you were hyperventilating. Your tongue became thick, your face numb, and your head throbbed.

Coughing, nosebleeds, bad breath, sneezing, visual impairment, appetite loss, hallucinations, jumbled words, and fragmentary sentences are other reactions to inhalants, and some children act violently.

Because inhalants are not "drugs"—that is, not intended for that purpose—it is a common misconception they are not harmful. Explain to your children that they can die from sniffing highly concentrated amounts of solvents or aerosol sprays, particularly when they are inhaled from a paper bag or cloth. In California in 1986, four adolescents paid with their lives after snorting typewriter correction fluid. Most overdose victims suffocate: Either they choke on their own vomit while unconscious, the vapors displace their lungs' oxygen supply, or their central nervous system is so depressed that they simply cease breathing.

Long-term Effects

Inhalants decimate brain cells and turn more kids into vegetables than any other drug. It is believed that between 40% and 60% of long-term users become brain damaged. The central nervous system is permanently harmed, diminishing mental and physical capacities, as are the kidneys, blood, and bone marrow. Further evidence of inhalant abuse that parents should watch for are pronounced weight loss, and mental and muscle fatigue.

SEDATIVE-HYPNOTICS

(Barbiturates, Tranquilizers, Methaqualone, Others)

Look like: white, red, blue, yellow, or red-and-blue capsules, sometimes sold as liquid, soluble powder, suppositories (barbiturates); tablets; capsules (tranquilizers and methaqualone).

135

Look for: slurred speech; poor reflexes; tremors; slow, unsteady gait; drunken behavior; longer sleep periods; constipation; skin abscesses, rashes and needle marks; long sleeves.

Related paraphernalia: small plastic bags or bottles of pills; syringes; spoons, bottle caps, and other drug-cooking implements; bloody cotton balls; matches and butane lighters.

Methods of ingestion: taken orally; barbiturates are sometimes crushed, dissolved, and heated in liquid, then injected.

Sedative-hypnotics slow down body functions, hence the street slang *downers*. They encompass six categories: barbiturates (brand names include Seconal, Nembutal, and others), benzodiazepines (Valium, Librium, others), methaqualone (Quaalude), ethchlorvynol (Placidyl), chloral hydrate (Noctec), and meprobamate (Miltown). First marketed in the U.S. in 1912, they are ordinarily prescribed for sleep or sedation but are highly abused, accounting for over three thousand accidental and intentional deaths yearly. The tranquilizer methaqualone was introduced as a sleeping medication in 1965 and enjoyed considerable popularity among young people a decade and a half later. Since the government choked off illicit production at home and importing from abroad, its use has dropped sharply since the beginning of the decade.

Immediate Effects

Twenty to forty minutes after a youngster swallows barbiturates, he feels intoxicated but more in control of himself than a drinker. He is tranquil and dreamy, with a general sense of well-being and a lack of inhibitions. Downers' action typically lasts four to six hours, but some work for more than twice that long. Though methaqualone has been mythologized as a matchless aphrodisiac, it is really no more so than a glass of wine.

Excessive doses of downers can cause slurred speech; staggering gait; lethargy; mental impairment; a rapid, involuntary oscillation of the eyeballs; blurred vision; a tingling sensation in the extremities; and alternating euphoria and depression. A real danger is that heavily sedated kids may be so confused that they forget how much of the drug they have ingested and take some more tablets—perhaps enough to overdose. Or, in a stupor, they drink. As with amphetamines, the availability of look-alikes further increases the potential for overdoses when the real thing is unknowingly introduced into his system.

Breathing, heart rate, and blood pressure are all diminished. In fact, sedative-hypnotics are such powerful respiratory depressants that a person who swallows too many may just stop breathing and die in his sleep.

Those who shoot up the drug for an intensified rush risk dangers such as skin abscesses, because unlike heroin and amphetamines, which cook down into a liquid, barbiturates remain thick and lumpy. I still have a scar on my arm from injecting barbiturates; my veins clogged up, and the surrounding tissue blew up like a golf ball.

Long-term Effects

Regular barbiturate use—for example, taking 400 milligrams, or four sleeping pills, daily for less than a month—brings on physical dependency. Tolerance also develops, and as youngsters require more of the drug to reach the same level of altered consciousness, the margin between intoxication and death narrows hazardously.

Behavior becomes more unpredictable and sometimes violent. One time when I lived in Florida, I got so zonked on downers that I jumped in my car and sped off down an intercoastal highway, with my father in pursuit on foot. I zigzagged across the grass median, crashing into other cars, glass busting around me, until finally I coasted to a halt and was dragged off to a hospital. At least, this is what I was told; my mind was so clouded from the drugs, I didn't remember a thing afterward.

When barbiturate and methaqualone use is decreased or discontinued, kids undergo a withdrawal even more racking than that of heroin. Symptoms include anxiety, restlessness, sweating, shaking, nausea, vomiting, and increased heart rate, accompanied by grand mal seizures and, possibly, convulsions much the same as delirium tremens.

LSD

Looks like: colorful tablets, saturated blotter paper and stamps, powder, thin gelatinoid squares, clear liquid.

Look for: dilated pupils, extremes of emotion, nervousness, erratic behavior.

Related paraphernalia: vials, small plastic bags and bottles of pills and liquid, eyedroppers.

Methods of ingestion: taken orally, licked off blotter paper, dropped in eyes (gelatinoid and liquid).

Lysergic acid diethylamide is one of several hallucinogens, which are, simply, drugs that induce hallucinations. Manufactured from lysergic acid found in the ergot fungus, it was synthesized accidentally in 1943 by Swiss chemist Albert Hofmann, who was searching for a migraine-headache remedy. To some proponents of the mind-expanding drug, his miscalculation was analogous to Columbus's chance discovery of America.

Immediate Effects

LSD, also referred to as *acid*, is colorless, odorless, and tasteless and is taken in average doses of between 50 and 250 micrograms. Once ingested, like a magic carpet it whisks a young person on a trip that can be either exhilarating or terrifying, depending on the amount ingested, his mood, his expectations, and the environment. The effects are usually felt within thirty to ninety minutes and last from six to twelve hours.

Physically, the child sweats, loses his appetite, his pupils dilate, his mouth becomes dry, and he may experience tremors or shaking. Body temperature, heart rate, and blood pressure all increase. It is believed doses as low as 10 micrograms can interfere with the traverse of messages across the narrow gaps between brain cells. Besides overstimulating those cells, LSD may also block the efficacy of serotonin, the nerve endings' natural transmitter.

Acid is a psychomimetic drug; that is, it produces a state mimicking a psychosis. The sensations are unpredictable, from rapid mood swings, to distortions of time, to *synesthesia*, where senses are translated into other senses: colors are "tasted," sounds are "seen." Those symptoms would constitute a good trip. On a bad trip, which can happen to first-time or seasoned users, the frightening sensations, panic, anxiety, and loss of control may last several minutes or up to twelve hours. So that you can appreciate how terrifying a bad trip can be, let me relate one of my own experiences.

I was doing acid many years ago at a friend's house. He owned this large white dog that closely resembled Spuds MacKenzie, and as my trip progressed the dog seemed to get bigger and bigger, his nose turning into a pile driver that bored through my leg and side, causing, I imagined, great pain. I screamed over and over, "Get this dog away from me!" while the poor animal looked about bewildered. It sounds comical now, but at the time, I was terrified.

After an acid trip, a child will usually feel exhausted, depressed, and unable to sleep. Brain waves may be abnormal for one or two days afterward. Trips can bring to the surface preexisting mental or emotional problems that were previously hidden, and suicides and accidental deaths sometimes ensue.

Long-term Effects

LSD does not lead to addiction, but tolerance can develop. Enthusiasts may suffer from flashbacks, experiencing the drug's effects without having taken it. These hallucinogenic phenomena have been reported to occur for as long as two years after a dose, with each flashback lasting anywhere from ten seconds to two hours. Signs of organic brain damage (confusion, shortened attention span, impaired memory, difficulty with abstract thinking) have been shown to develop in some heavy LSD users, though research has yet to conclude whether or not this is permanent.

PCP

Looks like: liquid, white powder, rock crystal, tablets.
Look for: confusion, agitation, and behavioral extremes.
Related paraphernalia: syringes, small plastic bags and bottles of pills, powder, and liquid; foil-wrapped marijuana cigarettes laced with the drug.
Methods of ingestion: taken orally, injected, smoked in cigarettes.

PCP (phencyclidine, better known as *angel dust*) was developed in the 1950s by the Parke-Davis Company as an animal and human anesthetic. It was taken off the market in 1965 because studies showed that when used on humans, one in six became severely psychotic for several hours. Even low doses of the drug could cause schizophrenia-like symptoms. It first appeared illicitly on the street in 1967 and has undergone brief revivals of popularity.

PCP powder is between 50% and 100% pure; in its other forms, between 5% and 35% pure, with the rest composed of potentially harmful contaminants. Because it can be produced inexpensively, it is often substituted for drugs with similar psychedelic powers: LSD, THC, mescaline, peyote and, sometimes, cocaine. Novice users, therefore, may take PCP unwittingly, which is like a boxer taking a blind-side punch.

Immediate Effects

If swallowed, PCP's high begins within about fifteen minutes; if smoked, within two to five minutes. No matter how it is ingested, the effects last from four to six hours, and a return to normalcy takes an additional twenty-four to twenty-eight hours. A typical dose is between 1 milligram and 5 milligrams, and is often taken in combination with other chemicals, including marijuana, amphetamines, opiates, cocaine, and barbiturates.

PCP is an extremely dangerous drug because its actions are so erratic, varying from person to person. A young user may become destructive, even if he never exhibited any violent tendencies in his life. Or he may withdraw completely, unable to communicate to others. Those under phencyclidine's influence may seem confused or have delusions of massive strength and invulnerability to pain. Consequently, they are occasionally victims of drownings, burns, falls, and car accidents. They can injure themselves severely and not even realize it until the drug has worn off.

The physical effects of PCP are just as impossible to predict. It can act as a stimulant in some and as a depressant in others. But typical symptoms include tearing of the eyes, lack of body control, sweating, cramps, nausea, and sometimes bloody vomiting from the contaminants. In large doses a child will feel drowsy, possibly suffer convulsions, or fall into a coma lasting for hours, sometimes for days. Death from respiratory failure can also transpire.

Long-term Effects

Three to four days after taking the drug, PCP psychosis may set in. One of the most dire drug-induced mental disorders, it consists of extreme depression, suicidal impulses, paranoia, and violence that persist for days, even weeks. Psychiatric treatment is often necessary. According to the National Institute on Drug Abuse, habitual users report slurred speech, problems with concentration and memory, as well as auditory delusions. They may hear these imaginary sounds or voices for as long as two years. Other long-term effects are extreme hypertension, multiple seizures, brain hemorrhaging, fever, and kidney failure. The drug produces both tolerance and psychological dependence.

MESCALINE, PEYOTE, PSILOCYBIN, AND OTHER HALLUCINOGENS

Look like: hard brown "buttons," tablets, and capsules (mescaline and peyote); fresh or dried whole, chopped, or ground brown mushrooms (psilocybin).

140

Look for: dilated pupils, tremors, sleeplessness, appetite loss.
Related paraphernalia: small plastic bags and bottles of substances.
Methods of ingestion: chewed (buttons); swallowed (mushrooms); taken orally or anally (mescaline).

Psilocybin, mescaline, and peyote are natural hallucinogens. The latter is derived from the crowns of the peyote cactus grown in the southwestern U.S. and Mexico, and has been used by the American Indians for centuries as part of religious rites. It is a legal sacrament for the quarter-million members of the Native American Church of North America.

After bringing on nausea and vomiting, peyote takes a youth on a trip similar to but milder than that of LSD, with illusions rather than hallucinations. Colors seems extremely radiant; sounds, crystal clear.

Mescaline is the psychoactive alkaloid found in the peyote cactus. It produces five to twelve hours of illusions and hallucinations but without the nausea, although users report such adverse effects as anxiety and depression. Tolerance to the drug can develop.

Psilocybin comes from twenty varieties of "magic" wild mushrooms cultivated throughout the U.S. The mushrooms are ground, soaked in methyl alcohol, and are usually taken orally. The effects of their two-to-six-hour trip are similar to LSD's but do not last as long.

Other hallucinogens, such as STP and DMT, are synthetic. The former combines the properties of LSD and amphetamines, giving its high a slight, protracted rush. DMT is usually a colorless, tasteless crystalline powder that may be snorted but is usually cooked down to a liquid, sprinkled on tobacco or marijuana, and smoked. Its high lasts only about an hour, which explains the origin of its nickname, "businessman's trip."

NARCOTICS

(Other than Heroin and Methadone)

Look like: liquid cough medicines, capsules, tablets (codeine); white crystals, tablets, liquid (morphine); white powder, tablets, solution (meperidine, or Demerol, its trade name); dark brown sticky bars, powder (opium); tablets, capsules, liquid (Percodan, Darvon, and other narcotics).
Look for: yawning, constant scratching, watery eyes, pinpoint pupils,

appetite loss, skin abscesses, needle marks, long sleeves, the sulfuric smell of burning matches.

Related paraphernalia: syringes; burnt spoons, bottle caps, and other cooking implements; skewers; cotton balls; tourniquets; eye droppers; small plastic bags and bottles of substances; matches and butane lighters.

Methods of ingestion: taken orally, injected (codeine); taken orally, injected, smoked (morphine); taken orally, injected (meperidine); smoked, eaten, injected (opium); taken orally, injected (Percodan, Darvon, and other narcotics).

The ancient Greek physician Hippocrates observed in 2,000 B.C. that opium users had great difficulty moderating their habit, and indeed, until the recent advent of crack, opiates were by far the most addictive of drugs. They are also among the most effective analgesics, or painkillers, and are used for controlling diarrhea and suppressing coughing.

Narcotics are made from opium, the natural product of the poppy plant. They may be semisynthetic (Dilaudid) or synthetic, such as the extremely potent, pure China White, and methadone, which is used in drug treatment and is described in detail in chapter 7. Until made illegal in 1914 opium was available in grocery stores, by mail order, and by doctor's prescription. It was also found in many patent medicines with such innocent names as Mrs. Winslow's Soothing Syrup and Ayers Cherry Pectoral. Unsuspecting men, women, children—even infants—became hooked.

Immediate Effects

Narcotics produce a euphoric state characterized by fantasy, torpor, and isolation, yet users feel more relief from anxiety than actual pleasure. They are likely to become restless, get nauseous and vomit, then turn drowsy and meander in and out of consciousness, or "nod off." Overdose victims may go into a stupor or a coma, as their respiration, body temperature, and blood pressure drop swiftly. As with barbiturate ODs, sometimes their breathing simply stops.

Long-term Effects

After approximately a month of heavy use or ten days of daily use, narcotics cause physical dependence. Addicts then continue taking them to avoid the unpleasant side effects. When deprived of opiates, an addict enters withdrawal four to six hours after his last dose. The symptoms include restlessness, diarrhea, cramps, tremors, sweating, chills, nausea, body pain, runny nose and eyes, and gooseflesh. *Cold turkey,* slang for withdrawal, stems from the way the skin resembles a plucked fowl's.

Withdrawal's extent and intensity hinge on which drug was taken, but usually the addict's agony peaks after two or three days. Then the symptoms subside within several days, sometimes a week. However, the National Institute on Drug Abuse contends that sleeplessness and drug craving can persist for months, as can feelings of despair, depression, and worthlessness. Withdrawing from the synthetic narcotics Dilaudid and methadone is even more torturous than from heroin.

Other long-term physical dangers are caused by needle use: infections or flooding of the heart lining and valves, skin abscesses, lung congestion, hepatitis, tetanus, liver disease, and AIDS, which is always fatal and for which there is no known cure.

HEROIN

Looks like: white to light brown powder, tarlike substance.

Look for: yawning, head nodding, constant scratching and sniffing, watery eyes, pinpoint pupils, powder on or around the nose, appetite loss, skin abscesses, needle marks, long sleeves, the sulfurous smell of burning matches.

Related paraphernalia: syringes, burnt spoons, bottle caps, and other cooking implements; straight-edge razor blades; cotton balls; tourniquets; eyedroppers; small plastic bags, glassine envelopes, bottles, and aluminum-foil packets; rolled-up dollar bills and straws for snorting; pipes; matches and butane lighters.

Methods of ingestion: mixed in water, heated, and injected into the flesh (skin popping) or a vein (mainlining); inhaled, smoked, taken orally.

The German Bayer Company blundered seriously when in 1898 it introduced heroin as a nonaddictive cough suppressant. Soon after it was discovered how addictive the narcotic truly was, regulation was enacted in 1914. Ten years later heroin was banned outright.

Immediate Effects

Heroin (junk, dope, smack, stuff) accounts for 90% of the opiate abuse in the U.S. and produces the absolute, ultimate high. Smack is *it.* And,

143

as ludicrous as it may sound, in the eyes of many other substance abusers, heroin addicts are the ultimate too. This is because a person caught in drugs' morass enters a world not unlike the Wonderland discovered by Alice when she crashed through the mirror: one of corrupt values and an upside-down social order. Here, junkies constitute the aristocracy, romanticized as valiants who hunger so greatly for the drug's transcendent high that they knowingly risk death each time they force the poison into their bodies.

It is estimated there are one million daily heroin users in the U.S. today, but I believe that figure will rise once cocaine users tire of their drug and aspire to more intense chemical thrills. According to Mark S. Gold, M.D., of Fair Oaks Hospital and Dr. Herbert Kleberg of Yale University Department of Psychiatry, stimulant epidemics such as crack use are followed by upswings in heroin use.

Those who mainline—inject into a vein—initially feel a wave of nausea, then, as the drug reaches the brain, a warm, enveloping rush. This is accompanied by itching, the result of the substances the narcotic is cut with: usually quinine, a bitter alkaloid often used in medicine, or lactose. Most heroin is between 3% and 5% pure—at the most, 20%—and its adulterants are sometimes toxins.

The rush lasts for less than a minute, but I can remember sitting with my legs crossed for as long as fifteen minutes, the syringe still stuck in my arm. That's how incapacitating it can be. Shooting up is like being suspended in midair over a precipice: While you're admiring the view below, you're praying you make it back to safety.

Heroin's high lasts from three to six hours and is distinguished by a sense of calm and well-being. In between nodding out, a junkie may babble incessantly, his pupils constrict noticeably, and his breathing turn shallow and sporadic.

Long-term Effects

Once physically addicted, users no longer feel the rush but desperately continue injecting the drug merely to ward off the symptoms of withdrawal, which are akin to those of other opiates. Obtaining heroin becomes an all-consuming passion, and addicts will go to extraordinary lengths to acquire it. Because an average 20-milligram dose costs approximately twenty-five dollars, their finances are soon drained. Few hard-core abusers can maintain jobs for long, so they often turn to crime. Heroin causes diminished sex drive, mood changes, and lethargy.

Overdose, convulsions, coma, and death occur because of impurities in the drug, contaminated needles, and excessive doses—always a possibility with addicts whose increasing tolerance forces them to up the ante. Reports have surfaced recently about fatalities from Black Tar, a highly potent but inexpensive form of heroin smuggled in from Mexico. Authorities believe it to be more than forty times purer than conventional powder.

Many heroin abusers become as psychologically addicted to the ritual of injecting the drug as they are physically hooked. They find it fascinating—*exciting*—to jab the needle in a vein, withdraw it, and see their own blood fill the syringe. Longtime users eventually exhaust the veins in their arms, their legs, and may have no alternative but to stick the needle in their groin, their neck, between their toes; wherever they can find a normal vein. When I was an addict I would rub cocoa butter into my skin to help heal the needle marks, even applying makeup to cover them up.

DESIGNER DRUGS

(Ecstasy, Eve)

Look like: white or white-gray powder, tablets, and capsules.
Look for: clenched teeth, sleeplessness, muscle tension.
Related paraphernalia: syringes, tourniquets, rolled-up dollar bills and straws for snorting, small plastic bags and small bottles.
Methods of ingestion: taken orally, injected, inhaled.

To bypass legal restraints, underground chemists have learned to alter the molecular structure of certain banned substances, creating synthetic compounds called "designer" drugs. It has been speculated that fear of AIDS from contaminated needles is at the root of this experimentation.

The best-known synthetic is MDA and its close relations MDMA and MMDA (Ecstasy), and MDEA (Eve), all analogs of amphetamines and methamphetamines. After the U.S. Drug Enforcement Administration declared Ecstasy a controlled substance in 1985, Eve turned up on the street as a substitute.

Immediate Effects

Early enthusiasts of Ecstasy called it the perfect drug, from its allegedly exhilarating rush to the way it invoked feelings of warmth and confidence, and seemed to enhance thinking. They neglected to mention adverse reactions such as confusion, depression, restlessness, anxiety, nausea, and faintness. Physically, kids who take Ecstasy endure increased heart rate and blood pressure, chills, sweating, and blurry vision.

Long-term Effects

Ecstasy is believed to cause permanent brain damage. Additionally, the *Journal of the American Medical Association* made public in March 1987 that five deaths in Texas had been linked to Ecstasy and Eve, while according to the Cocaine Hotline, overdose cases are being reported by hospital emergency rooms. Making the drugs additionally dangerous is the common practice among dealers of peddling other drugs—for example, LSD and PCP—as Ecstasy. Or they are combined with other substances.

Too little is known definitively about these synthetics, but given what research has uncovered about other drugs once thought to be harmless, children should be warned to avoid them. Remind your youngsters that at one time virtually every illegal substance—marijuana, cocaine, PCP, heroin—was legal and considered safe for consumption.

IN AN EMERGENCY*

A drug overdose; unusual and severe reactions to a pill; symptoms of drug withdrawal. These are life-threatening drug emergencies and require immediate medical attention. Knowing what to do, staying calm, and acting fast can save a life—perhaps your child's.

General Rules for All Drug Emergencies

Don't delay in phoning for help: If the area where you live has a special number to call in an emergency, dial it and describe the situation. Or dial "0" (operator), tell the operator it's an emergency call, and ask to be connected to Poison Control. Or find the number for Poison Control in the White Pages (under *P* and in the Community Services Numbers listings) and call it directly. When you reach Poison Control, be prepared to tell the person who answers: your location; what was taken and how much; the victim's condition; his age and weight; if he has any chronic

---

*Adapted from "In an Emergency," from *The Little Black Pill Book*, Lawrence D. Chilnick, ed. (New York: Bantam Books, Inc., 1983), © The Food & Drug Book Co., Inc.

medical conditions, such as diabetes, epilepsy, or high blood pressure; and what medicines, if any, the victim takes regularly.

Never use a second drug: Don't give a stimulant, not even coffee, to a drug-overdose victim who seems to be extremely tired, for instance. The combination can be more dangerous than the original overdose drug.

Assume the worst: Even if you aren't certain that a youngster is suffering from an overdose or drug withdrawal, assume he is and get medical help immediately.

Don't be afraid to try to help: You won't be arrested or otherwise penalized for trying to help during what you believe is a genuine emergency. It's better to apologize later—if you made a mistake by rushing a child to the hospital who didn't really have to be treated—than to take a chance on letting him suffer or possibly die. Even if a kid doesn't think he needs help, or doesn't want it, call for help anyway if *you* think it's needed.

Don't try to force an unconscious child to drink or eat: He could accidentally choke if you do.

If the Victim Is Conscious

Ask the victim if an overdose could have occurred, or whether withdrawal from drugs is the likely cause of the symptoms: If there is any doubt whether overdose or withdrawal is responsible, proceed as though an overdose has occurred. If you are positive that withdrawal is the cause, but *only* if you are positive, then rush the victim to a hospital immediately.

Phone for help right away: Call Poison Control, a hospital, or a doctor. Tell them, if you know, what drug is involved and describe the symptoms as well as you can (dizziness, slow or rapid breathing, pinpoint pupils, general weakness, and so on). Follow the instructions you receive.

Induce vomiting: Although in general you should not cause vomiting for poisoning (because some poisons, such as lye, can be more damaging if they are regurgitated), overdoses of most medicines are best treated by forcing the child to empty his stomach.

Vomiting can be induced by making the victim swallow a spoonful of ipecac syrup—a teaspoon for a child, a tablespoon for a young adult—followed by two to three glasses of water (one glass for a young child). Ipecac syrup is available from most pharmacies and is often included in first-aid kits. If vomiting does not occur within fifteen minutes, repeat the dose once.

Vomiting can sometimes be caused by tickling the back of the victim's throat while he is in a "spanking" position; that is, lying face-down across your lap. You should use a spoon or similar household implement. If you use your finger, be careful, since you might receive a painful bite should the victim gag.

Do not force the child to swallow mustard powder or large amounts of table salt. Neither method works reliably, and excessive salt can worsen the victim's condition.

Administer an antidote: Activated charcoal is the only safe substance useful as an antidote to pill overdoses. When swallowed, it absorbs some of the drug remaining in the stomach after vomiting. However, charcoal is unpleasant to take. It stains the gums and mouth black, feels gritty, and tastes bitter. To make it more palatable, it can be mixed with a small amount of cocoa and swallowed dry, or mixed with water in a dark-colored glass, so that it doesn't look so bad.

Phone for help again if it has not arrived.

Talk to the child reassuringly, to help keep him conscious and to lessen his fears: Give as much emotional support as you can and maintain what is called a "reality base" by identifying yourself over and over, so that he knows who you are and understands you are trying to help. Maintain eye contact, hug the youngster occasionally, and repeatedly tell him he will be all right. Keep him abreast of what's happening around him: "The ambulance will be here any minute"; "The neighbors are waiting outside to bring in the medics."

If help does not arrive and you have good reason to believe it will not come soon: Take the victim to the nearest hospital yourself—by car, taxi, or any other way you can arrange.

If the Victim Is Unconscious or Having Convulsions

Do not try to make the child vomit: An unconscious person can choke to death on his own vomit, or on food or liquid he is being forced to ingest.

Find out if the victim is breathing: Listen closely to the nose, mouth, and chest. If you hear no sound and see no chest movement, he has probably stopped breathing. The skin turning blue (initially under fingernails and toenails) is another sign that breathing has stopped or is severely restricted.

If the child is breathing, phone for help immediately.

If he is not, perform mouth-to-mouth resuscitation: Doing so is easier than you think. Lay the victim on his back. Force the mouth open and check that there are no visible obstructions. Pull the tongue forward if it blocks the throat.

Move the victim's head so that the chin juts out, to help open the airway. With one hand, pinch the nose closed. With the other hand holding the chin firmly, keep the mouth open. Take a deep breath and press your lips to the child's. Force your air into his lungs as if inflating a balloon. If there is a lot of resistance, and his chest does not expand, check inside the mouth again for obstructions. If you are alone, continue mouth-to-mouth for at least ten minutes before phoning for help, or until the victim starts breathing on his own.

While calling for assistance at the same time you're helping the victim breathe, do not stop mouth-to-mouth for more than a few seconds at a time. You can grab the phone, dial "0," then fill the victim's lungs a few more times. Pause again, begin describing the emergency, then go back to your mouth-to-mouth resuscitation. Complete your explanation between breaths. If you can, carry the child close to the phone to minimize time lost in administering mouth-to-mouth.

If possible, have someone else phone for medical help while you continue mouth-to-mouth resuscitation. Do not stop until help arrives, until you are too exhausted to continue, or until someone takes over from you.

If convulsions occur (muscle spasms throughout the body, or suddenly rigid muscles): Lay the victim on his stomach, and turn the head to one side to keep him from inhaling anything he might vomit up. Keep him warm with a blanket, and push away from the immediate area anything he might bump into during severe spasms.

Phone again for help if it has not arrived.

If help does not arrive and you have good reason to believe it will not come soon: Take the victim to the nearest hospital yourself—by car, taxi, or any other way you can arrange. Try keeping an unconscious or convulsive child lying face-down during transport, to lessen the chance of choking.

How You Can Help Medical Personnel

Collect information about the kind of drug involved—whether it's a barbiturate, amphetamine, tranquilizer, narcotic, or some other substance: This can be vital to a doctor trying to decide on the proper emergency treatment. If possible, find a sample of the drug to bring to the emergency room or give to ambulance attendants. Or try finding an empty pill bottle.

Was the drug legitimate? Try learning if the drug was purchased from a pharmacy or bought on the street. There are often big differences between legitimate drugs and street drugs, and the source can be important to a doctor's decision on how to treat the victim.

What was taken with the drug? If you can discover whether the drug was used with another substance, tell the medical personnel.

How much was taken? Try determining how much of the drug was used, and how recently.

What is the victim's drug history? This can be extremely important to a doctor deciding how tolerant the child is to the drug involved in the emergency. If you know how long the victim has been using a specific drug, and the amounts, such information may save his life.

Be Prepared

Every household should be ready for a drug emergency. Now is the proper time—before a crisis arises—to do the following:

- Write down the phone number of your local Poison Control Center and keep it near your telephone.
- Find out which hospital is closest to you, and think about how you can get there quickly in an emergency.
- Buy a one-ounce bottle of ipecac syrup at your pharmacy and make sure you understand how to use it properly. Ask the pharmacist. Keep it where you can find it quickly in an emergency.
- Learn how to give mouth-to-mouth resuscitation. Practice at least once with your spouse or a friend.
- Never remove the labels from pill containers. They can provide vital information in case of an emergency.

KEY POINTS

- Physical evidence of substance abuse:
1. packets of rolling papers
2. roach clips
3. water pipes, or "bongs"
4. more conventional pipes made of wood, metal, plastic, and paper
5. syringes
6. coke spoons

7. small plastic bags, Baggies, Zip-loc pouches, glassine envelopes, aluminum-foil strips, small bottles, boxes, and vials
8. desktop scales
9. razor blades
10. "cookers": kitchen spoons and soda-bottle caps burnt black on the bottom
11. bloodstained pieces of cotton
12. over-the-counter eye drops
13. containers of rubbing alcohol
14. butane lighters and matches
15. burn holes on clothing and furniture from dropped joints and marijuana seeds

● Maintain careful inventory of alcohol and prescription drugs in your home. Mark levels on the back of liquor bottles with a grease pencil; count the number of pills in a bottle. Better yet, install locks on both medicine and liquor cabinets.

● Be cognizant of smells such as marijuana's and hashish's sweet scents; the acrid odor of burnt cooking implements; the pungency of sulfur from spent matches; incense and room deodorizers, for masking alcohol and smoke; and mouthwash on your youngster's breath, for covering up alcohol, pot, and hashish.

● Behavioral evidence of substance abuse:

1. long periods spent in the bathroom
2. sudden, unexplained availability of money
3. secretive behavior
4. changes in friends and hangouts
5. mercurial mood changes
6. irresponsibility at home and at school
7. preoccupation with drugs and drug culture
8. deteriorating health and physical appearance
9. loss of ambition

● Whenever a youngster of drug-vulnerable age seems to be acting peculiarly—or he just doesn't seem "like himself"—jot down in a notepad your impression and what triggered it. Then date the entry. If the unusual

151

conduct reoccurs you can at least rest assured your imagination is not playing tricks on you.

● America's Top Ten list of abused substances, according to 1986 high-school seniors:

1. alcohol
2. tobacco
3. marijuana/hashish
4. stimulants
5. cocaine/crack
6. inhalants
7. hallucinogens
8. sedative-hypnotics/tranquilizers
9. opiates other than heroin
10. heroin

Chapter Six

Confronting a Drug- or Alcohol-Abusing Child

You're standing in the middle of your child's room, hands on hips, exasperated. You had reminded him earlier to put away his freshly laundered clothes before going out with his friends, but there they lie in a heap on his bed, untouched. With a sigh, you scoop up several shirts, open a dresser drawer, and place them inside, when your hand brushes against something cold and metallic. You remove a pipe that is unlike any you have ever seen. Feeling around in back, you pull out a small plastic bag containing marijuana, and a glass vial of brightly colored pills. You collapse on the bed, your head in your hands.

"I don't believe it," you mutter. But you had better believe it. Your kid is using drugs. And I'm going to tell you what to do.

First, however, I'm going to tell you what *not* to do and how to avoid the mistakes parents commonly make when challenged by this unsettling, trying situation.

Don't deny the obvious: Here is a classic initial reaction to the discovery of substances or paraphernalia: "It's not his, it must belong to somebody else." Possible but not probable. The odds are slim that a youngster associates with drug users—even holds their illicit substances for them— but does not actively engage in drug use.

Abuse and addiction are diseases of denial, for drinkers, for drug users, *and* for their families. Parents often turn a blind eye to the crisis because they are afraid they won't know what to do, how to intervene. Maybe if

153

they ignore the problem, it will go away. But instead it perpetuates. "Johnny's been a good boy all his life," they rationalize. "I can't believe he would do drugs." So they don't believe it. Perhaps Johnny has been a good boy, or Mary a good girl. But even good kids do drugs. The issue isn't whether a child is good or bad, it's that he is abusing himself with chemicals, and you have to get him help.

For years my parents refused to face up to my heroin addiction, making constant excuses for their errant son's behavior. Michael, who was also a teenage addict, laughs dryly as he recalls "constantly leaving clues about my drug habit all over the house, like a dirty cooker [spoon] on the dresser or a syringe under the bed. I knew my mother would find them, because she's a cleaning fanatic. And she did. For months she just kept throwing them away, never saying a word to me. Of course, she did it out of love; she just could not accept that I was putting a spike in my arm."

Don't be an enabler: That is the term used to describe someone like Michael's mother: someone who consciously or unconsciously supports a drug user's deviant behavior. They do so in a variety of ways.

One way is by bargaining with the abuser to stop: "If you quit using drugs/drinking, we'll get you that new car/guitar/outfit you've been asking for." Cut a deal with a kid on drugs, and you'll make out about as well as the Indians who unloaded Manhattan island. When the youngster eventually violates the agreement, both sides feel more disillusioned and discouraged than before.

Drug users are magnificent manipulators. I say that recalling my own behavior when I was addicted and from having worked with thousands of youths in rehabilitation. Drug users view kindness as weakness and will exploit the guilt almost any parent will feel, that somehow he or she was neglectful. The abuser doesn't even have to say it but simply imply, "If you had paid more attention to me, if you really loved me, I wouldn't be this way."

Another method of enabling is by protecting the abuser from shouldering responsibility for himself, in the end sanctioning further misconduct: A youngster smashes up the family car while out on a drunken joyride, his parents hurry to the police station to fetch him, pay for the repair bill, and several weeks later he's cruising around town again. Where is the motivation for him to change, when he knows that Mom and Dad will be there to bail him out of trouble (figuratively or literally)? In chapter 3 I stressed the importance of imparting to kids that they are accountable for their actions, and it is even more crucial now that you do so. Place responsibility where it belongs: on the abuser.

Don't point fingers haphazardly: Parents contending with a youngster's drug problem often give way to panic. Frustrated, desperately seeking answers and anxious to lay blame somewhere, they heap it upon their spouse. Sometimes siblings absorb the brunt of it. Or "bad influences" such as the substance abuser's friends and steady dates. No matter who plays the scapegoat, blaming others succeeds only in turning family members against one another at a time when they need mutual support. It squanders precious time and constitutes yet more denial: the refusal to admit that ultimately the child drank or took drugs *of his own volition.*

That can be a hard fact to swallow. I've worked with kids whose parents' method of dealing with their addictions was to shuttle them from school to school. When they flunked out or were suspended, their families would pull up stakes and move to another town. "Don't worry," these children were told, "we'll start over again somewhere else." The results were always the same, of course, because no attempt was made to rectify the insecurities, the deficient values, and so forth that accompanied their youngsters to each new situation.

Kids can be corrupted by morally impoverished surroundings, but rarely will shifting them to more wholesome environments alone rehabilitate substance abusers. Once a child has been in the drug cultrue, the motivation to drink or to use chemicals is more internal than external. Previous experience has reinforced in his mind that drugs abet peer acceptance, relieve boredom, make him feel grown up—all of the reasons reviewed in chapter 3. No matter where their families relocate, drug-using youngsters will track down others like them. When I was nineteen I fled to Florida from New York for the sole purpose of leaving behind my druggie friends and getting clean. Within weeks I was part of an even seamier crowd, and my habit worsened.

Here is one other place not to lay blame: on yourself. It is an unnecessary burden that too many parents willingly bear, wringing their hands and imploring, "Where did we go wrong?" Did you make some mistakes raising your child? Of course, just like all parents do—including those whose kids are delightfully drug-free.

Don't fool yourself that the problem's solution is simple and painless: Shortly after I admitted being addicted to heroin, at my parents' insistence I visited a psychiatrist. This relieved them tremendously. One day, concluding a lengthy, grim discussion about my future, my father said to me as he stood up to go, "Well, I feel much better now, and I think you're going to be all right." I was racked with guilt and kept apologizing to him profusely. "I'll straighten up, Dad, I promise.'

"And by the way, can I borrow twenty dollars?"

My father handed me the bill. He walked away feeling encouraged about the situation, while I went out to score some dope and get high. Spending a whole hour talking about my problems—feeling so ashamed—was just too much for me to handle without drugs.

My chemical dependency was not going to be solved with a single psychiatric session or a heart-to-heart with my dad. But my folks, having refused to acknowledge its mere existence for so long, were now denying its severity and the reality that rehabilitation would be a lengthy, often grueling process.

HOW TO RAISE THE ISSUE WITH YOUR YOUNGSTER

It is extremely important that you do not act rashly. Before broaching the subject with your child, discuss the crisis and your intervention strategy with your spouse, for unity is critical.

Ask yourselves, How long has this been going on?, the prime consideration in determining whether or not professional attention is needed. The answer is easier to ascertain than you might think. Once you accept that your child is drinking or taking drugs, you'll recollect seemingly innocent remarks and episodes from months past that will fill in the puzzle's missing pieces: his new cast of companions assembled virtually overnight, which at the time you attributed to the transient nature of youthful friendships; the drop in grades he claimed was due to incompetent teachers who "have it in for me"; the defensiveness at the dinner table whenever the subject of drugs or his friends is brought up. Refer again to chapter 5's roll call of substance-abuse indicators.

If you don't feel confident in your ability to piece together the evidence, call any drug-information hotline or chemical-dependency treatment center. Ask to speak to a counselor, who can help evaluate the problem's extent and offer relevant referrals. However, most will refrain from rendering a conclusive diagnosis over the telephone and will suggest you bring the child in for evaluation.

I do not recommend traditional information sources such as family doctors and clergy. Though M.D.'s can readily identify the physical symptoms of abuse, not all are familiar with the behavioral signs. And while a minister, priest, or rabbi may be able to offer comforting words, few are adequately informed on the subject. Upon learning of my affair with drugs, my parents sought counsel from some rather unorthodox "experts." One was a psychic, who predicted my torment would eventually end and that it would provide me with a valuable lesson for the future. As it turned out, he was far more accurate than the many psychiatrists who dismissed me as hopeless.

Wait a day or two before confronting your youngster. Allow yourselves sufficient time to read this chapter thoroughly, to rehearse what to say and how to say it, and to get over your initial shock, dismay, outrage, hurt, resentment—there is no telling what your emotions may be. Sometimes mothers and fathers react differently to the discovery of a child's substance use, with one showing extreme concern and the other brushing it off as an adolescent rite of passage. This, too, must be vented between couples and resolved before sitting the youngster down. I say that it is always better to overreact in this situation than to underreact, for the stakes are so high. Trust yourself and your instincts. If you feel in your gut that something is wrong with your child, it probably is.

Select a time, preferably a weekend afternoon, when interruptions will be minimal. Take the phone off the hook and, if possible, send the other kids to a movie. Confronting a child about suspected drug use is draining enough—for both parties—without distractions. And if your youngster appears to be inebriated, wait for the next available opportunity.

Make your best effort to keep your emotions in check. Confrontation is not meant to be punitive, it is a fact-finding mission.

What Not to Do

Do not accuse before you have *all* the facts ("We know you're doing drugs!"): An innocent kid who is unjustly pronounced guilty may decide to take part in the wrongful behavior after all. Why serve the sentence without getting to commit the crime?

Do not get angry or belittle ("If I catch you smoking pot, I'll smack your face," or "What are you, stupid?"): Doing so will only send him back to his drug-using peers with a ready rationalization for getting stoned: "Nobody cares about me anyway." When you ridicule a child, he is made to feel like an irresponsible kid. Inadvertently, you've granted him license for more irresponsible, kidlike misconduct.

Do not load on the guilt ("You're going to give your father a heart attack."): Drinkers and drug users already feel encumbered by remorse and worthlessness. Their way of coping with the distress they have caused is to become intoxicated.

Do not say, "How can you do this to us?" You will only reinforce what he probably believes already: that you are more concerned about yourselves, your reputation, and so forth than about his welfare.

Speak calmly, compassionately, and in your own language, which you tailor to his age. "We'd like to talk to you about a problem we think this family is having and that we all have to work at," you begin. Not *your problem*, but *this family's problem*, for substance abuse is indeed a family crisis that demands everybody's cooperation.

"We've noticed some changes in you lately." Name them. "We love you and sense something is troubling you, in which case we want to help. We understand that you want to keep some things private, which is fine, but we think this problem is too big for you to work out by yourself." Express your concern not just about his possible drug use but about other things that might be bothering him. Ask questions, so that he has to answer you: "Do you know what we're talking about?"

Some kids will blurt out the truth right then and there. Most will not.

Some Possible Responses

Your child may become defensive, deny anything is the matter, and try turning the tables, acting hurt that you could even suspect him of using alcohol or drugs.

He may feign innocence, looking you right in the eye when he says, "I've never taken drugs in my life." If he does admit to sporadic use, he minimizes it. "Don't worry," he assures you, "it's no problem. Besides, I was going to give it up." Delivered so sincerely, it is a response that some parents are all too eager to accept at face value. End of discussion, and the child slips past the checkpoint on his journey down drugs' destructive path.

Not all promises to straighten up are deceptions; some kids really mean it. But they may be in too deep to quit without professional help.

He may become antagonistic and bolt out of the house. "I don't have to listen to this." Assure him he most certainly does, and that the conversation will resume the next day. And, if necessary, the day after that, "until we get to the truth." Make a hostile youngster understand in no uncertain terms that you mean business.

He may act sarcastic and call you hypocrites, sneering, "How come you can drink, but I can't?" Your reply is simple: "You are a minor for whom alcohol and drugs are illegal. So long as you live under this roof, drinking and drugging will not be tolerated under any condition." Kids may also accuse you of ignorance ("You don't know what you're talking about."), further underscoring the importance of boning up on your facts. Don't be taken in by this and other diversionary tactics.

A basic guideline: Expect to hear a bunch of lies, for substance-using kids are con artists who will say anything to get you off their back. I used to placate my parents with all sorts of baloney, from "But I never inhaled" to "I tried it just once" to "It made me so sick, I'll never do it again." In order to cover up my lies, I was forced to tell many more, until even I could not discern truth from fiction. The longer a child has been able to elude you with his drug use, the smarter he thinks he is, and the more fabrications he will feed you.

If you don't make any progress in the confrontation's early stages, take a breath, compose yourself, and probe further in a firm tone of voice:

"We have to disagree with you that no problem exists. Your grades have gone down, you're hanging out with a different element of friends, and you seem out of it half the time—as if you're drunk or stoned."

Should you have drug experiences of your own, call on them, to break down his wall of denial. "We're not stupid. We know how people who are high look and act, and we're reasonably sure that you are hurting yourself with chemicals. Now, how about being honest with us so that we can help you help yourself?"

The child's response? Possibly still more disavowals, in which case curtail the discussion. The parent with whom the child feels closest should suggest the conversation be continued the next day, perhaps over lunch. A variation on the good-cop/bad-cop mode of interrogation, it can work to gain the child's trust—and subsequent confession.

Another technique is to confront him with the physical proof. This way:

"If, as you insist, you are not using drugs, then we're sure you won't mind if we search your room. Not behind your back, but right in front of you." Thrusting evidence at the youngster only allows him to sidestep the real issue at hand and make you the culprit. "You went snooping through

159

my drawers? I can't believe it! How could you do a thing like that?" Give him the option of retrieving it himself: "You can either bring the drugs and paraphernalia down here yourself, and we can discuss what to do next, or you can accompany us to your room, and we'll see what we can find."

Even if he finally admits to concealing substances, prepare yourself for another barrage of lies. The standard is, "That stuff's not mine, I'm holding it for a friend." Don't fall for it. Ask him about the furtive phone calls, and he might tell you, straight-faced, "We were planning a surprise anniversary party for you guys." Expect to hear some pretty preposterous stories. In general, the older the abuser and the more persistent the abuse, the more resistance you will face.

INCREASED DISCIPLINE OR DRUG REHABILITATION?

Continuing this scenario, let's assume your child has confessed. (When kids have deluded themselves into believing they have no problem, parents must resort to what is called an intervention, explained later in this chapter.) Now it's time to establish exactly how long he has been a user and of what substances. At Cenikor, our method was to ask a new patient about his dependency's duration—then multiply his answer by ten. I've never known a drug abuser who was an accurate bookkeeper or who overreported the extent of his habit. If he claimed he'd been a cocaine addict for a month, it was probably closer to a year. If he insisted he used only cocaine, we could be sure he'd turned to other chemicals too.

I recommend immediate professional treatment for *all second-time offenders*, for first-time offenders whose use of *any* substance except tobacco is chronic, and for first-time offenders found to be taking cocaine, crack, hallucinogens, PCP, or narcotics, or who are polydrug abusers.

For argument's sake I'm going to assume that your child's use is limited to experimentations with tobacco, alcohol, marijuana, hashish, uppers, or downers; possibly more than one. (A youngster ingesting all of the above substances certainly would fit my definition of a polydrug user and is in need of rehabilitation.) The problem is not so out of hand that you cannot respond to it at home. However, it calls for your accepting the role of disciplinarian—no matter how uncomfortably it fits at first—and putting into effect a new Family Contract:

Family Contract II

I, _____*(child's name)*, pledge to abide by the following rules:

1. No use of alcohol or drugs, ever.
2. No tobacco use.
3. No associating with known drug users or hanging out where drugs are used.
4. Obeying all school regulations and remaining on school grounds during the day.
5. At the end of the day, returning directly home from school.
6. No going out on school nights, unless to an activity approved by Mom and Dad.
7. Completing all homework assignments, which will then be shown to Mom and Dad. In return, Mom and Dad promise their assistance as much as possible.
8. No attending parties without adult supervision or parties held at the homes of children unknown to Mom and Dad.
9. All callers must identify themselves to Mom and Dad, or they will not be put through.
10. A weekend-eveing curfew will be adhered to:
    - for twelve-to-fourteen-year-olds: 10 p.m.
    - for fifteen- and sixteen-year-olds: 12 a.m.
    - for seventeen- and eighteen-year-olds: 1 a.m.

Date effective: _____

Signed:

_____
(Child's name)

_____
(Parent's name)

_____
(Parent's name)

The penalties, which are also written into the contract, depend on the infractions. If the child breaks any of rules 2 through 10, the contract is made more stringent. If he is caught drinking or drugging, it is mutually understood that he will be enrolled in some form of drug treatment, depending on the nature of the abuse.

For kids who follow the contract, standards can be relaxed after a month and adjusted every two months after that: curfew extended by a half hour, more approved activities for weeknights, and so forth. Noncompliance is punished; responsibility is rewarded.

Other tacks parents should take to help discourage future violations:

- Limit the child's access to money; grant a small allowance contingent upon completion of chores and schoolwork.
- Restrict car access to sanctioned activities only.
- Lock up all liquor, medicine, and potential inhalants.
- When he has friends over, insist the door to his room be kept open at all times.
- Leave him at home alone as seldom as possible until he earns your trust.

Another option is to submit kids to random drug testing. Because of the sensitive nature of this issue—not to mention the time and expense (anywhere from twenty-five to one hundred dollars) involved—I advocate it only in instances where a child's use of alcohol, marijuana, hashish, uppers, or downers has been regular (three to five times a week) and on the verge of meriting treatment. Urinalysis should be performed not more than once a week and not less than once a month at a local laboratory, which you can locate by looking under "Laboratories—Medical" in the Yellow Pages.

There are several different tests for measuring the presence of alcohol or drugs. Generally, if a urine specimen tests positive, it will be checked a second time. Parents can rest assured that the results are highly accurate, if not 100% without error. Fortunately, the mere threat of urinalysis is often enough to intimidate kids into staying straight—especially once they learn that traces of THC from marijuana can remain in their fatty tissues for as long as thirty days.

No matter what threats you make, be prepared to carry them out if household rules are defied. And if your kid drinks or drugs again, you must follow through on entering him in a rehabilitation program, for at this stage the problem is too severe for you to contend with alone.

Professional treatment is also appropriate if

- drug use has taken its toll on a youngster's physical or psychological well-being;
- it is recommended by another authority, including school counselors, teachers, and police;
- a child's drug use threatens to destroy the family—for example, if he seems to be a negative influence on his siblings;
- *if you've done everything you can and no longer feel capable of coping with the problem in a way benefitting your child.*

Getting a Second-Time Offender into Treatment

Once again you confront him with his transgressions, only this time more directly. If you happen upon physical evidence, set it down in front of him and demand an explanation. Probably you'll hear more of the same excuses. But sometimes even kids realize their habits are out of control and may welcome your interceding.

Helen, one of the former drug users we spoke to, intentionally left drug-related implements around her mother's apartment. "It was my way of crying for help," she says. When Darrell's parents finally challenged him about his crack addiction, "I just spilled my guts out to them and told them I needed help. I couldn't stand all the lies and deceptions anymore. I felt ashamed, but mostly I felt like a huge weight had been lifted from my shoulders." The twenty-one-year-old was then persuaded by his mother and father to enroll in New York's Daytop Village chemical-dependency program.

Seriously addicted kids who refuse to seek help are confronted through an approach called intervention, which involves siblings, relatives, neighbors, and friends—anyone concerned enough about a drug-abusing youth to rebuke him en masse for his destructive habit and to induce him into getting the proper care. Its effectiveness lies in its shock value, for few drug users, in their delusions of grandeur, believe anyone is wise to them.

To conduct an intervention, a group of between six and ten people is gathered on an evening when you know your youngster will be home. Explain during your initial phone call the visit's purpose and what is expected of everyone. For example, the uncle for whom the drug user works on weekends might stand up among the group and address him directly: "You haven't been showing up to your job on time, when you do show up at all. Last Saturday you stayed home because you claimed you were sick, but I found out differently from your parents. So where were you that day, and what were you doing?"

A brother or sister might stand up next. "You've been stealing money from me to pay for your cocaine, and I'm really angry. What are you going to do about your problem?"

Enlisting the help of those his own age is a tricky proposition, since the majority of a substance abuser's companions share the same vice. Rely instead on former friends the abuser has since deserted for the drug crowd: the ex-steady who tired of his constantly being stoned; the onetime best buddy who no longer comes around.

Intervention shatters the user's ego—he isn't as clever as he thought— and sets him thinking that while he is not fooling anyone else, perhaps he is fooling himself. Essentially, through the confrontation of others, he is forced to confront himself. It can be easier to get a drug-dependent person to concede he has a problem than an alcohol-dependent person, since drinking is more socially acceptable in our culture than drug abuse. For that reason, it may be harder gaining the support of others. If they themselves drink socially, they may feel uncomfortable accusing someone else of imbibing too much.

Most parents will not feel at ease in an intervention, which of course can and will do more harm than good. If that is the case, contact a professional alcohol- and drug-abuse counselor. Some will come to the home for what is called a family therapy session, but most prefer the child be brought to the treatment facility.

Interventions have an excellent success rate of getting resisters into treatment; once youthful drug users reconcile their feelings of hurt and humiliation, the caring shown by friends and loved ones often moves them to consent to rehabilitation. However, what happens when all of the aforementioned measures fails?

Paul, then twenty, agreed to placement in Odyssey House's Manhattan therapeutic-community program only because the alternative was prison. He'd been arrested five times for grand larceny. "I never would have admitted to myself that I needed help," he says a year later, adding that he plans on remaining in the program even once his probation is up.

If you are the parent of a youngster like Paul—who declines treatment but presents an obvious danger to himself and to his family—you probably feel powerless. How can you get him into rehabilitation if he won't go? By utilizing the juvenile court system. In many states parents can consign drug-abusing minors to substance-dependency programs without their consent. As for what effect involuntary commitment has on patients, National Institute on Drug Abuse director Dr. Charles Shuster confirms the studies that show "there is no difference between the outcomes of people forced into treatment and those who enter of their own free will."

According to the Juvenile Justice Center at the American Bar Association, restrictions for involuntary commitment vary from state to state. Minnesota is comparatively lenient, whereas New Jersey is more stringent. Generally, parents will face fewer obstacles if they can obtain the approval of a physician, or if the juvenile in question has been previously involved with the delinquency system; for example, if he has been arrested for drunken driving, shoplifting, and so on.

The recommended procedure is for parents to contact their county's department (also called a division or unit) of social services or department of health and human services, both found in the Goverment Offices listings of the White Pages. They request formally that their child be committed to substance-abuse treatment. A caseworker assembles the details of the case, which is then brought before a judge in the family court's juvenile unit. If it can be proved to the court's satisfaction that the youngster is not competent to decide in his own best interest, he will be ordered into drug-free care. Before instigating this action, it is suggested parents retain an attorney's services, though the court assigns counsel to those who cannot afford representation.

An alternative is to file a PINS (*persons in need of supervision*) petition, also through the county family court's juvenile unit. For its telephone number, look under "Family Court" in the County Government Offices listings of the White Pages. The names vary (CHINS, of children in need of supervision, is one), but all states have similar legal processes. Again, if it can be shown that a minor is not competent to decide in his own best interest, the court assumes responsibility for him and can place him in rehabilitation.

Initiating a PINS petition takes anywhere from twenty-four hours to thirty days, depending on court gridlock. For some parents it is the answer to getting their child the help he needs. One cautionary word, however: Such a course should be followed only when all other attempts have failed. In some cases a child may be referred to state-run mental facilities and hospitals that often do nothing more than warehouse patients until they are physically drug-free. These programs last from one to two weeks, which is appallingly insufficient for attending to young people's psychological needs.

Something else to be aware of: If you are the parent of a substance-dependent child, you know that time is of the essence. When you contact government social-services agencies for assistance, it is natural to expect immediate answers and a clear-cut plan of action. Unfortunately, the majority of these offices are understaffed and overwhelmed by cases. Prepare youself to occasionally have your telephone call passed from staff member to staff member like a hockey puck. No matter how infuriating, don't get discouraged and *stay on that line*. Remember, with most bureaucracies the wheels of progress turn s-l-o-w-l-y.

Getting Legal-Age Kids into Treatment

The majority of parents reading this book will not have to exercise PINS petitions and the like, for most minors enter rehabilitation voluntarily. According to a survey published by the National Institute on Alcohol Abuse and Alcoholism, the referral sources to outpatient and inpatient drug-free programs for seventeen-year-old boys and girls were:

- male outpatients: self, 10%; family and friends, 28%; criminal-justice system, 22%; medical, 4%; community, 13%; school, 21%;
- female outpatients: self, 9%; family and friends, 38%; criminal-justice system, 17%; medical, 8%; community, 11%; school, 18%;
- male inpatients: self, 8%; family and friends, 25%; criminal-justice system, 47%; medical, 8%; community, 12%; school, 0%;
- female inpatients: self, 15%; family and friends, 35%; criminal-justice system, 20%; medical, 10%; community, 21%; school, 0%.

The sources are somewhat different for eighteen- and nineteen-year-olds. Though nearly twice as many refer themselves, they are less likely to accept the suggestions of family and friends, and a significantly greater number wind up in treatment through the criminal-justice system.

When resisters are of legal age, parents cannot rely on the courts; they have to act as their own judges. Therefore, if an emancipated youngster refuses to stop using drugs and to seek help, give him a choice of *getting clean or getting out of the house*.

Too tough? Sooner or later, parents of chronic substance abusers have to consider their self-preservation. One child's drug habit can wreck havoc on famly life, strain marriages, and unsettle siblings. Think of the dependent person as being afflicted with a contagious disease. Unless he is

166

quarantined from the other, healthy family members, everyone eventually becomes contaminated in some way.

Here are some typical scenes from households bedeviled by a child's substance abuse:

Family dynamics are knocked off-axis, with everything and everybody revolving around him. Alcoholics and drug users may not be able to manage their own lives, but they have a remarkable propensity for gaining control over loved ones.

Enabling parents are always on the alert for substances, emptying bottles of liquor down the sink, flushing drugs down the toilet, hoping that way to rid the abuser of his habit.

Whenever the child is out of the house and the phone rings, his parents shiver with fear. Has he gotten into trouble with the law? Been in a car accident?

Strange, unsavory characters show up at the home to buy or sell drugs. If a deal turns sour, there may be threatening phone calls—or threats that are carried out against the child or the family.

A valiant effort is made to maintain some semblance of normality, but gradually routines such as family meals and holiday celebrations break down. The substance abuser frequently misses dinner and may not come home at all some nights. The rest of the family functions as if on tenterhooks, trying its best to suppress feelings of anger and resentment toward the problem kid. At intervals, the friction ignites in explosions of tempers and arguments.

The mother and father, frustrated, nerves frayed, argue between themselves, each blaming the other that the problem is not being handled properly. They also feel ashamed about their family's crisis and worry other adults will regard them as "bad" parents. Socializing is avoided so as not to contend with the possibility that the subject may be raised.

Having to play caretaker eventually exacts its toll physically and psychologically on parents. A Fair Oaks Hospital study of mothers and fathers whose children had substance-abuse problems showed that many suffered from psychiatric disturbances, while nearly half complained of physical ailments such as hypertension, arthritis, and diabetes.

Siblings often feel ignored and that all of the parents' attention is focused on the troublemaker. It seems to them as if he is being rewarded for his misbehavior. They may also harbor feelings of guilt, that somehow they too failed their brother or sister.

* * *

It is important that you try not to neglect your other kids during this time of emergency. And while of course you should remain loyal to your troubled child and make every reasonable effort to help him, *don't neglect your own needs.* Don't be a martyr. Yes, you will be affected by a youngster's drug habit, but the damage doesn't have to be extreme or permanent. Protect yourself from the promises that will only be broken. Come to the hard realization that you cannot make a drug user stop simply by loving him enough. Learn to separate yourself emotionally from his self-created misery. This will not come easy, for a parent's natural instinct is to run to his child and cradle him when he is hurting. Besides, what if detachment is interpreted as abandonment?

Most likely it will be, because your kid is used to your responding immediately to his every whim. Understand that drugs strip people of their consciences. They become selfish, self-obsessed—*different human beings*—who secretly delight in your anguish every time they stagger home intoxicated or get into trouble. They relish the attention. During the years that I was strung out on junk, I didn't care a whit about the heartache I was causing my parents, my wife, even my baby daughter. All I cared about was getting high. Only when I sobered up would I grasp what I had done and the monster I'd become—which merely sent me back to using drugs, to alleviate the guilt.

Parents who detach break that ruinous pattern. Sometimes, when drug-using kids see they can no longer manipulate, they realize the game is up, cave in, and are finally ready to accept professional help for their problem.

You have to be able to deal with your youngster's substance dependency rationally. Of what use is a parent incapacitated by a crisis? If someone is drowning in a churning surf, you don't leap in blindly after him, which results in two persons' endangerment. You analyze the risks and formulate a safer plan for saving him.

Get Help for Yourself

There is an old saying that when a kid is a drug user, his parents love him but hate to see him coming. How true. For some parents, used to loving their youngster unconditionally, it is a new and uncomfortable sensation to manage; just one of many. If you are undergoing a child's drug-related crisis, some of the emotions you may be feeling right now are:

- anger and resentment—over the time and energy expended on the drug user; over the way he is frittering away his life;

- frustration and helplessness—Your child seems beyond your control;
- loneliness—The kid living in your home might as well be a total stranger;
- hurt—Is his substance abuse a rejection of you?
- embarrassment—Perhaps you wonder if his problem is reflective of your parenting abilities;
- guilt—Though you will always love your kid, at the moment you don't particularly like or respect him. You also feel that you somehow have failed him.

It is natural to have difficulty coming to terms with any or all of the above feelings, in which case I recommend family support groups such as Al-Anon, Families Anonymous, Drug-Anon, and Toughlove. Also called self-help and peer counseling, these fellowships address addictions ranging from overeating to chronic gambling. There are more than five hundred thousand chapters and fifteen million members nationwide.

All are made up of lay therapists; that is, everyday people who share a common experience. The four abovementioned groups provide mutual support, understanding, and education among relatives and friends of drug abusers. Parents often ask me if professional treatment is preferable to self-help. I advise starting with a program such as Al-Anon first, then supplementing it with professional therapy if you feel you need it. But support groups have long been documented to benefit millions of people. One distinct advantage over counseling is that there is no charge, although voluntary contributions are accepted. Most are based on the principles of Alcoholics Anonymous (AA), which is covered in chapter 7.

Al-Anon, in fact, was founded in 1950 by families of alcoholics who had found sobriety in AA. It now has thousands of groups in over eighty countries. As with any "Anonymous" organization, members are nameless if they wish to be. Meetings are held weekly, or as determined by group consensus. The goals of Al-Anon and kindred societies include

- sharing ways for parents to adjust to a child's dependency by learning to detach, to focus inward rather than outward, and to stop assuming responsibility for them;
- offering a variety of perspectives on the same problem;
- helping parents understand that addiction is a compulsive illness and that the young person can not refrain from his habit;
- giving parents the courage to balance their lives once again, to resume former friendships and form new ones.

It is always recommended that both parents attend meetings, though not necessarily in the same group; some adults are less self-conscious when their spouses are not present. The abuser's siblings are also encouraged to attend, with separate Alateen groups available for young people from twelve to twenty.

Do not expect to learn in Al-Anon, Families Anonymous, Drug-Anon, or Toughlove how to deter your child from using substances; this group is for *you* and for your feelings.

KEY POINTS

● Upon discovering a child's drug dependency, ask yourselves, How long has this been going on? If you don't feel confident in your ability to piece together the physical and behavioral evidence, consult a counselor at any drug-information hotline or chemical-dependency treatment center.

● How to raise the issue with your child:

1. Select a time, preferably a weekend afternoon, when interruptions will be minimal. Take the phone off the hook and, if possible, send the other kids to a movie.
2. Do not accuse before you have all the facts, get angry, belittle your youngster, or load on the guilt.
3. Speak calmly and in your own language about "the *family's* problem," not "*your* problem."
4. Express your concern not just about his possible drug use but about other things that might be bothering him.
5. Ask questions, so that he has to answer you.
6. If necessary, confront him with physical evidence of substance abuse.

● A basic guideline when confronting a suspected drug abuser: Expect to hear a bunch of lies. Substance-using kids are con artists who will say anything to get you off their back.

● First-time offenders whose use is limited to experimentations with tobacco, alcohol, marijuana, hashish, uppers, or downers should be made to abide by a new, more stringent Family Contract. Other tacks parents should take to help discourage future violations:

1. Limit the child's access to money; grant a small allowance contingent upon completion of chores and schoolwork.
2. Restrict car access to sanctioned activities only.
3. Lock up all liquor, medicine, and potential inhalants.
4. When he has friends over, insist the door to his room be kept open at all times.
5. Leave him at home alone as seldom as possible until he earns your trust.
6. Submit him to random drug testing.

● Methods of getting second-time offenders into treatment against their will:

1. Conduct an intervention, either on your own or, preferably, with the help of a professional drug-rehabilitation counselor.
2. Take your child to family court, juvenile unit. Request that he be committed to substance-abuse treatment. Or make him a ward of the state by filing a PINS/CHINS petition, also through family court's juvenile unit.
3. When resisters are of legal age, give them the choice of getting clean or getting out of the house.

● Learn to detach from your child's addiction, to focus inward rather than outward, and to stop assuming responsibility for him.

● Substance-dependency treatment is recommended

1. for all second-time offenders;
2. for first-time offenders whose use of *any* substance except tobacco is chronic;
3. for first-time offenders found to be taking cocaine, crack, hallucinogens, PCP, or narcotics, or who are polydrug abusers;
4. when drug use has taken its toll on a youngster's physical or psychological well-being;
5. when it is suggested by another authority, including school counselors, teachers, and police;
6. when a child's drug use threatens to destroy the family; for example, if he seems to be a negative influence on his siblings;
7. when you've done everything you can and no longer feel capable of coping with the problem in a way benefiting your child.

RECOMMENDED RESOURCES

If you've observed signs of drug abuse but need help in determining conclusively whether or not a child has a substance-abuse problem, contact:

Cocaine Hotline
(800) COC-AINE

National Federation of Parents for
Drug-Free Youth
(800) 554-KIDS

National Institute on Drug Abuse
Drug-Referral Helpline
(800) 662-HELP

National Parents' Resource Institute for
Drug Education
Drug Information Line
(800) 241-7946

Parents' Association to Neutralize Drug
and Alcohol Abuse
The Listening Ear
(703) 750-9285

Other sources: For alcohol- and drug-treatment centers, look under "Alcoholism Information and Treatment Centers" and "Drug Abuse and Addiction Information and Treatment" in the Yellow Pages. Or, for referrals, contact your state's alcohol- and drug-abuse agency, the address and telephone number of which are in Appendix A.

If you or other family members need the support of a self-help group, or fellowship, for coming to grips with a child's substance abuse, contact the following organizations' headquarters to be referred to the chapter nearest you:

Al-Anon/Alateen
1372 Broadway
New York, NY 10018
(212) 302-7240

Drug-Anon
P. O. Box 473
Ansonia Station
New York, NY 10023
(212) 874-0700

Families Anonymous
P. O. Box 528
Van Nuys, CA 91408
(818) 989-7841

Toughlove
P. O. Box 1069
Doylestown, PA 18901
(215) 348-7090

Confronting a Drug- or Alcohol-Abusing Child

For referrals to self-help organizations of any type, contact:

National Self-Help Clearinghouse
33 West 42nd Street
Room 620N
New York, NY 10036
(212) 840-1259

Other sources: In the Yellow Pages, look under "Alcoholism Information and Treatment Centers" and "Drug Abuse and Addiction Information and Treatment"; look alphabetically in the White Pages.

Chapter Seven

Seeking
Professional
Treatment

So that he doesn't have time to back out, once your child agrees to undergo treatment, bring him to a chemical-dependency program within thirty-six hours. With over ten thousand rehabilitation centers nationwide, selecting the appropriate one for your youngster is going to require a great deal of time, thought, and research.

Therefore, parents should begin this process as soon as they detect a drug or alcohol problem. If your child had a stubborn cold, you would get him medical attention at once, not wait until it turned into pneumonia. The same forethought applies to the disease of substance abuse. In the event that his habit worsens, you'll be prepared to enter him promptly into a program that has earned your full confidence. Procrastinating until the family is embroiled in a drug-related emergency culminates in hasty and at times ill-conceived decisions that ultimately hamper a youngster's recovery.

Professional alcohol- and drug-abuse care can successfully treat problems as comparatively minor as pot smoking and as critical as prolonged heroin addiction. Claims of recovery fluctuate between 40% and 90%; however, the U.S. Office of Technology Assessment puts the average rate in the vicinity of 67%. The implication that treatment fails with one out of every three drug users is indeed chilling, but, fortunately, teens and preteens usually adapt more quickly to change than do adults.

Prior to World War II neither the government nor the public was sympathetic toward addicts, who were "treated" by being incarcerated in sanitariums. In 1935 the first of a scattering of federally sponsored narcotics farms opened in Lexington, Kentucky, and though residents underwent psychoanalysis, group therapy, and vocational training, the ambience was that of prison, with iron bars on the windows. Drugs were dispensed for the purpose of detoxification, inciting then-Commissioner of Narcotics Harry J. Anslinger to call these rehabilitation centers nothing more than supply houses for their "so-called patients." His callous remark contained an unintended truth: Whatever they were, the facilities rarely rehabilitated. In fact, the recidivism rate among ex-patients was believed to be as high as 98%.

In the 1950s and 1960s, more enlightened approaches to treating substance abusers gained acceptance. None has had a more lasting impact than the therapeutic doctrine that tending to a person's psychological conflicts is as imperative as arresting his physical dependency. Today that philosophy informs all treatment modes: self-help peer-group counseling, outpatient care, inpatient care, long-term residential (therapeutic-community) care, and methadone maintenance. We review each one as it pertains to the progressive stages of drug use.

If a child violates Family Contract II by continuing to occasionally (once, twice a month or less) use alcohol, marijuana, or inhalants:

Peer-counseling, by way of groups such as Alcoholics Anonymous, Drugs Anonymous, Cocaine Anonymous, and Narcotics Anonymous, is effective for stemming incipient substance use. (The latter two organizations are for abusers of *all* drugs, not just cocaine and narcotics.)

AA serves as the cornerstone for the other three. It is a fellowship of alcoholics begun in 1935 by an Akron, Ohio, surgeon known only as Dr. Bob S., and a prosperous New York stockbroker, Bill Griffith Wilson, whose name was divulged after his death in 1971. Both were chronic drinkers. Through word of mouth and eventually press coverage, by 1941 membership stood at six thousand; by 1950, at one hundred thousand. Today, with thirty-eight thousand U.S. and Canadian chapters, the society claims over one million constituents. One-third of them are women, and one-fifth are young people, nearly three times as many as there were in 1968. Groups are racially, ethnically, and generationally mixed, but some communities host meetings geared specifically toward adolescent alcoholism and codependency.

Members are not health-care/mental-health-care professionals, yet AA's recovery rate is alleged to be 75%. The program is based on twelve steps, or principles, stressing abstinence, service to others suffering from the same disease, and spirituality, though it is nondenominational. Meetings are held weekly or more frequently, according to each group's discretion. Members may also attend as many other chapters' meetings as they wish. In New York City there are an estimated two thousand AA meetings per week.

What do drinkers derive from AA? For one thing, shared strength. Men and women talk candidly about how alcohol adversely affected their lives, about their former drinking habits, and about how they are fighting to overcome their addiction. When kids see others with the same affliction successfully refrain from drinking, they are heartened and inspired to stay sober themselves. Moreover, for perhaps the first time they feel others understand them and are concerned about their welfare.

Support does not end with the conclusion of meetings, as each person selects a sponsor: a veteran same-sex group member who has maintained his sobriety. He or she becomes a trusted friend that can be called on twenty-four hours a day, whenever the abuser feels his resolve slipping or just needs someone to talk to. Members also regularly exchange phone numbers and are encouraged to call one another. In fellowships such as AA, children never need feel alone.

The atmosphere at a closed AA session—that is, closed to nonalcoholics—is comfortable and nonjudgmental. Posted on the walls are signs bearing reminders ("Easy Does It," "One Day at a Time") that staying temperate can be a struggle. When a youngster nervously walks in to his first meeting, it's usually a matter of minutes before others introduce themselves, offer him a cup of tea or coffee, and attempt to put him at ease.

"Hello, I'm _____, and I'm an alcoholic," is how each person introduces himself when speaking to the assemblage. All information revealed within the confines of the public or private building in which meetings are held is strictly confidential. Members typically go by first names only, so parents need not worry that family business is being aired to the community. Age and economic status are meaningless; lank-haired teenagers in torn jeans and conservatively shorn businessmen in handsomely tailored suits sit together, "identifying and comparing," as they say in AA parlance: learning from and finding strength in one another.

For many alcoholics the fellowship is a lifeline to emotional stability, enabling them to come to terms with feelings previously buried by booze. The only point on which I disagree with AA is its conviction that once an alcoholic, always an alcoholic. The rationale makes sense: Alcoholism is a disease of denial; thus, admitting to being an alcoholic is the first step toward sobriety. But since substance abusers are treated like second-class citizens in our society, I question how productive it is to hang albatrosses around the necks of people already suffering from poor self-image. That philosophical difference aside, I strongly recommend all four fellowships. None requires dues, although voluntary contributions are accepted.

AA suggests members attend ninety meetings in their first ninety days. However, for children whose use of alcohol, pot, and inhalants is still experimental or occasional, one to two per week is sufficient. Parents should accompany their youngster to an open meeting (for alcoholics, friends, relatives, and interested parties) once a week to begin with, then decrease gradually. Read all organizational literature as well, to get a sense of the fellowship's objectives and how it works. Certainly before you enter your kid in either Alcoholics Anonymous, Drugs Anonymous, Cocaine Anonymous, or Narcotics Anonymous, it is wise to sit in on an open meeting.

If a child violates Family Contract II by continuing to regularly (three to five times a week) use alcohol, marijuana, or inhalants:

I am partial to professional outpatient care, which, according to a National Institute on Alcohol Abuse and Alcoholism survey, is how as many as 78% of all substance abusers obtain treatment. Taking the definition of rehabilitation literally, its purpose is to restore the youngster to his former state, or his norm. A more regimented program is necessary for regular alcohol, pot, and inhalant users because their norm is *abnormal*: getting high. Especially if they are quite young—in their early teens or preteens—they've had little experience living straight, and their thought and maturation processes have been stunted by chemicals.

In a short-term four-to-six-month outpatient arrangement, kids attend school during the day and report afterward to the clinic, which may be either freestanding, in mental-health centers, or in general hospitals. (Hospital daycare is often referred to as partial hospitalization.) Evening-hour programs, or nightcare, may also be available. Though there are many excellent daycare facilities nationwide, Phoenix House is a first-rate model. Founded in 1967, it has both outpatient and residential centers in New York and California.

When a young person is first brought to the admissions unit, he undergoes an extensive screening to evaluate the extent of his drug use. Counselors then devise a personalized program encompassing individual, group, and family counseling. All three therapies are standard for each treatment mode.

In individual therapy youngsters work one-on-one with a counselor, learning to identify what caused their substance abuse and establishing goals leading to more productive lives. For example, the counselor—usually trained in chemical dependency or a former substance abuser himself—will help the child restructure his free time around new interests and friendships, to fill the void formerly occupied by getting stoned.

Some kids are less inhibited about revealing themselves to an older confidant than to a peer group, while other kids may see him as an authority figure and clam up. It is essential parents understand the counselor is not a spy who will report back to them. Neither will he act as the parents' disciplinary substitute. Generally, therapists contact the home only if advised of a situation that may be harmful to the child: talk of suicide, admission of having committed a serious crime, and so on. If progress is to be made, kids must feel they can trust their counselor.

Group therapy consists of approximately eight participants and one or two adult leaders. The principle is similar to that of self-help, with kids learning from and psychoanalyzing one another. Therapists function as moderators, redirecting tangential discussions, but mainly distancing themselves and allowing the patients to control the dynamics. Because they share the same experiences and language, many kids feel more comfortable opening up before a group of equals than in a one-on-one setting. Observing others express themselves frankly influences them to air their own feelings.

In addition, listening to other youths' drug histories yields insights into one's own motives for using chemicals. Ira, whose background contrasts radically with those of many addicts in his therapeutic-community program, says, "The parallels between their stories and mine scared the hell out of me. I heard the same anger, fear, loneliness, and lack of self-esteem."

Helen recalls feeling "overwhelmed" at her first group-therapy session "because I had thought I was the only person who felt the way I did, you know? Seeing that I wasn't so unique, so *weird*, was a big relief. When it came my turn to talk about my past, I didn't feel so awkward. Everyone else was telling the truth; I figured, why shouldn't I?" When among substance abusers, no one has to be ashamed of his habit.

At an encounter session, a youngster may say to the group, "This boy whose locker is next to mine at school always hits on me to smoke grass with him. What should I do? I've got to admit, sometimes it's tempting." His peers will advance suggestions on how to handle the situation, one that many of them contend with every day.

However, this kind of counseling is not all slaps on the back and words of encouragement. Group, as it is called, can be rough on the ego, especially for someone trying to perpetrate his self-deceptions on other drug users—who at one time or another probably rationalized their own substance problems in much the same way. That person will find himself quickly challenged, in language that is harsh and sometimes downright abusive.

"Everyone in the group sees right through a bullshitter," says Paul, "because we're all bullshitters, okay? We've been on the street and conned people, so we know when we're being conned. If somebody says, 'I never needed to smoke angel dust, I only did it when it was around,' I'll say, 'Bullshit, man, you were addicted to it, just like I was. Nobody does dust *occasionally.*' He's forced to admit that he has a real problem."

As the group evolves, however, such verbal sparring becomes accepted as part of the treatment, not a personal attack. Warm friendships often develop among kids whose former relationships were founded merely on a mutual interest in getting high. For some, their newfound acceptance and respect is so alien, they have difficulty adjusting.

"When things get good," Ira explains, "you become afraid because you're conditioned to always screwing up. And you feel guilty, as if you don't deserve happiness. Strange, isn't it? You're pulled in two directions at the same time."

As patients make strides in the program, staying straight and resolving emotional problems, they show one another by example that rehabilitation is possible; conversely, those who have relapsed can warn about the danger signs and situations to avoid. Naturally, the success of group therapy hinges on the rapport among the youngsters and on the counselor's expertise. Personally, I've seen few fail to accomplish their goals if they are allowed to last several sessions and find their rhythm.

Other types of therapy employed by drug-treatment facilities include:

Relaxation training: to provide kids with alternatives for coping with pressure. One of these may be biofeedback, which is conducted by a schooled therapist. It incorporates electrodes, which are devices that sense and register imperceptible electrical impulses, such as those occurring in the brain. Essentially, biofeedback trains people to relax without drugs. It has both its proponents and detractors, and studies on its effectiveness are inconclusive. Critics claim it is the caring of the therapist, not the hardware, that makes the treatment *sometimes* successful.

Recreational therapy (encompassing music, dance, arts and crafts, supervised sports activities): to provide new interests, new areas of self-discovery and accomplishment, enhanced self-esteem, and pride in a healthy body.

Psychodrama groups: in which patients role-play before a videotape camera. When conducted correctly by an experienced professional, the abuser is able to explore his feelings and learn new methods of coping with old situations.

Assertiveness training: to master problem-solving techniques that can be applied in daily life.

You will notice that these therapies basically employ the same prevention principles covered in chapter 3: rearranging preconceived notions of self, instilling confidence, alleviating boredom, encouraging responsibility, and so forth.

After approximately four to six months as an outpatient, the child is reevaluated. If he is declared recovered, he enters an aftercare program for a period of six months to a year. Weekly counseling may be conducted either at the facility itself or through one of the self-help fellowships described earlier in this chapter. Eventually his visits are tapered to monthly, then perhaps quarterly, until he is discharged from the program.

If a child violates Family Contract II by continuing to regularly use stimulants or depressants; if he is a first-time offender regularly using

hallucinogens or occasionally using cocaine, crack, PCP, or narcotics; if
alcohol abuse is chronic; or if self-help and/or outpatient care has failed:

He needs to be taken out of his environment and placed in an inpatient or residential facility, which may be freestanding or in a general hospital. Many are located in bucolic settings. For example, at the well-known Hazelden rehabilitation program, walking trails wind their way through the abundant greenery of its 288-acre campus in Center City, Minnesota. Although the 203-bed facility was founded in 1949 as an alcoholism treatment center, 80% of its present clientele suffer from drug abuse. Half are women. With a recovery rate of approximately 65%, Hazelden has been referred to as the "Minnesota Model" on which numerous rehabilitation centers worldwide have based their treatment procedures.

Hazelden maintains a separate 64-bed facility for young people between the ages of fourteen and thirty: Pioneer House, located on Medicine Lake, in Plymouth, Minnesota. Upon entering the program, each youngster is given a thorough intake evaluation by the nursing staff, observed over a period of not less than twenty-four hours.

Serious chemical dependency may warrant detoxification, the planned withdrawal from substances. It is necessary in about one-tenth of all cases.

The patient is detoxed gradually over a period of two to fourteen days, with medication generally administered in decreasing doses. If no drugs are prescribed, he goes through cold turkey, which, though agonizing, serves as an effective deterrent for some addicts. So contended the late medical physiologist Hardin B. Jones and his nutritionist wife, Helen C. Jones, acclaimed experts in the field of drugs and drug treatment. They theorized that a person willing to kick drugs cold turkey had made "a stronger commitment." Certainly once you experience it, as I have, you are forever reminded that you *never* want to feel that wretched again. Most substance dependents, however, opt for gradual detox. Besides briefly enabling them to continue getting high, drug users fear that once their chemical crutches have been snatched away, they will be nothing more than empty shells emotionally.

Withdrawal for a youngster abruptly quitting marijuana—or hallucinogens, which rarely bring about tolerance in children—is relatively mild and lasts only a day or two. But kids detoxifying from stimulants and cocaine can suffer for two weeks or more from terrifying hallucinations, heart palpitations, diarrhea, vomiting, loss of consciousness, severe depression, and suicidal thoughts. Consequently, they must always be under strict medical supervision. The racking withdrawal symptoms heroin addicts endure have been widely documented in literature, film, and popular music. However, most agonizing of all are those common to alcohol and, especially, depressant detoxification: aches and pains, weakness, dizziness, hyperanxiety, the shakes, delusions, hallucinations, and hostile, violent behavior.

After detox it is typical for the patient to feel physically weak, depressed, sometimes sexually dysfunctional, for his mind and body have been thrown into disorder by months or years of abuse. His "pleasure mechanisms," as the Joneses called them, may need time before they are capable of functioning minus the stimulus of mind-altering drugs. It makes the patient extremely vulnerable to a regression, as he wonders if he'll ever feel good again without chemicals. Consequently, therapists generally counsel clients about the debilitating effects of the substances they took and how long it will take until they become healthy. Drug users should always be informed about what to expect during treatment so that they do not become frustrated with themselves or the program and backslide.

Facilities that don't perform on-premises detoxification usually contract with a nearby hospital or outpatient clinic.

Once the youngster's physical condition is stabilized, at Hazelden a team of counselors, psychologists, medical doctors, therapists, and clergy puts him through a battery of psychological, personality, intelligence, behavioral, and performance tests. What is his self-esteem? How does he relate to others? If there is evidence of a psychosis (paranoia, delusions), is it chemically induced or a preexisting disorder? Based on this detailed portrait, they devise a treatment plan and assign the child a counselor.

The Pioneer House program runs six weeks; the primary-facility program, twenty-nine days, which is the yardstick for residential care. Youngsters room with members of the same sex and eat all their meals on campus. Emphasis is placed on good nutrition, for many of these kids have neglected their health for years. They attend daily lectures on substance abuse, group-therapy sessions, and individual counseling with certified chemical-dependency specialists. Time is also appropriated for physical activities such as volleyball, cross-country skiing, and Nautilus exercise, and residents are free to use meditation rooms, a library, and a bookstore.

Just prior to reentry, the child and his counselor formulate an aftercare program, for easing the transition back to home and school. It usually consists of six to twelve months in a Twelve Steps group or in outpatient counseling. Because many of their clients do not live within commuting distance, inpatient programs often affiliate themselves with outpatient clinics around the country.

If other forms of treatment have failed, or if a child is a first-time offender regularly using cocaine, crack, PCP, designer drugs, or narcotics:

When a youngster's dependency is so advanced, parents can be reasonably sure it has been festering for at least a year. The longer youths abuse substances, the longer it takes to get them off, as undesirable behavioral and social patterns have become ingrained. Not only do they need to be set free from drugs, they must be directed toward an alternative life-style that does not revolve around getting high. Such a radical reformation cannot be achieved overnight; it requires long-term residential care in a therapeutic community.

The first therapeutic community in the U.S. was Synanon, started in Santa Monica, California, in 1958 by Charles Dederich, a onetime alcoholic who attributed his sobriety to AA. Synanon's concept—having people with similar problems treat each other while living in a communal, extended-family setting—was revolutionary. And widely suspect, especially among members of the psychiatric profession. Some of their criticisms were justified.

In the 1960s and 1970s, for example, several therapeutic-community leaders were guilty of abusing their power, converting their rehabilitation centers into quasi-religious cults. Unfortunately, many residents were easily manipulable, transferring their dependencies from drugs to these therapists-turned-gurus. But one should not denounce the entire field any more than one should discredit organized religion because of the improprieties of a few. Today there are over seven hundred inpatient and outpatient therapeutic communities in the country, and the National Institute on Drug Abuse declares their comprehensive treatment is effective even for hard-core drug abusers.

Although there are many splendid TCs, I've selected Straight as a model. It is a twelve-to-eighteen-month family-oriented program for youngsters from twelve to twenty-one. You read right: twelve to eighteen months, and each day of treatment is essential. (Rehabilitation at other therapeutic communities, such as Texas's Cenikor Foundation, can take as long as two and a half years.) Straight was called "the best drug-abuse program I have seen anywhere" by former White House drug chief Dr. Robert L. Dupont, Jr. I concur, having visited several of its eight facilities—in Florida, Georgia, Massachusetts, Michigan, Ohio, Texas, and Virginia—some with First Lady Nancy Reagan.

The Straight program has five phases, the first of which is fourteen days or more of self-analysis with the aid of counselors and therapists. New arrivals' clothing and personal articles are searched for substances, and until they prove their trustworthiness, other youngsters escort them *everywhere*. When I entered Cenikor, it took three months before I was allowed to walk around by myself. I had to request somebody usher me to breakfast, to therapy sessions, even to the bathroom, which, though demeaning, was effective in shattering my ego. Doing drugs while out on the street, I had acted like a real big shot. But not there. I was completely dependent on others.

Through nearly eighty hours a week of counseling, held individually and in groups as large as three hundred, Straight kids learn why they needed to get high. They examine their deficiencies and fears, and rediscover emotions shunted aside for so long. "It's like being reintroduced to yourself," says Ira, who is a resident at another highly recommended therapeutic community, New York's Daytop Village, founded in 1963. Children find support at Straight, which calls itself a community of tough love. But they are also held accountable for their progress and are made to understand that ultimately no one can help them but themselves.

When phase-one kids leave the Straight center at night, they reside in a "host" home. These are families whose own youngsters are either in the program's advanced stages or are graduates. House rules are strict: beds must be made every morning; dishes washed; showers are military style; socks, shoes, and pants must be worn at all times; and lights are out at eleven-thirty, after which children may not leave their rooms till morning.

Straight is unorthodox in that by phase two, which lasts a minimum of one week, youngsters are permitted to return home at night. Meanwhile they continue to work on improving family relationships. In this sense, Straight is a kind of outpatient therapeutic community. The majority of TCs are residential.

Next, phase three, also for a one-week minimum: Kids go to school or to work during weekdays, then report to the center, which is also where they spend Saturdays and Sundays. During the minimum ninety days in phase four, youngsters begin their staged withdrawal from the program, required to come to the center only three weekdays and on Saturday or Sunday. Counselors aid them in finding constructive ways to utilize leisure time, and on a written-permission basis they may accompany family or program peers to recreational activities.

Finally, reentry, which incorporates social responsibility, to further bolster self-confidence. Children are at the center three days a week, assisting the staff and working with other kids. After sixty days they are fully released from Straight but must attend six months of aftercare. There, with a counselor, they work out problems: dating, forming new friendships, positive thinking, and, especially, coping with the pressures of their new, sober life-style.

In residential therapeutic communities such as Pennsylvania's Abraxas I, kids live on a campus and continue their education in a state-certified school. The ideal environment is comfortable but not too luxurious. They must abide by a fixed system of discipline, comply with orders, and learn to take initiative. It's early to bed and early to rise, as illustrated by the typical daily routine at Florida's Palmview Hospital, a short-term therapeutic-community program for kids eleven to eighteen:

6:00 a.m.	Wake-up, hygiene, rooms cleaned
7:00 a.m.	Breakfast
7:30–8:30 a.m.	Community meeting for all patients and staff, to discuss unit business, special problems, introducing new patients
8:30–9:00 a.m.	Exercise
9:00–9:50 a.m.	School
9:50–10:00 a.m.	Break (movement exercise)
10:00–10:50 a.m.	School
10:50–11:00 a.m.	Break (movement exercise)
11:00–11:50 a.m.	School
11:50–12:00 noon	Free time
12:00–12:30 p.m.	Lunch
12:30–1:15 p.m.	Group (Mondays, Wednesdays, Fridays, chemical-dependency education group; Tuesdays, Thursdays, group therapy; those not in chemical-dependency education group attend group therapy instead)
1:15–2:00 p.m.	School
2:00–2:30 p.m.	Free time
2:30–4:00 p.m.	Occupational therapy/recreational therapy

4:00–5:00 p.m.	Social-skills group, for discussing issues such as relationships, sexuality, expressing feelings, self-image, self-esteem, and independent-living skills
5:00–5:30 p.m.	Dinner
5:30–6:00 p.m.	Quiet time
6:00–7:00 p.m.	Visitation or family tapes
7:00–7:15 p.m.	Preparation for next activity
7:15–8:00 p.m.	Physical conditioning
8:00–9:00 p.m.	Study time (Fridays, movie and snacks, 8:00–9:30)
9:00–9:30 p.m.	Community meeting (Fridays, 9:30–10:00)
9:30–10:00 p.m.	Snacks and chores (Fridays, 10:00–10:30)
10:00–10:30 p.m.	Bedtime/lights-out (Fridays, 10:30–11:30)

The days are so full, that come lights-out, youngsters are ready for a good night's sleep. In addition to attending education classes, therapy sessions, and so on, community residents are assigned chores. This is not punishment but an integral part of treatment, for some kids have never completed a task before or learned to work alongside others. For perhaps the first time, they see it is possible to excel without chemicals.

If it all sounds a lot like boot camp, believe me, it is. But children with long-standing habits sorely need rigidly structured order and rule enforcement. Therapeutic communities have occasionally been accused of being too harsh on kids and brainwashing them. Frankly, habitual drug users *should* have their brains washed; they need them good and scrubbed. I won't deny that punishments are sometimes onerous—I remember once being banished to the roof of the Cenikor building to "sweep the sun off of it"—but they are rarely physical, and then only to restrain kids from leaving without parental consent (in some programs).

All of this is necessary to rebuild the foundation of values eroded by years of drug use. Youngsters must be taught accountability to themselves and to others, and they must be allowed to suffer the consequences of their actions. However, patients are not solely dictated to; they are actively involved with planning their own rehabilitation agenda and determining which personal problems to work on: "I'm finding it hard to say no to people," they may tell their counselor, or "I need to become more disciplined."

The ratio of patients to total staff is usually four to one, and of patients to counselors, ten to one. Counselors either hold academic credentials or are program graduates. They befriend the children but are rarely manipulable, having heard drug users' plethora of excuses and lies before. Each youngster is encouraged and expected to perform to the best of his abilities and to take pride in himself. Those who do not may be discharged from the program. At California's Impact therapeutic community for persons eighteen and older, grounds for dismissal are

- drug or alcohol use while a resident, or reasonable suspicion of use;
- violence or threats of violence;
- sexual activity;
- theft or other crimes;
- four disciplinary actions in one week;
- becoming a detriment to other residents;
- poor response to treatment;
- leaving the facility without permission.

For many kids, being sent to a therapeutic community is the shock of a lifetime, for they are long accustomed to deceiving others, shirking responsibility, and getting away with misconduct. Parents who place substance-abusing youths in long-term residential treatment can anticipate having their sympathies played on at first. "They treat me terribly," a kid will whine on a phone call home. "Please, get me out of here." If this happens to you, don't allow yourself to be fooled—again. He is simply frustrated because both counselors and peers call his bluffs, and he is angry at having to follow rules for a change. Naturally he wants out. Of the nine Daytop Village and Odyssey House residents we spoke with, all contemplated quitting at some point, and two actually did.

"Sometimes," says Anthony, "I go through entire weeks when I want to leave. The reason I don't?" He lapses into silence for a moment, then continues in a quiet voice. "Well, it's not because I was probated here; I'd only have to do thirty days in jail, and that doesn't mean a thing to me.

"I stay here because I remember how bad I was before I came in. I think of my mother's face and how I was killing her with my drug use. See, now I value my health and my parents. Before, I didn't value anything."

After approximately six to nine months, children go on to the reentry phase. Their residence is often a separate dormitory, called a halfway house, for those preparing to return to society. They are encouraged to mend fractured family relationships at home and to either return to school or get a job with the aid of a vocational counselor. According to the Abraxas Foundation, because of the work ethic extolled in its program, many of its residents even find employment in areas where jobs are scarce. Many times their marketable skills were gained in rehabilitation. At

Cenikor, for example, we developed several businesses staffed and supervised by patients: landscaping, auto detailing, a service station, data processing, and football-equipment manufacturing.

Reentry's three to six months is followed by an undetermined period of aftercare, which may be held on an outpatient basis at the therapeutic community, at an outpatient clinic, or through a self-help group. Then comes graduation day, which is a joyous occasion. I remember many of them at Cenikor, parents beaming proudly in the audience, eyes glistening with tears. The graduates' mood was equally emotional; for most of them it was the first time they'd accomplished something in their lives.

Methadone Maintenance

Probably the most flaring controversy in the drug-rehabilitation field is over methadone maintenance as a viable method of treating narcotics addicts. I should preface my remarks on the subject of methodone by noting that during my years as a heroin abuser, I underwent methadone maintenance four times, all unsuccessful.

A white crystalline powder, methadone is a synthetic opiate and antagonist (a drug that blocks the effects of another) used for weaning addicts off heroin. It was originally a painkiller christened Dolophine, after Adolf Hitler, by the German chemists who developed it during World War II, when morphine was scarce. In the 1950s, American state and federal hospitals began employing the drug to ease heroin withdrawal symptoms.

Taken orally as prescribed by a licensed physician or nurse, methadone eliminates the "narcotic hunger," as it was characterized by pioneering researchers Drs. Marie Nyswander and Vincent Dole in their 1965 *Journal of the American Medical Association* report. Whereas heroin's euphoria lasts but three to six hours, methadone's effects work for twenty-four, and another synthetic, called LAMM, for up to seventy-two. Through the mid-1960s, detoxification by way of methadone was the only medically approved procedure of kicking heroin, even though its long-term success rate was a dismal 10%.

Methadone's withdrawal symptoms are much less debilitating than those of heroin. The theory behind maintenance is to transfer the patient's addiction from the natural narcotic to the synthetic, so that he can continue leading a productive life. And indeed, studies have shown that most methadone-maintenance recipients can perform as well on the job as the average worker.

So what exactly is my objection to maintenance through methadone or other synthetic antagonists such as clonidine and naltrexone? The treatment essentially substitutes one substance for another, keeping the addict chemical dependent and divorced from his emotions. Because he must come to the clinic for his daily dose, it is difficult for him to elude his old crowd. Certainly methadone maintenance does little to enhance a person's self-esteem.

Originally, almost no attempt was made to treat the psychological origins of substance dependency, but in recent years significant strides have been made in combining social rehabilitation and chemical maintenance. According to Dr. Robert Newman, head of New York's Beth Israel Medical Center's methadone program, the nation's largest, "All programs incorporate counseling, either by the clinic staff or through an outside agency. It is a federal regulatory requirement."

But because maintenance is conducted strictly on an outpatient basis, there is great potential for abuse. I remember one methadone program I attended in Florida. The procedure was, wait in line, then when it was your turn, walk up to the thick glass window. There a white-uniformed nurse dispensed small cups of 100-milligram doses. Each was enough to incapacitate Bigfoot, but not necessarily enough to keep him off heroin. I'd look in my cup, and there they were: sixteen little pills. Enterprising spirits that we were, many of us addicts schemed up ways to swallow just a few. Then we'd stroll out of the clinic and head back to the street, where we'd exchange methadone for the real thing.

Because of the recent AIDS epidemic, it has been suggested in some quarters that sterile syringes be distributed to addicts in lieu of methadone maintenance. I find *neither* solution acceptable. One possible answer to the problem has been proposed by Peter Bell, executive director of Minneapolis's Institute on Black Chemical Abuse: furnish addicts a new type of syringe that can be used only once. Certainly it would help to curb the number of AIDS cases transmitted by contaminated needles.

If your child is a narcotics addict, the preferred treatment consists of detoxification under medical supervision and long-term therapeutic-community care. The only form of drug therapy I advocate is the use of alcohol antagonists such as Antabuse, which when combined with alcohol makes the drinker nauseous; soon he associates alcohol with unpleasant side effects. It has been shown to be an effective deterrent.

QUALITY DRUG TREATMENT: WHERE TO LOOK, WHAT TO LOOK FOR

When seeking professional care, call your state's alcohol- and drug-abuse agency (see Appendix A) for referrals to programs in your area. Explain your child's problem, the type or types of treatment you are interested in researching, and request addresses and telephone numbers for roughly a half-dozen programs. Call them, asking to speak to an admissions counselor. By using the following checklist as a guide, you should be able to screen out several over the phone. Then visit the remaining programs under consideration. Tour the facilities—Do they appear clean and professional?—and talk to counselors and patients at random.

Inquiries Checklist

What is the program's recovery rate? This should be based on a one-, preferably two-year follow-up poll of graduates. About 67% is average; claims of 80% or more are suspect.

Is detoxification conducted on the premises? If it is not, are arrangements made with another clinic or hospital?

Is their policy one of total abstinence? If they go on about allowing patients to continue using any substance "in moderation," steer clear of that program.

What is the ratio of counselors to clients? Ideally, it should be no less than one to ten.

How many counselors are ex-addicts or program graduates? Generally, former drug abusers relate well to kids with substance-abuse problems. About half the counselors should be onetime users, and most should be state certified.

What are the credentials of other personnel? An M.D. *and* a Ph.D. should be available at all times, at the very least for consultation. At Second Genesis, which runs therapeutic communities in the District of Columbia, Maryland, and Virginia, the staff includes master's-degree mental-health and vocational-rehabilitation counselors, learning-disabilities specialists, family therapists, addiction specialists, and a research analyst.

If a freestanding facility, is it affiliated with a nearby hospital for emergency treatment and diagnostic, lab, X-ray, and pharmacy services?

190

For example, the Impact therapeutic community in Pasadena, California, maintains working agreements with two city hospitals.

How long is the program? Outpatient care is typically four to six months; inpatient, four to six weeks; and therapeutic communities, six to twenty-four months. Be wary of any treatment center that claims a miracle cure.

Is aftercare part of the program, conducted either on the premises or through a self-help, Twelve Steps–type group? A six-month minimum of aftercare is essential.

Is the program state licensed or approved?

Are academic programs state licensed? Residents of Philadelphia's The Bridge therapeutic community attend The Bridge School, which is licensed by the Pennsylvania Department of Education, the State Board of Private Academic Schools, and is approved for regular secondary education, special education, and summer remedial programs. It is also a member of the United Private Academic Schools Association of Pennsylvania.

If an outpatient program, are youngsters given urine tests at least twice a week? It has to be known if a client is slipping at any point during treatment.

If outpatient or inpatient rehabilitation is administered in a general hospital, is it accredited by the Joint Commission on Accreditation of Hospitals? The JCAH is a private, nonprofit organization committed to upholding high-quality health care through an extensive, voluntary survey conducted every three years. Currently five thousand hospitals, more than seven hundred of which have substance-dependency treatment units, are JCAH accredited. (Another organization, the Commission on Accreditation of Rehabilitation Facilities [CARF], accredits mostly other kinds of rehabilitation programs and will not be an especially useful resource for parents of children with drug or alcohol problems.)

Ask about the facility's background. How many years has it been operating? Ask to see its yearly or biyearly financial report. If the institution is financially unstable, the possibility exists of its shutting down while your child is in midtreatment—obviously a devastating disruption to his progress.

Are there girls-only therapy groups? Boys typically outnumber girls in treatment by as many as ten to one. Women substance abusers have often lead sexually promiscuous life-styles, and it may be difficult for them to discuss such personal issues honestly if men are present.

Is family therapy part of the program? This vital aspect of the recovery process is examined extensively later in this chapter.

What is the total cost? Sometimes rehabilitation centers neglect to paint a complete picture of their cost. It is the difference between ordering a meal in a restaurant a la carte or on the dinner plan. Total expenses include detoxification, if necessary; family counseling, if billed separately; and aftercare. Be sure to inquire about private-insurance and Medicaid coverage, as well as payment schedule. Some programs require a 50% deposit, others a full deposit, with the unused balance refunded after completion, or if the person leaves the program prematurely.

Cost, Insurance, Medicaid

Parents of drug-abusing children pay a steep price both emotionally and financially, for quality drug treatment is not inexpensive. Certainly you cannot put a price tag on your child's well-being, but it is only natural to want to keep expenditures down as much as possible.

Fees for each treatment mode vary widely and are constantly changing. Therefore I am reluctant to cite too many figures, since they will soon be outdated. But just to give you an idea of the approximate cost, here are the fees, circa late-1987, of this chapter's model programs.

Self-help/peer-counseling groups: Twelve-Steps fellowships such as Alcoholics Anonymous, Cocaine Anonymous, Drugs Anonymous, and Narcotics Anonymous are free, although members may contribute on a pass-the-hat basis to meet the costs of meeting-place rental, refreshments, and literature. To reduce the expense of outpatient, inpatient, and therapeutic-community care, I recommend requesting aftercare be provided through a self-help fellowship.

Outpatient care: Parents can expect to pay between $1,200 and $3,200 for a four-to-six-week program. At Phoenix House, for example, the following costs are incurred: $200 for onetime-only admission assessment; $80 a week for four group-therapy sessions (the number varies according to the individualized treatment plan developed by the staff), and $40 for each family-counseling visit. Required tests are billed per laboratory charge.

Residential care: Because bed, board, educational curriculum, and vocational counseling are provided, the cost of inpatient facilities is roughly double that of outpatient clinics. Some twenty-eight-day adolescent programs, however, come to as much as $12,000. The average four-week stay at Hazelden's primary facility is significantly less: approximately

$4,400, plus $222 for twelve outpatient aftercare visits and $400 for twenty-five family sessions. Parents can expect to assume other, incidental costs such as for books and personal items during their child's stay.

Long-term therapeutic-community care: Straight, which is nonresidential, charges $6,000 for a one-year minimum stay; other programs that provide bed, board, educational curriculum, and vocational counseling can cost as much as $20,000.

Methadone maintenance: New York's Beth Israel Medical Center's fee is $2,200 per year, which is on a par with other methadone-maintenance outpatient programs throughout the country.

Detoxification: When conducted in a hospital, from $300 to $500 daily. Some patients require just a day or two of hospitalization, others up to two weeks.

As is true of most health-care services these days, the figures seem astronomical. However, virtually all literature from drug-rehabilitation facilities contains the addendum "No one will be turned away because of an inability to pay." Many work out sliding-scale fees based on family income, which is another vital point to raise when inquiring into programs. Treatment may be covered by health insurance, although most private health insurers' current policies regarding alcohol- and drug-abuse treatment are unconscionably deficient.

Private health insurance supplies coverage for nearly 85% of the population. Despite the fact that substance abuse is the number one health danger facing our kids, according to a report issued by the National Association of State Alcohol and Drug Abuse Directors,

- only ten states mandate insurers cover alcohol- and drug-dependency treatment: Kansas; Maine; Michigan, as an inpatient only; Minnesota, group policy only; Montana; Nevada; North Dakota; Oregon, group policy only; Virginia, as an inpatient only; and Wisconsin;
- only thirteen states mandate benefits for the treatment of alcohol dependency: Connecticut, as an inpatient only; Illinois; Maryland; Massachusetts; Mississippi; Missouri; New Jersey; New York, as an outpatient only; Ohio; Rhode Island; Texas; Vermont; and Washington;
- only nine states require insurers to offer purchasable policies for alcohol-dependency treatment: California; Colorado; Connecticut, as an outpatient only; Kentucky; Michigan, as a hospital inpatient only; New Mexico; New York, as an inpatient only; South Dakota; and Virginia, as an outpatient only;

- only two states require offers of purchasable policies for drug-dependency treatment: Maryland and Missouri;
- only nine states require offers of purchasable policies for both alcohol- and drug-dependency treatment: Alabama; Florida; Louisiana; Minnesota, individual policy only; Nebraska; North Carolina; Oregon, individual policy only; Tennessee; and Wyoming.

Such practices are indicative of a societal double standard that recognizes abuse of only one drug—alcohol—as requiring medical or psychological attention. But even alcohol-dependency treatment is provided for in fewer than half the states. Furthermore, rarely can individuals purchase policies, and only certain types of rehabilitation programs are covered. Typically, health insurers explicitly identify hospitals as the single appropriate treatment setting, excluding entirely therapeutic-community care. As a rule, inpatient rehabilitation is favored over outpatient, though twenty-nine states' statutes do specify coverage for outpatient treatment.

Each state has its own minimum or limit on money spent on and time spent in rehabilitation. Rhode Island, for example, covers a minimum of just 30 hours yearly, while in Minnesota insurers must provide for at least 130. Ohio guarantees an alcohol-dependent child a mere $500 per year—barely one-eighth the cost of a quality inpatient program—while in Oregon a youngster is entitled to a minimum total of $6,000, encompassing inpatient, residential, and outpatient care.

For information about your individual coverage, contact your insurer. For information about your state's insurance-coverage laws, contact

- your state's department of insurance, which is in the State Government Offices listings of the White Pages;

- your state's alcohol- and drug-abuse agency (see Appendix A);

- the National Association of State Alcohol and Drug Abuse Directors.

The following chart detailing the policies of each state has been adapted and updated from the NASADAD January/February 1986 special report on private health-insurance coverage for alcoholism- and drug-dependency treatment services.

ALABAMA

Requires insurers and health-maintenance organizations (HMOs) offer purchasable group alcohol- and drug-dependency treatment coverage.

Annual minimum benefits: based on a formula where one inpatient day equals two residential days or three outpatient visits. Therefore: 30 inpatient days or equivalent, 60 residential days, or 90 outpatient sessions. No dollar minimum or limit.

ALASKA

No legislation enacted.

ARIZONA

No legislation enacted.

ARKANSAS

No legislation enacted.

CALIFORNIA

Requires insurers but not HMOs offer purchasable group alcohol-dependency treatment coverage. No annual minimum benefits and treatment settings are specified.

COLORADO

Requires insurers but not HMOs offer purchasable group alcohol-dependency treatment coverage.

Annual minimum benefits: 45 inpatient days, $500 for outpatient care. Benefits are not payable unless the patient completes full continuum of care, encompassing detoxification and rehabilitation.

CONNECTICUT

Mandates insurers and HMOs (by insurance-department action) provide group and individual inpatient alcohol-dependency treatment coverage, and requires they offer purchasable group and individual outpatient alcohol-dependency treatment coverage.

Annual minimum benefits: 45 inpatient or residential days.

DELAWARE

No legislation enacted.

DISTRICT OF COLUMBIA

No legislation as of January 1, 1986, but since then mandatory coverage for alcohol-, drug-dependency, and mental-illness treatment has been enacted.

FLORIDA

Requires insurers and HMOs offer purchasable group alcohol-dependency and drug-dependency treatment coverage.

Annual minimum benefits: 44 outpatient visits at $35 per; $2,000 lifetime.

GEORGIA

No legislation enacted.

HAWAII

No legislation enacted.

IDAHO

No legislation enacted.

ILLINOIS

Mandates insurers but not HMOs provide group alcohol-dependency treatment coverage.

Annual minimum benefits: 10 inpatient days.

INDIANA

No legislation enacted.

IOWA

No legislation enacted.

KANSAS

Mandates insurers but not HMOs provide group alcohol-dependency and drug-dependency treatment coverage.

Annual minimum benefits: 30 inpatient days, $500 for outpatient care.

KENTUCKY

Requires insurers and HMOs offer purchasable group alcohol-dependency treatment coverage.

Annual minimum benefits: 3 detoxification or inpatient days at $40 per, 10 residential days at $50 per, 10 outpatient visits at $10 per.

LOUISIANA

Requires insurers and HMOs offer purchasable group alcohol-dependency and drug-dependency treatment coverage. No annual minimum benefits are specified.

MAINE

Mandates insurers and HMOs provide group alcohol-dependency and drug-dependency treatment coverage.

Annual minimum benefits: 30 days residential, 60 days residential lifetime, $1,000 for outpatient care, $25,000 for all lifetime benefits. The state requires that a written treatment plan be filed by a physician or registered substance-abuse counselor employed by a certified or licensed substance-abuse agency. Health insurers are required to report annually the amount of claims paid.

MARYLAND

Mandates insurers and HMOs provide group alcohol-dependency treatment coverage, and requires insurers but not HMOs offer purchasable group drug-dependency treatment coverage.

Annual minimum benefits: 7 days detoxification, 30 days residential, $1,000 for 30 outpatient visits; 120 total lifetime inpatient/residential days and outpatient visits.

MASSACHUSETTS

Mandates insurers and HMOs provide alcohol-dependency treatment coverage.

Annual minimum benefits: 30 inpatient or residential days; $500 for outpatient care, which must be provided by a physician or psychotherapist who devotes time to psychiatry and treating alcoholics.

MICHIGAN

Mandates insurers and HMOs provide group and individual outpatient and intermediate-residential alcohol-dependency treatment coverage, and requires insurers but not HMOs offer purchasable inpatient alcohol-dependency and drug-dependency treatment coverage.

Annual minimum benefits: The rate for residential and outpatient care is currently $1,996 and is adjusted annually.

MINNESOTA

Mandates insurers and HMOs provide group alcohol-dependency and drug-dependency treatment coverage, and requires insurers but not HMOs offer purchasable individual alcohol-dependency and drug-dependency treatment coverage.

Annual minimum benefits: under group coverage, 28 inpatient or residential days; under individual coverage, 130 hours of outpatient care. Coverage must exceed at least 20% of the total patient days allowed by the policy and must exceed 28 days per benefit year.

MISSISSIPPI

Mandates insurers but not HMOs provide group alcohol-dependency treatment coverage.

Annual minimum benefits: $1,000 for inpatient care. Only inpatient hospital care is mandated, and treatment must be administered by a physician.

MISSOURI

Mandates insurers and HMOs provide group and individual alcohol-dependency treatment coverage, and requires insurers and HMOs offer purchasable group and individual drug-dependency treatment coverage.

Annual minimum benefits: 30 inpatient or residential days, or 30 outpatient visits; $2,000 total.

MONTANA

Mandates insurers but not HMOs provide group alcohol-dependency and drug-dependency treatment coverage.

Annual minimum benefits: 30 inpatient or residential days; $1,000 for outpatient care, $4,000 biannually, $8,000 lifetime.

NEBRASKA

Requires insurers and HMOs offer purchasable group alcohol-dependency treatment coverage.

Annual minimum benefits: 30 inpatient days, $1,000 for outpatient care.

NEVADA

Mandates insurers and HMOs provide group and individual alcohol-dependency and drug-dependency treatment coverage.

Annual minimum benefits: 7 detoxification days at $1,500, $9,000 for inpatient or residential care, $2,500 for outpatient care, $39,000 lifetime.

NEW HAMPSHIRE

No legislation enacted.

NEW JERSEY

Mandates insurers but not HMOs provide group and individual alcohol-dependency treatment coverage. No annual minimum benefits are specified, except to say they should be the same as those granted for any other illness.

NEW MEXICO

Requires insurers but not HMOs offer purchasable group alcohol-dependency treatment coverage.

Annual minimum benefits: 30 inpatient or residential days, 30 outpatient visits.

NEW YORK

Mandates insurers and HMOs provide group outpatient alcohol-dependency treatment coverage, and requires both offer purchasable group inpatient or residential alcohol-dependency treatment coverage.

Annual minimum benefits: 7 detoxification days, 30 residential days, 60 outpatient visits, including up to 20 visits for family members, who are entitled to as many as 5 outpatient visits even if the covered alcoholic has never received treatment.

NORTH CAROLINA

Requires insurers and HMOs offer group alcohol-dependency and drug-dependency treatment coverage.

Annual minimum benefits: the same as for any other medical illness, which is $6,000 biennially "of which not more than one-half . . . shall be paid . . . in any 30-consecutive-day period" and not more than $5,000 per calendar year; $12,000 contract lifetime; $15,000 lifetime.

NORTH DAKOTA

Mandates insurers and HMOs provide group alcohol-dependency and drug-dependency treatment coverage.

Annual minimum benefits: 70 inpatient days, 140 partial hospitalization days, 52 outpatient visits.

OHIO

Mandates insurers but not HMOs provide group alcohol-dependency treatment coverage.

Annual minimum benefits: $500 total. Treatment plan must be provided.

OKLAHOMA

No legislation enacted.

OREGON

Mandates insurers but not HMOs provide group alcohol-dependency and drug-dependency treatment coverage, and requires insurers but not HMOs offer purchasable individual alcohol-dependency and drug-dependency treatment coverage.

Annual minimum benefits: $6,000 total biennially, including $1,500 for outpatient care, $3,000 for full- or part-time (at least four hours daily and four days weekly) residential care, $4,500 for inpatient care. According to the mandate, "to the greatest extent possible, the least costly settings for treatment, outpatient services and residential facilities" are to be used. Oregon is one of the few states to recognize both alcoholism and drug abuse as illnesses and declares that deductibles and coinsurance "shall be no greater than for other illnesses."

PENNSYLVANIA

No legislation as of January 1, 1986, but since then mandatory coverage for alcohol-dependency treatment has been enacted.

RHODE ISLAND

Mandates insurers and HMOs provide group alcohol-dependency treatment coverage.

Annual minimum benefits: 21 inpatient days; for detoxification, up to three 7-day episodes; 30 residential days; 30 hours of outpatient care, plus 20 hours for family members; 90 inpatient days over contract lifetime.

SOUTH CAROLINA

No legislation enacted.

SOUTH DAKOTA

Requires insurers and HMOs offer purchasable group and individual alcohol-dependency treatment coverage.

Annual minimum benefits: 30 inpatient or residential days in any six-month period, 90 inpatient or residential days in lifetime.

TENNESSEE

Requires insurers and HMOs offer purchasable group alcohol-dependency and drug-dependency treatment coverage. No annual minimum benefits are specified, although they are subject to the same durational and monetary limits, and deductibles and coinsurance factors that apply to any other disease.

TEXAS

Mandates insurers and HMOs provide group alcohol-dependency treatment coverage. Annual minimum benefits are the same as Tennessee's.

UTAH

No legislation as of January 1, 1986, but since then required-offer coverage for alcohol-dependency treatment has been enacted.

VERMONT

Mandates insurers and HMOs provide group and individual alcohol-dependency treatment coverage.

Annual minimum benefits: 5 detoxification days; 28 inpatient days; 56 partial institutional rehabilitation days, lifetime (when combined, one inpatient day equals two partial institutional rehabilitation days); 90 hours of outpatient care, including family visits; 100 hours of outpatient care, lifetime. To be eligible for coverage, benefits must be rendered by either a state-approved substance-abuse counselor or institution, and a rehabilitation program must be provided.

VIRGINIA

Mandates insurers but not HMOs provide group and individual inpatient alcohol-dependency and drug-dependency treatment coverage, and requires insurers offer purchasable outpatient alcohol-dependency and drug-dependency treatment coverage.

Annual minimum benefits: 30 inpatient or residential days at $80-a-day indemnity; 90 inpatient or residential days, lifetime; 45 outpatient visits at $1,000; 45 intermediate or residential days.

WASHINGTON

Mandates insurers and HMOs provide group alcohol-dependency treatment coverage. No annual minimum benefits are specified.

WEST VIRGINIA

Requires insurers but not HMOs offer purchasable group alcohol-dependency treatment coverage.

Annual minimum benefits: 30 inpatient days; $750 for outpatient care; $10,000, lifetime, or 25% of the policy lifetime limit, whichever is less.

WISCONSIN

Mandates insurers and HMOs provide group alcohol-dependency and drug-dependency treatment coverage.

Annual minimum benefits: 30 inpatient days at $6,300, $900 for outpatient care, $7,300 total.

WYOMING

No legislation enacted.

Clearly, substance abusers are discriminated against by health insurers—not to mention legislators—in many states. Because dependency is oftimes viewed cynically as a self-imposed problem, many people remain uncompassionate to the addict's plight. One reason given for limiting coverage is that mandatory benefits would drive up the price of individual and group policies until they were unaffordable.

However, quite the opposite is true. A study published by the National Institute on Alcohol Abuse and Alcoholism shows that providing benefits actually lowers the cost because abusers are so prone to injury, illness, and accidents. Once the surveyed alcoholics entered treatment, their health-care claims decreased dramatically: Outpatient medical visits alone dropped by nearly half.

Too, there is little basis to opponents' questioning the efficacy of chemical-dependency treatment programs. The majority of them, including therapeutic communities, are reviewed and licensed by the state alcohol- and drug-abuse agencies, and are subject to accreditation by the Joint Commission on Accreditation of Hospitals and the Commission for Accreditation of Rehabilitation Facilities.

Unfortunately, parents do not fare much better if they are eligible for Medicaid, a state-administered assistance program for low-income families unable to afford medical care. Coverage for dependency treatment varies greatly.

In New York, for example, alcohol and drug rehabilitation are paid for, though treatment can be conducted only on an inpatient basis at an acute-care hospital or on an outpatient basis at a hospital or freestanding clinic. California's Medi-Cal program covers outpatient alcohol-abuse treatment but no drug treatment except for outpatient heroin detoxification. Iowa and Louisiana remit for kids needing alcohol- and drug-abuse treatment, but as hospital inpatients only. In no instances are therapeutic communities covered.

To learn the specifics about your state's Medicaid coverage, contact Medicaid, listed in the White Pages under *M* or in the Community Services Numbers. In some states, Medicaid operates under the auspices of the department of social services or the department of health and human services, both found in the Government Offices listings of the White Pages.

Legislative measures to improve public and private health-care coverage of substance-abuse treatment are currently under way. Hopefully, in the next few years the grave injustice being done to our country's alcohol- and drug-addicted population will be corrected. Especially for the children's sake.

FAMILY INVOLVEMENT IS CRUCIAL

No matter what type of treatment you select for your child, family involvement is vital to his recovery. According to research made public by the National Federation of Parents for Drug-Free Youth, it improves a youngster's chances ten times; and studies conducted by Straight show that rehabilitation programs have a mere 2% to 3% success rate without family interaction.

For that reason, Straight will not even accept youths unless accompanied by a parent, for one of its primary therapeutic goals is to rejuvenate the family system. In the program's early stages families are required to attend open meetings twice a week. There, in front of a mass of children and adults, they praise their kids' progress: "Jim, we heard you're doing really well, and we just want you to know we're proud of you and love you." Or they express their disappointment: "Judy, we've been told you were caught drinking, and we're very hurt and angry." As you might imagine, these face-to-face encounters provoke both tears and laughter, as parents and kids say, "I love you"—words that sometimes have not been articulated in ages.

Family visits usually begin one to three months after entry at most residential programs, depending on the youngster's progress. At first an attempt is made to insulate him from his parents, who in many cases acted as codependents, or enablers. They have to learn the rules of the program and what is expected of their child, as well as how they can aid the rehabilitation process.

All treatment types insist on family involvement, usually through a combination of private parents-and-siblings therapy and joint counseling with the family and patient. The fee is either included in the overall cost or is separate, ranging from $25 to $100 per session. In Phoenix House's

IMPACT outpatient program, parents are encouraged to attend six weekly education seminars, followed by full-family visits with a therapist. There they learn about issues having to do with substance abuse and parenting, how to improve intrafamily communications, and how to effectively set limits. Each visit is $40. At Hazelden parents may attend an optional but recommended $540 five-day residential program. And no-cost self-help for family members is available by way of the peer-counseling groups touched upon in chapter 6: Al-Anon, Drug-Anon, Families Anonymous, and Toughlove.

"But I don't have a problem, my kid does," a parent might ask. "Why do I need counseling? And why do my other kids need counseling? They're not doing drugs."

When one child uses drugs, *every* family member gets pulled against his will into the vortex of substance abuse. As stated before in these pages, it is a family disease. Siblings typically react to a brother's or sister's habit one of several ways:

- They deny his problem, pretending that nothing is wrong.
- They fear for themselves, asking questions such as, "Will I start using drugs too?"
- They isolate themselves from the problem kid, or from the entire family.
- They become angry and reject the substance abuser.
- They identify with his misconduct and engage in drinking, drugging, or other delinquent behavior.

Why do you need counseling? To help you come to terms with your feelings. In chapter 6 we examined the many emotions parents experience upon discovering a child's substance abuse. As his treatment proceeds, demanding time, energy, and money, the anger, resentment, frustration, helplessness, loneliness, hurt, embarrassment, and/or guilt may intensify. The result is yet another concern: confusion. You are likely to have many questions. Will the family ever return to normal? Will you be able to trust your child again?

The support of other parents and experienced counselors can help you to resolve these issues and calm the emotional tempest that has shaken you and your family. It is vital that preexisting conflicts be attended to before your youngster completes rehabilitation. He has learned new ways of coping, and so must you. His returning to a household where the atmosphere hangs heavy with resentment will only impede his staying straight. What is the point of abstaining if parents and siblings are upset with him anyway? By the same token, incessant parental guilt can be just as damaging, once again enabling him to manipulate. Past mistakes should be learned from, not repeated.

Counseling can also quell your anxiety over the rapidly approaching day that your child's program ends. You need to know beforehand what to expect from yourself, what to expect from him, and what daily life with a still-recovering alcohol or drug abuser is like.

KEY POINTS

● So that he doesn't have time to back out, once your child agrees to undergo treatment, bring him to a chemical-dependency facility within thirty-six hours.

● Begin researching treatment programs immediately after detecting your child is drinking or taking drugs. In the event that his habit worsens, you'll be prepared to enter him promptly into a facility that has earned your full confidence.

● Extent of abuse and recommended form of treatment:

1. Continued occasional (once, twice a month or less) use of alcohol, marijuana, or inhalants: peer counseling, by way of groups such as Alcoholics Anonymous, Drugs Anonymous, Cocaine Anonymous, and Narcotics Anonymous.
2. Continued regular (three to five times a week) use of alcohol, marijuana, or inhalants: professional outpatient care.
3. Continued regular use of stimulants or depressants; if he is a first-time offender regularly using hallucinogens or occasionally using cocaine, crack, PCP, or narcotics; if alcohol abuse is chronic; or if self-help and/or outpatient care has failed: inpatient or residential care.
4. If other forms of treatment have failed, or if a child is a first-time offender regularly using cocaine, crack, PCP, designer drugs, or narcotics: long-term residential care in a therapeutic community.

● To find quality professional care, call your state's alcohol- and drug-abuse agency (see Appendix A) for referrals. Appendix A also contains personally recommended treatment programs around the U.S.

- What to look for in a chemical-dependency program:

1. Recovery rate of at least 67%.
2. Detoxification, either on-site or at another facility.
3. Total-abstinence policy.
4. At least a one-to-ten counselor-to-client ratio. Half the counselors should be former drug abusers, and most should be state certified.
5. M.D. and Ph.D. available at all times, at the very least for consultation.
6. Affiliation with nearby hospital if emergency treatment and diagnostic, lab, X-ray, and pharmacy services are not available on the premises.
7. Aftercare, either at the facility or through a Twelve Steps–type group.
8. State license or approval; if in a hospital, JCAH accreditation.
9. State license for academic programs.
10. Weekly urine tests for outpatients.
11. Girls-only therapy groups.
12. Family therapy.

- To reduce the expense of inpatient, outpatient, and therapeutic-community care, request aftercare be provided by a self-help group.

- No matter what mode of treatment you select for your child, your involvement is vital to his recovery. According to National Federation of Parents for Drug-Free Youth research, family interaction improves a youngster's chances ten times; and studies conducted by Straight show that rehabilitation programs have a mere 2% to 3% success rate without it.

- Families must resolve preexisting conflicts while their drug-dependent child is receiving treatment. He has learned new ways of coping; so must his parents and siblings.

RECOMMENDED RESOURCES

If the children you love need professional drug- or alcohol-dependency treatment, contact the following organizations for referrals to programs in your area:

Cocaine Hotline
Provided by Fair Oaks Hospital
19 Prospect Street
Summit, NJ 07901
(800) COC-AINE

National Institute on Drug Abuse
Drug-Referral Helpline
5600 Fishers Lane
Rockville, MD 20857
(800) 662-HELP

Therapeutic Communities of America
54 West 40th Street
New York, NY 10018
(212) 354-6000

National Clearinghouse for Drug and
Alcohol Information
P. O. Box 2345
Rockville, MD 20852
(301) 468-2600

The Clearinghouse makes available an approximately three-hundred-page *National Directory of Drug Abuse and Alcoholism Treatment and Prevention Programs.* Its most recent edition was published in 1984 and as of this writing was no longer in stock. However, most public libraries' reference sections should have a copy.

For referrals to accredited hospital inpatient and outpatient programs only, contact:

Joint Commission on Accreditation of
Hospitals
875 North Michigan Avenue
Chicago, IL 60611
(312) 642-6061

Other sources: In the Yellow Pages, look under "Drug Abuse and Addiction Information and Treatment" for the names of nearby drug-abuse rehabilitation centers; under "Crisis Intervention Service" for referrals. In the White Pages, look under "Drug Abuse" in the Community Services Numbers, or under "Youth Board" in the County Government Offices listings. Some employee-assistance plans may also make treatment referrals.

Personally recommended treatment programs are in Appendix A, which also contains the address and telephone number of your state's alcohol- and drug-abuse agency, for referrals to professional help.

To learn about private health insurance coverage for alcoholism and drug-dependency treatment programs, contact:

National Association of State Alcohol
and Drug Abuse Directors
444 North Capitol Street N.W.
Suite 520
Washington, DC 20001
(202) 783-6868

Other sources: Contact your state's department of insurance, the address and telephone number of which are in the State Government Offices listings of the White Pages, or your state's alcohol- and drug-abuse agency.

If the children you love need the support of a self-help group, or fellowship, for coming to grips with their substance abuse, contact:

Alcoholics Anonymous
P. O. Box 459
Grand Central Station
New York, NY 10163
(212) 686-1100

Cocaine Anonymous
World Services, Inc.
P. O. Box 1367
Culver City, CA 90232
(213) 559-5833

Drugs Anonymous
World Services
P. O. Box 473
Ansonia Station, NY 10023
(212) 874-0700

Narcotics Anonymous
World Service Office, Inc.
P. O. Box 9999
Van Nuys, CA 91409
(818) 780-3951

Other sources: In the Yellow Pages, under "Alcoholism Information and Treatment Centers" and "Drug Abuse and Addiction Information and Treatment"; alphabetically in the White Pages.

For referrals to self-help organizations of any type, contact:

National Self-Help Clearinghouse
33 West 42nd Street
Room 620N
New York, NY 10036
(212) 840-1259

Chapter Eight

Aftershocks:
When Treatment Ends

With the termination of rehabilitation, it is natural for parents to assume their family ordeal is behind them. Not entirely. Certainly the worst is over, and the youngster is finally drug-free. But keeping him that way entails several more months to a year of attentive supervision and discipline while he is in aftercare. Having already expended so much time, tears, and money, some mothers and fathers find that hard to accept.

"He's straightened up his act. What problems could we possibly face now?" It would seem that way: Their child looks and acts like he did before delving into the drug culture. He is once again well groomed, agreeable, and he doesn't withdraw from the rest of the family. His parents survey the scene at the dinner table and smile to themselves; at last, life is back to normal.

But roiling beneath the calm surface are undercurrents of conflict. When a recovering addict returns home, it can be an uneasy transition for everyone.

FEELINGS PARENTS MAY EXPERIENCE

Abandonment, emptiness: We are all creatures of conditioning. Over the course of a child's substance dependency, his parents frequently assumed the roles of saviors—a polite euphemism for enablers. They grew

210

accustomed to constant crises, and might have even secretly thrived on being needed so much and so often. Now that their youngster is healthy and more self-sufficient, they may feel rejected and aimless, as if stripped of their purpose in life.

Resentment: "How long is this going to take? Haven't we been through enough?"

Disappointment: A child's drug abuse seriously disrupts home life. Other problems arise due to neglect, for so much energy and emotion have been consumed by his addiction. Parents sometimes delude themselves into believing that all family issues will be resolved upon their kid's recovery. But each one must be settled individually.

There is no telling just how parents and siblings will cope. It is always recommended that while the abuser undergoes aftercare counseling, family members continue receiving either outpatient or self-help therapy. I suggest starting with weekly sessions for a half year, then cutting back to monthly attendance. Continue until the child's rehabilitation is completed or until family members are satisfied that all discord is reconciled.

FEELINGS RECOVERING KIDS MAY EXPERIENCE

Pressure: Youngsters on the wagon may feel constantly under surveillance or that others have little faith in their commitment to sobriety. After spending weeks or months in a supportive therapeutic environment, they are now back among peers who may entice them with alcohol and drugs. Even though treatment shored up their self-esteem and refusal skills, they still worry. How will they react the first time someone offers them a drink or a joint? What will happen when they are confronted by their former crowd?

It took me nearly *five years* before I absolutely believed I could abstain from drugs. Until I reached that point, I was visibly tense whenever out in public. On the average, it takes a recovering substance abuser twelve to eighteen months to be able to mingle comfortably among intoxicated persons. Doing so is still risky; another roll of the dice.

The anxiety a former addict feels is as likely to be internal as external. He may be so sensitive about his alcoholism or drug dependency that he misinterprets encouragement from friends and loved ones as pressure, believing their love is not unconditional but a reward for staying straight.

Ironically, some former drinkers and drug users find that psychological burden too great to bear, leading to a relapse.

Guilt: Substance dependents never give much thought to the pain they bring to others. However, once their minds clear, they see the torment they caused and are properly ashamed. Not that parents should summarily pardon a former addict for his transgressions, but they should refrain from dredging up the past. As an ex-addict who wrestled with his conscience for a long time afterward, I can assure you that recovering youngsters realize what they did and feel extremely guilty.

Loneliness: The convalescing child is faced with the daunting prospect of having to establish a new network of non-drug-using friends. He may feel like an outsider among his peers, particularly if he encounters his former gang or is taunted for resisting propositions to get high. In addition, he must find drugless activities and interests. An aftercare counselor can help to ease his discouragement and suggest constructive ways of filling up his spare time, but he also needs support at home.

Apprehension: Kids need to be reassured that, just as they have changed, so has the home situation, which was often fraught with strife. That is why family counseling is so essential to treatment, to remedy negative patterns of communication. Yet it is common for returning youngsters to worry about whether or not the situation will be improved.

"I think about it a lot," says Carl, who entered treatment only after his teenage girlfriend died of a drug overdose. "I hope things are going to be different at home, but I can't really say. If anything, I have a feeling they're going to be even worse; my mother's drinking, the arguments."

I don't mean to imply that all recovering substance abusers return home as emotional time bombs ready to explode. Rehabilitation inspires in many children the confidence to go back to the same home, the same streets, and still uphold their sobriety. All of the kids we spoke with expressed optimism for the future:

"I've learned not to compromise myself anymore. For the first time in my life, I have principles, which are going to keep me from getting into drugs again."

—*Ira*

"I can't go back home, because my mother still smokes reefer. I haven't heard from her since I've been in treatment, and I know that straightening myself out won't stop her from using drugs. So I'm going to move out on my own, and I think I'll be able to make it."

—*Helen*

212

"Instead of hanging out with my old friends, I'm going to get together with the people I met here in the program. I feel good about making it because I feel good about myself."

—*Anthony*

HELPING YOUR CHILD REMAIN STRAIGHT

The first reality parents have to accept is that they will not be able to shield a recovering child from all negative influences and temptations. At the same time, to remove all restraints may place too much pressure on him too soon. Accordingly, I recommend providing some disciplinary structure by way of yet another contract, which should be renegotiated every two months until aftercare is completed. Incorporate the following provisions:

Family Contract III

I, _____*(child's name)*, pledge to abide by the following rules:

1. No use of alcohol or drugs.
2. No tobacco use.
3. No associating with known drug users or hanging out where drugs are used.
4. Obeying all school regulations, remaining on school grounds during the day, and maintaining satisfactory academic grades.
5. Must attend individual and family therapy.
6. Must perform certain household chores, for which an allowance will be granted.
7. Must complete all homework assignments, which are to be shown to Mom and Dad. They promise their assistance as much as possible.
8. Mom and Dad will provide transportation to a reasonable number of activities.
9. A curfew (based on the type of neighborhood in which you live) will be adhered to:

- for twelve-to-fourteen-year-olds: 9 p.m. on school nights; 10 p.m. on weekends
- for fifteen- and sixteen-year-olds: 9 p.m. and 12 a.m.
- for seventeen- and eighteen-year-olds: 10 p.m. and 1 a.m.

10. Mom and Dad must always be notified of my whereabouts.

Date effective: _____

Signed:

_____
(Child's name)

_____
(Parent's name)

_____
(Parent's name)

What else can you do? Basically, employ the preventative techniques described in chapter 3, which are reprised here briefly:

- Praise your youngster when appropriate, to help boost self-esteem and to demonstrate that dependability, honesty, obedience, and so forth are rewarded.
- Through a combination of structured and unstructured activities, help him to cultivate new interests. Even before a child finishes treatment, parents should be investigating prospects. Ask some of your other kids' straight friends what they do in their spare time. One of the goals of family therapy, incidentally, is to suggest ways all family members can utilize this new time creatively.
- Encourage alternative means of handling stress and feeling good without chemicals.
- Promote individuality, so that he has other outlets of self-expression besides misbehaving.

214

- Without pushing, direct him toward long-range goals; for example, helping him with career orientation.
- Reassure him you can be counted on at all times for support and advice.
- Continue coaching him on his refusal skills.

WHEN A CHILD SUFFERS A RELAPSE

Probably the greatest danger any substance abuser faces is the self-deception that he can trifle with drugs "just this once." When I was a counselor at Cenikor, we saw innumerable cases of patients successfully completing the program only to wind up back in treatment some time later. They would always lament, "I thought I had it licked, so I figured that one joint couldn't hurt . . ."

That same rationalization continually prevented me from escaping my addiction. When I was living in Dallas, impending marriage and father-hood motivated me into actually staying sober for four or five months. Until I went back to Florida to pick up some personal items and ran into some of my former "friends." When they invited me to their house, I knew what was in store but was drawn like a moth to a flame. They were preparing to inject a newly discovered synthetic narcotic called Numor-phan—tiny blue pills that packed a tremendous punch and could be dissolved in water for injections. "Want some?" they offered.

"No, man," I declared sanctimoniously. "I'm staying straight. I'm getting married to a great girl."

"But this isn't heroin," one of my buddies reasoned. To an addict, eager to explain away his habit, it was incentive enough for me to pocket about two hundred dollars' worth of the drug before returning to Texas. *Just this last time*, I lied to myself. There were hundreds more "last times" to follow.

A youngster's temporary relapse is often compounded by parental denial. The parents revert to their old enabling ways, as if his dependency had never happened. Understandably, mothers and fathers are terrified by the prospect of a child becoming readdicted. But by ignoring harbingers that the beast still lurks around, they only feed its voracious appetite. One or two flirtations, and a recovering youth's sobriety can be salvaged. But if his substance use is permitted to continue, he backslides completely. As I emphasize throughout this book, *trust your instincts and act upon them.*

However, if your child does regress to his previous behavior, neither you nor he should throw up your hands in defeat. This reaction, called Abstinence Violation Effect (AVE), is endemic to recovering addicts, who experience guilt, feelings of failure, self-loathing, and hopelessness about ever being cured. Therefore, some come to believe, why resist it? Why not surrender without a struggle? And so they go back to abusing substances. Through counseling, both youngsters and their parents must appreciate that while breaches of temperance should always be staunchly discouraged, they do not negate the entire treatment. I hesitate to say they should be expected, which connotes approval, so let me put it this way: Lapses should not be *un*expected.

Most of the former drug users we spoke with admitted to having backslid at some point. Some briefly resumed smoking marijuana or drinking before realizing they were headed for disaster and quitting. Others, like Darrell, slipped back until they were all the way at the bottom, even dropping out of rehabilitation.

"I started hanging around with the old gang again," he says, "and at first I was able to handle it. I'd think, *I can just talk to them, I don't have to get high with them,* but, to be honest, I felt like an outsider. Finally, one day I said the hell with it and smoked some reefer. As soon as I smoked some reefer I wanted cocaine. Then I wanted to hit the crack pipe. A couple of hits, and I was back to blowing my biweekly pay—eight hundred dollars—in one night. I began missing work, got fired, and was ready to start stealing again. Luckily, I woke up in time. *Wait a minute. What am I doing? I'm going back to the way I was.* I hated the way I was. At that point I called the program and told them I wanted to return."

WORST-CASE SCENARIO

If all treatment fails to break your child of his habit, or if he completes treatment but regresses to regular use of alcohol or drugs:

The hard truth is that not all kids are going to make it through chemical rehabilitation. Those over eighteen may drop out midway through, and of those who do stick it out, approximately one in three eventually becomes a habitual user again. Why didn't treatment work for them? It is hard to say. You can fault the program's efficiency, but ultimately it comes down to the fact that the child did not truly want to be helped.

Parents who find themselves in such a predicament will probably recoil at what I am about to propose: When *all* courses have been exhausted, they should not permit the drug abuser back into the home until he proves he has stopped using all drugs and is attending outpatient care; or, if his use has advanced to the point where he is physically dependent, he must undergo detoxification followed by residential or inpatient treatment, in the same facility as before. *And this time, at his expense.* Since most facilities operate on a sliding scale, he will be charged a fee he can afford through working.

Throwing a kid out of the house—sounds heartless, doesn't it?

Not when you consider the alternative: to facilitate his drug use at home, where habits can be sustained—and overdoses can occur—just as readily as on the street. *You must allow him to suffer the consequences of his actions.* Let him see what life is like without financial support, alone on the streets, without a roof over his head. For many chronic drug users, such an extreme measure is necessary to force them to confront the truth about themselves and their life-style. That was certainly the case for me.

"Let's go, your things are packed. We want you out of here." My parents were waiting for me at a friend's house in Florida. I was so stoned at the time that I barely comprehended them much less believed them; after all, I'd been threatened similarly before but had always managed to prey upon my parents' sympathies. This time, however, my father meant it. He was literally red-faced with anger. In retrospect I can see that throwing me out was the hardest—and most courageous—thing he'd ever done in his life.

In my father's trembling hands were two hundred dollars and two airplane tickets, which he gave to my then wife, Sarah. At the time, I was grateful to leave, since my next residence in Florida seemed destined to be a prison cell. But I should have been thankful for another reason: Forcing me out on the streets was the kindest, most loving act my parents could have performed. It was what eventually led me to straighten out my life.

But first I had to hit rock bottom: with just rags on my back and on the verge of dying. Like most hard-core addicts, I wanted out of my dreary life but didn't wish for my ticket to be one-way. Once I was forced into a decision between life and death, I had no choice but to accept the sacrifices I needed to make in order to become drug-free. In all likelihood, your child won't have to plunge to the depths that I did. He may bottom out in a treatment program. Or in a jail cell after being arrested for driving under the influence. But if the situation demands getting tough, get tough.

It will not be easy. You will feel like an ogre, a terrible parent; just two

217

of the accusations you can expect your child to cast at you. You will need a great deal of support during this time and should attend support-group meetings, where other parents who have undergone similar situations will understand your agony. Certain relatives and neighbors may not, however, and those in your self-help group can assist you in learning to steel yourself against their disapproval. Just remember that only you and your spouse know the anguish of living with a child intent on destroying himself and his family through alcohol or drugs—and that only parents who truly love their child would risk losing his love so that he may live.

I remember the day I stood at the canopied entrance of the Cenikor building, waiting to greet the presidential motorcade. Ronald Reagan, the fortieth president of the United States, was about to arrive for a tour of the facility. The quiet afternoon was interrupted by the cacophony of helicopter blades slicing the air, wailing sirens, and thundering motorcycle engines.

Between the time the president stepped out of his limousine and walked up to where I stood—no more than thirty seconds—in my mind I saw faces from my past: my wife, Maria, and my sons; my ex-wife, Sarah, and my daughter, Dawn; my parents; friends who had been hooked on drugs but managed to overcome them; and those who did not.

I reflected on how perilously close I had come to winding up just another drug casualty. Also, how ironic it was that I started using drugs as a teenager because I felt I was nothing without them; I believed I couldn't reach myself or feel good without them. For years I fooled myself into thinking chemicals held the key to the world, when in reality they imprisoned me, robbing me of my free will.

Many things have changed since I first became involved with drugs. Although the problem has intensified, so has the resolve of parents to protect their children from this menace. As for the future, I am hopeful. Thanks to the efforts of so many people who have experienced the tragedy of substance abuse, and through the leadership of First Lady Nancy Reagan, we now understand the problem better and know that it is too dangerous to neglect. Today's parents are better informed and have the added advantage of numerous supportive private and public resources.

This book is one. Apply its tools, and you stand a good chance of keeping the wily beast drug abuse at bay.

KEY POINTS

● Feelings parents may experience once their child completes his treatment program:

1. *Abandonment and emptiness:* Now that they are no longer needed to constantly bail their child out of trouble, they feel stripped of their purpose in life.
2. *Resentment:* They feel the family has been put through enough and want the crisis to end.
3. *Disappointment:* Parents sometimes delude themselves into believing that all family problems will be resolved upon their kid's recovery and are let down when they are not.

● It is always recommended that while the abuser undergoes aftercare counseling, family members continue receiving either outpatient or self-help therapy. Start with weekly sessions for a half year, then cut back to monthly attendance. Continue until the child's rehabilitation is completed or until family members are satisfied that all discord is reconciled.

● Feelings recovering kids may experience:

1. *Pressure:* They feel constantly under surveillance or that others have little faith in their commitment to stay straight. They worry about how they will react when someone offers them a drink or a joint and about what will happen when they are confronted by their former crowd. On the average, it takes recovering substance abusers twelve to eighteen months to be able to mingle comfortably among intoxicated persons.
2. *Guilt:* Once their minds clear, former substance abusers see the heartache they have caused and are properly ashamed.
3. *Loneliness:* Recovering drug users must establish a new network of non-drug-using friends and may feel like outsiders among their peers. In addition, they need to find drugless activities and interests to occupy their time.
4. *Apprehension:* Kids need reassurance that, just as they have changed, so has the situation at home.

● Youngsters who have completed their programs should receive six to twelve months of aftercare therapy, either at the facility or through Twelve

219

Steps groups such as Alcoholics Anonymous, Cocaine Anonymous, Drugs Anonymous, and Narcotics Anonymous.

● In addition to instituting a new Family Contract, parents can aid their child's commitment to sobriety by

1. praising him when appropriate;
2. helping him to cultivate new interests through a combination of structured and unstructured activities;
3. encouraging alternative means of handling stress and feeling good without chemicals;
4. promoting his individuality, so that he has other outlets of self-expression besides misbehaving;
5. directing him toward long-range goals such as career orientation—but without pressuring him;
6. reassuring him they can be counted on at all times for support and advice;
7. continuing to coach him on his refusal skills.

● One in three kids who complete chemical-dependency rehabilitation will relapse.

● In the worst-case scenario, if treatment fails, or if a child completes rehabilitation but regresses to regular use of alcohol or drugs, parents should not permit him in the home until he proves he has stopped using all substances and is attending outpatient care. If his use has advanced to the point where he is physically dependent, he must undergo detoxification followed by residential or inpatient treatment, in the same facility as before—this time at his expense—before he may return home.

Appendix A

Treatment and Counseling

If the children you love need professional drug- or alcohol-dependency treatment, contact the following organizations for referrals to programs in your area:

Forty-six states and the District of Columbia have combined alcohol- and drug-abuse agencies; four states have separate agencies for each. All twelve Canadian provinces have similar agencies.

ALABAMA

Division of Mental Illness and
  Substance Abuse Community
  Programs
Department of Mental Health
200 Interstate Park Drive
P.O. Box 3710
Montgomery, AL 36193
(205) 271-9209

ALASKA

Office of Alcoholism and Drug Abuse
Department of Health and Social
  Services
Pouch H-05-F
Juneau, AK 99811
(907) 586-6201

ARIZONA

Office of Community Behavioral
  Services
Arizona Department of Health
  Services
701 East Jefferson
Suite 400A
Phoenix, AZ 85034
(602) 255-1152

ARKANSAS

Arkansas Office on Alcohol and Drug
  Abuse Prevention
1515 West 7th Avenue
Suite 300
Little Rock, AR 72202
(501) 371-2603

CALIFORNIA

Department of Alcohol and Drug
  Programs
111 Capitol Mall
Suite 450
Sacramento, CA 95814
(916) 445-0834

COLORADO

Alcohol and Drug Abuse Division
Department of Health
4210 East 11th Avenue
Denver, CO 80220
(303) 331-8201

CONNECTICUT

Connecticut Alcohol and Drug Abuse
  Commission
999 Asylum Avenue
Third Floor
Hartford, CT 06105
(203) 566-4145

DELAWARE

Bureau of Alcoholism and Drug Abuse
1901 North DuPont Highway
Newcastle, DE 19720
(302) 421-6101

DISTRICT OF COLUMBIA

Health Planning and Development
1875 Connecticut Avenue N.W.
Suite 836
Washington, DC 20009
(202) 673-7481

FLORIDA

Alcohol and Drug Abuse Program
Department of Health and
  Rehabilitative Services
1317 Winewood Boulevard
Tallahassee, FL 32301
(904) 488-0900

GEORGIA

Alcohol and Drug Services Section
878 Peachtree Street N.E.
Suite 318
Atlanta, GA 30309
(404) 894-6352

HAWAII

Alcohol and Drug Abuse Branch
Department of Health
P.O. Box 3378
Honolulu, HI 96801
(808) 548-4280

IDAHO

Bureau of Substance Abuse and Social
  Services
Department of Health and Welfare
450 West State Street
Seventh Floor
Boise, ID 83720
(208) 334-5935

ILLINOIS

Illinois Department of Alcoholism and
  Substance Abuse
100 West Randolph Street
Suite 5-600
Chicago, IL 60601
(312) 917-3840

INDIANA

Division of Addiction Services
Department of Mental Health
117 East Washington Street
Indianapolis, IN 46204
(317) 232-7816

IOWA

Iowa Department of Public Health
Division of Substance Abuse and
    Health Promotion
Lucas State Office Building
Fourth Floor
Des Moines, IA 50319
(515) 281-3641

KANSAS

Alcohol and Drug Abuse Services
Biddle Building
2700 West 6th Street
Topeka, KS 66606
(913) 296-3925

KENTUCKY

Division of Substance Abuse
Department for Mental Health-Human
    Resources Services
275 East Main Street
Frankfort, KY 40621
(502) 564-2880

LOUISIANA

Office of Prevention and Recovery
    from Alcohol and Drug Abuse
P.O. Box 53129
Baton Rouge, LA 70892
(504) 922-0730

MAINE

Office of Alcoholism and Drug Abuse
    Prevention
Bureau of Rehabilitation
State House Station Number 11
Augusta, ME 04333
(207) 289-2781

MARYLAND

Alcoholism Control Administration
201 West Preston Street
Fourth Floor
Baltimore, MD 21201
(301) 225-6542

Maryland State Drug Abuse
    Administration
201 West Preston Street
Baltimore, MD 21201
(301) 225-6926

MASSACHUSETTS

Division of Substance Abuse Services
150 Tremont Street
Boston, MA 02111
(617) 727-8614

MICHIGAN

Office of Substance Abuse Services
Department of Public Health
3500 North Logan Street
Lansing, MI 48909
(517) 335-8809

MINNESOTA

Chemical Dependency Program
    Division
Department of Human Services
Centennial Building

Fourth Floor
658 Cedar
St. Paul, MN 55155
(612) 296-4610

MISSISSIPPI

Division of Alcohol and Drug Abuse
Department of Mental Health
1500 Woolfolk Building
Jackson, MS 39201
(601) 359-1297

MISSOURI

Division of Alcohol and Drug Abuse
Department of Mental Health
1915 South Ridge Drive
P.O. Box 687
Jefferson City, MO 65102
(314) 751-4942

MONTANA

Alcohol and Drug Abuse Division
State of Montana Department of
   Institutions
Helena, MT 59601
(406) 444-2827

NEBRASKA

Division of Alcoholism and Drug
   Abuse
Department of Public Institutions
P.O. Box 94728
Lincoln, NB 68509
(402) 471-2851

NEVADA

Bureau of Alcohol and Drug Abuse
Department of Human Resources

505 East King Street
Carson City, NV 89710
(702) 885-4790

NEW HAMPSHIRE

Office of Alcohol and Drug Abuse
   Prevention
Health and Welfare Building
Hazen Drive
Concord, NH 03301
(603) 271-4627

NEW JERSEY

New Jersey Division of Alcoholism
129 East Hanover Street
Trenton, NJ 08625
(609) 292-8947

Division of Narcotic and Drug Abuse
   Control
129 East Hanover Street
Trenton, NJ 08625
(609) 292-5760

NEW MEXICO

Substance Abuse Bureau
Behavioral Health Services Division
P.O. Box 968
Sante Fe, NM 87504
(505) 827-0117

NEW YORK

Division of Alcoholism and Alcohol
   Abuse
194 Washington Avenue
Albany, NY 12210
(518) 474-5417

Division of Substance Abuse Services
Executive Park South
P.O. Box 8200
Albany, NY 12203
(518) 457-7629

NORTH CAROLINA

Alcohol and Drug Abuse Section
Division of Mental Health and Mental
  Retardation Services
325 North Salisbury Street
Raleigh, NC 27611
(919) 733-4670

NORTH DAKOTA

Division of Alcoholism and Drug
  Abuse
North Dakota Department of Human
  Services
State Capitol
Judicial Wing
Bismarck, ND 58505
(701) 224-2769

OHIO

Bureau on Alcohol Abuse and
  Recovery
Ohio Department of Health
170 North High Street
Third Floor
Columbus, OH 43266
(614) 466-3445

Bureau of Drug Abuse
170 North High Street
Third Floor
Columbus, OH 43215
(614) 466-7893

OKLAHOMA

Alcohol and Drug Programs
Oklahoma Department of Mental
  Health
P.O. Box 53277
Capitol Station
Oklahoma City, OK 73152
(405) 521-0044

OREGON

Office of Alcohol and Drug Abuse
  Programs
301 Public Service Building
Salem, OR 97310
(503) 378-2163

PENNSYLVANIA

Deputy Secretary for Drug and
  Alcohol Programs
Pennsylvania Department of Health
P.O. Box 90
Harrisburg, PA 17108
(717) 787-9857

RHODE ISLAND

Department of Mental Health, Mental
  Retardation and Hospitals
Division of Substance Abuse
Substance Abuse Administration
  Building
Cranston, RI 02920
(401) 464-2091

SOUTH CAROLINA

South Carolina Commission on
  Alcohol and Drug Abuse
3700 Forest Drive
Columbia, SC 29204
(803) 734-9520

SOUTH DAKOTA

Division of Alcohol and Drug Abuse
Joe Foss Building
523 East Capitol
Pierre, SD 57501
(605) 773-3123

TENNESSEE

Alcohol and Drug Abuse Services
Tennessee Department of Mental
   Health and Mental Retardation
706 Church Street
Fourth Floor
Nashville, TN 37219
(615) 741-1921

TEXAS

Texas Commission on Alcohol and
   Drug Abuse
1705 Guadalupe Street
Austin, TX 78701
(512) 463-5510

UTAH

Division of Alcoholism and Drugs
150 West North Temple
Suite 350
P.O. Box 2500
Salt Lake City, UT 84110
(801) 533-6532

VERMONT

Office of Alcohol and Drug Abuse
   Programs
103 South Maine Street
Waterbury, VT 05676
(802) 241-2170/241-1000

VIRGINIA

Office of Substance Abuse Services
State Department of Mental Health
   and Mental Retardation
P.O. Box 1797
109 Governor Street
Richmond, VA 23214
(804) 786-3906

WASHINGTON

Bureau of Alcoholism and Substance
   Abuse
Washington Department of Social and
   Health Services
Mail Stop OB-44W
Olympia, WA 98504
(206) 753-5866

WEST VIRGINIA

Division of Alcohol and Drug Abuse
State Capitol
1800 Washington Street East
Room 451
Charleston, WV 25305
(304) 348-2276

WISCONSIN

Office of Alcohol and Other Drug
   Abuse
1 West Wilson Street
P.O. Box 7851
Madison, WI 53707
(608) 266-3442

WYOMING

Alcohol and Drug Abuse Programs
Hathaway Building
Cheyenne, WY 82002
(307) 777-7115

CANADA

ALBERTA

Alcoholism and Drug Abuse
  Commission
10909 Jasper Avenue
Edmonton, Alberta T5J 3M9
(403) 427-7301

BRITISH COLUMBIA

Alcohol-Drug Education Services
96 East Broadway
Suite 302
Vancouver, British Columbia B6J 4S5
(604) 731-9121

MANITOBA

Alcoholism Foundation of Manitoba
1031 Portage Avenue
Winnipeg, Manitoba R3G OR8
(204) 944-6200

NEW BRUNSWICK

Alcoholism and Drug Dependency
  Commission of New Brunswick
65 Brunswick Street
Fredericton, New Brunswick E3B 5H1
(506) 453-2136

NEWFOUNDLAND

Alcohol and Drug Dependency
  Commission of Newfoundland and
  Labrador
Prince Charles Building
Suite 105
St. Johns, Newfoundland A1C 1B1
(709) 737-3600

NORTHWEST TERRITORIES

Department of Social Services,
  Alcohol and Drug Program
Government of the Northwest
  Territories
Yellowknife, Northwest
  Territories X1A 2L9
(403) 873-7155

NOVA SCOTIA

Commission on Drug Dependency
5675 Spring Garden Road
Suite 314
Halifax, Nova Scotia B3J 1H1
(902) 424-4270

ONTARIO

Addiction Research Foundation
33 Russell Street
Toronto, Ontario M5S 2S1
(416) 596-6000

PRINCE EDWARD ISLAND

Queens County Addiction Services
P.O. Box 1832
Charlottetown, Prince Edward Island
  C1A 7N5
(902) 892-4265

QUEBEC

Ministry of Social Affairs
1075 Chemin Ste. Foy
Quebec City, Quebec G1S 2M1
(418) 643-3380

SASKATCHEWAN

Alcohol and Drug Abuse Commission
3475 Albert Street
Regina, Saskatchewan S4S 6X6
(306) 787-4085

YUKON

Royal Canadian Mounted Police,
  M Division
N.C.O. in Charge, Drug Section
4100 Fourth Avenue
White Horse, Yukon Y1A 1H5
(403) 667-5577

NATIONAL REFERRAL AGENCIES

Cocaine Hotline
Provided by Fair Oaks Hospital
19 Prospect Street
Summit, NY 07901
(800) COC-AINE

National Institute on Drug Abuse
Drug-Referral Helpline
5600 Fishers Lane
Rockville, MD 20857
(800) 662-HELP

Therapeutic Communities of America
54 West 40th Street
New York, NY 10018
(212) 354-6000

National Clearinghouse for Drug and
  Alcohol Information
P.O. Box 2345
Rockville, MD 20852
(301) 468-2600

The Clearinghouse makes available an approximately three-hundred-page *National Directory of Drug Abuse and Alcoholism Treatment and Prevention Programs*. Its most recent edition was published in 1984 and as of this writing was no longer in stock. However, most public libraries' reference sections should have a copy.

Other sources: In Yellow Pages, look under "Drug Abuse and Addiction Information and Treatment" for the names of nearby drug-abuse rehabilitation centers; look under "Crisis Intervention Service" for referrals. In the White Pages, look under "Drug Abuse" in the Community Services Numbers, or "Youth Board" in the County Government Offices listings.

For referrals to accredited hospital inpatient and outpatient programs only, contact:

Joint Commission on Accreditation of
  Hospitals (JCAH)
875 North Michigan Avenue
Chicago, IL 60611
(312) 642-6061

Recommended drug-treatment programs, by state:

Briefly, the criterion used in singling out these substance-dependency treatment facilities was to provide readers with a range of program types (outpatient, short- and long-term hospital inpatient, short-term residential, and therapeutic community). Another consideration was to cover as broad a geographical area of the U.S. as possible. There are many other exemplary programs around the country, but for obvious reasons not all could be included.

Please note that for most inpatient and residential facilities, the approximate length of stay is specified and does not reflect outpatient aftercare. For therapeutic communities, except where indicated, the length of stay can be from six to twenty-four months.

ALABAMA

BIRMINGHAM

The University of Alabama at Birmingham Substance Abuse Programs
3015 7th Avenue South
Birmingham, AL 35233
(205) 934-2118

Program type: Outpatient for persons 13 to 17

DECATUR

Charter Retreat Hospital
P. O. Box 1230
Decatur, AL 35602
(205) 350-1450

Program type: Short-term (45-day) inpatient for persons 12 to 18; short-term (4-week) inpatient for persons 18 and older

DOTHAN

Charter Woods Hospital
700 Cottonwood Road
Dothan, AL 36301
(205) 793-6660

Program type: Inpatient for persons 11 and older

MOBILE

Charter Academy of Mobile
251 Cox Street
Mobile, AL 36604
(205) 432-4111

Program type: Therapeutic community for persons 12 to 18

Charter Southland Hospital
5800 Southland Drive
P.O. Box 9699
Mobile, AL 36691
(205) 666-7900

Program type: Outpatient and short-term (4-week) inpatient for persons 13 and older

ALASKA

ANCHORAGE

Charter North Hospital
2530 Debarr Road
Anchorage, AK 99514
(907) 258-7575

Program type: Short-term (30-day) inpatient for persons 12 to 18; outpatient and short-term (4-week) inpatient for persons 18 and older

ARIZONA

CHANDLER

Charter Hospital
2195 North Grace Boulevard
Chandler, AZ 85224
(602) 899-8989

Program type: Short-term inpatient for
persons 13 to 18; short-term (approximately 3-week) inpatient for persons 18
and older

GLENDALE

Charter Hospital of Glendale
6015 West Peoria
Glendale, AZ 85302
(602) 878-7878

Program type: Short-term (4-week) inpatient for persons 12 to 18; short-term
(approximately 30-day) inpatient for
persons 18 and older

PHOENIX

St. Luke's Behavioral Center
1800 East Van Buren
Phoenix, AZ 85006
(602) 251-8535

Program type: Short-term (2-to-3-
month) inpatient for persons 13 to 17

ARKANSAS

FAYETTEVILLE

Charter Vista Hospital
4253 Crossover Road
Fayetteville, AR 72702
(501) 521-5731

Program type: Outpatient for persons 18
and older; short-term (60-to-90-day) inpatient for persons 13 to 18; short-term
(4-week) alcohol inpatient for persons
18 and older

CALIFORNIA

AUBURN

Sierra Family Services
219 Maple Street
Auburn, CA 95603
(916) 885-0441

Program type: Outpatient for all ages

CARNELIAN BAY

Sierra Family Services
3080 North Lake Boulevard No. C
Tahoe City
P.O. Box 383
Carnelian Bay, CA 95711
(916) 581-4054

Program type: Outpatient for all ages

CORONA

Charter Grove Hospital
2005 Kellogg Street
Corona, CA 91719
(714) 735-2910

Program type: Outpatient and short-
term (30-day) inpatient for persons 13
to 18; outpatient and short-term (30-
day) inpatient for persons 18 and older

COVINA

Charter Oak Hospital
1161 East Covina Boulevard
Covina, CA 91724
(818) 915-8711

Program type: Outpatient and short-term (6-week) inpatient for persons 13 to 17; outpatient and short-term inpatient for persons 18 and older

DESCANSO

Phoenix House Academy
23981 Sherilton Road
Descanso, CA 92016
(619) 445-0405

Program type: Residential high school for persons 13 to 18

GARDENA

South Bay Chemical Dependency and Family Treatment Center
15519 Crenshaw Boulevard
Gardena, CA 90249
(213) 679-9031

Program type: Outpatient for all ages

HAWTHORNE

Pacifica House
2501 West El Segundo Boulevard
Hawthorne, CA 90250
(213) 538-5568

Program type: Therapeutic community for persons 18 and older

HOLLYWOOD

Hollywood Community Recovery Center
1857 Taft Avenue
Hollywood, CA 90028
(213) 461-3161

Program type: Outpatient for all ages

INGLEWOOD

Inglewood Community Recovery Center
279 Beach Avenue
Inglewood, CA 90302
(213) 673-5750

Program type: Outpatient for all ages

LONG BEACH

Charter Hospital of Long Beach
6060 Paramount Boulevard
Long Beach, CA 90805
(213) 408-3100

Program type: Short-term (3-to-4-week) inpatient for persons 18 and older

Patterns
2246 Earl Avenue
Long Beach, CA 90806
(213) 595-9542

Program type: Residential for alcoholic mothers 18 and older

Redgate Memorial Hospital
1775 Chestnut Avenue
Long Beach, CA 90813
(213) 599-8444

Program type: Alcoholism inpatient for persons 18 and older

LOS ANGELES

East L.A. Chemical Dependency and Family Treatment Center
3421 East Olympic Boulevard
Los Angeles, CA 90023
(213) 262-1786

Program type: Outpatient for chemically dependent mothers or mothers-to-

231

be 18 and older; accepts 17-year-olds, but they must be accompanied by parent

El Sereno Chemical Dependency and Family Treatment Center
4837 Huntington Drive North
Los Angeles, CA 90032
(213) 221-1746

Program type: Outpatient for chemically dependent mothers or mothers-to-be 18 and older; accepts 17-year-olds, but they must be accompanied by parent

MOUNTAIN VIEW

Comadres
Family Service Association
655 Castro Street
Mountain View, CA 94041
(415) 968-3371

Program type: Outpatient for women 16 and older

POMONA

American Hospital
2180 West Valley Boulevard
Pomona, CA 91768
(714) 865-2336

Program type: Long-term (9-to-18-month) inpatient for persons 18 and older

PASADENA

Impact Drug and Alcohol Treatment Center
1680 North Fair Oaks Avenue
P.O. Box 93607
Pasadena, CA 91109
(213) 681-2575

Program type: Therapeutic community for persons 18 and older

REDWOOD CITY

Serenity
2893 Spring Street
P.O. Box 5070
Redwood City, CA 94603
(415) 368-1437

Program type: Therapeutic community for persons 12 to 18

ROSEVILLE

Sierra Family Services
424 Vernon Street
Roseville, CA 95678
(916) 783-5207

Program type: Outpatient for all ages

SAN FRANCISCO

Delancey Street Foundation
2563 Divisadero Street
San Francisco, CA 94115
(415) 563-5326

Program type: Therapeutic community for persons 18 and older

Haight-Ashbury Free Medical Clinic
529 Clayton Street
San Francisco, CA 94117
(415) 621-2014

Program type: Outpatient for persons 12 and older

Haight-Ashbury Free Medical Clinic
Bill Pone Memorial Unit
531 Clayton Street
San Francisco, CA 94117
(415) 621-2036

Program type: Bilingual outpatient for persons 12 and older

SAN JOSE

Comadres
Family Service Association
55 East Empire Street
San Jose, CA 95112
(408) 288-6200

Program type: Outpatient for women 16
and older

SANTA ANA

Phoenix House
1207 East Fruit Street
Santa Ana, CA 92701
(213) 305-0170

Program type: Therapeutic community
for persons 12 and older

SANTA MONICA

Delancey Street Foundation
1344 16th Street
Santa Monica, CA 90404
(213) 393-2657

Program type: Therapeutic community
for persons 18 and older

TARZANA

Tarzana Treatment Center
18646 Oxnard Street
Tarzana, CA 91356
(818) 996-1051

Program type: Outpatient for persons 12
to 18; short-term (30-to-90-day) residential for persons 18 and older; therapeutic community for persons 18 and
older

TORRANCE

Charter Pacific Hospital
4025 West 226th Street

Torrance, CA 90509
(213) 373-0261

Program type: Short-term (90-day maximum) inpatient for persons 14 and
older; short-term (4-week) inpatient for
persons 18 and older

TURLOCK

Phoenix House/Tuum Est
219 South Broadway
Turlock, CA 95380
(209) 668-0771

Program type: Therapeutic community
for persons 18 and older

VENICE

Phoenix House/Tuum Est
503 Ocean Front Walk
Venice, CA 90291
(213) 392-3070

Program type: Therapeutic community
for persons 12 to 17½

COLORADO

LAKEWOOD

Cenikor
1533 Glen Ayr Drive
Lakewood, CO 80215
(303) 234-1288

Program type: Therapeutic community
for persons 18 and older

CONNECTICUT

NEW HAVEN

Connecticut Mental Health Center/
APT Foundation
Substance-Abuse Treatment Center
285 Orchard Street
New Haven, CT 06511
(203) 789-7387

Program type: Drug- and alcohol-out-patient for persons 18 and older

Connecticut Mental-Health Center/
APT Foundation
Substance-Abuse Treatment Center
Park Institute
1401 Chapel Street
New Haven, CT 06511
(203) 624-0840

Program type: Outpatient for persons 18 and older

Connecticut Mental Health Center/
APT Foundation
Substance-Abuse Treatment Center
SOS Substance-Abuse Treatment
Center
904 Howard Avenue
New Haven, CT 06519
(203) 789-7817

Program type: Outpatient for persons 18 and older

Crossroads
48 Howe Street
New Haven, CT 06511
(203) 865-3541

Program type: Therapeutic community for persons 18 and older

NEWTOWN

Connecticut Mental Health Center/
APT Foundation
Substance-Abuse Treatment Center
Alpha House
Mile Hill Road
Newtown, CT 06470
(203) 776-1600

Program type: Therapeutic community for persons 14 to 18; some 19 and 20

Connecticut Mental Health Center/
APT Foundation
Substance-Abuse Treatment Center
Daytop
Mile Hill Road
Newtown, CT 06470
(203) 776-1600

Program type: Therapeutic community for persons 21 and older; some 19 and 20

NORWALK

Connecticut Renaissance
83 Wall Street
Norwalk, CT 06850
(203) 866-2541

Program type: Outpatient for persons 17 and older

STAMFORD

Liberation Clinic
125 Main Street
Stamford, CT 06901
(203) 324-7511

Program type: Outpatient for persons 6 and older

Liberation House
119 Main Street
Stamford, CT 06901
(203) 325-4161

Program type: Therapeutic community
for persons 16 and older

Connecticut Renaissance
31 Wolcott Street
Waterbury, CT 06702
(203) 753-2341

Program type: Therapeutic community
for persons 18 and older

DISTRICT OF COLUMBIA

Second Genesis
1320 Harvard Street N.W.
Washington, DC 20009
(202) 234-6800

Program type: Therapeutic community
for persons 14 and older

FLORIDA

FORT LAUDERDALE

Spectrum
Financial East Building
2801 East Oakland Park Boulevard
Fort Lauderdale, FL 33306
(305) 564-2266

Program type: Outpatient for all ages

FORT MYERS

Charter Glade Hospital
3550 Colonial Boulevard
Fort Myers, FL 33912
(813) 939-0403

Program type: Short-term (45-to-50-
day) inpatient for persons 13 to 18;
short-term (4-week) alcohol inpatient
for persons 18 and older; short-term (6-
week) inpatient for persons 18 and older

JACKSONVILLE

Gateway Community Services
4814 Lexington Avenue
Jacksonville, FL 32210
(904) 384-8669

Program type: Outpatient for persons 13
and older

Gateway Community Services
580 West 8th Street
Jacksonville, FL 32209
(904) 798-8255

Program type: Short-term (6-to-9-week)
residential for persons 13 to 17

Gateway Community Services
1105 Edgewood Avenue
Jacksonville, FL 32208
(904) 765-4633

Program type: Outpatient for persons 18
and older

LAKELAND

Palmview Hospital
2510 North Florida Avenue
Lakeland, FL 33805
(813) 682-6105; in Florida,
   (800) 282-3480

Program type: Outpatient for all ages;
short-term therapeutic community for
persons 11 to 18

235

MIAMI

Charter Hospital of Miami
11100 N.W. 27th Street
Miami, FL 33172
(305) 591-3230

Program type: Outpatient and short-term (4-week) inpatient for persons 18 and older

New Horizons Community Mental
  Health Center
1469 N.W. 36th Street
Miami, FL 33142
(305) 635-0366

Program type: Outpatient for persons 13 to 30

Spectrum Dade Chase House
140 N.W. 59th Street
Miami, FL 33127
(305) 754-1683

Program type: Therapeutic community for persons 18 and older

Spectrum
11055 N.E. 6th Avenue
Miami, FL 33161
(305) 754-1683

Program type: Outpatient for all ages

Spectrum
Glades Professional Building
8353 S.W. 124th Street
Miami, FL 33156

Program type: Outpatient for all ages

OCALA

Charter Springs Hospital
3130 S.W. 27th Avenue

P.O. Box 3338
Ocala, FL 32678
(904) 237-7293

Program type: Outpatient and short-term (6-to-8-week) inpatient for persons 10 to 17; short-term (3-to-4-week mini-mum) inpatient for persons 18 and older

ORLANDO

Straight
2400 Silver Star Road
Orlando, FL 32804
(305) 291-HELP

Program type: Long-term outpatient, termporary residential for persons 12 to 21

ST. PETERSBURG

Straight
3001 Gandy Boulevard
St. Petersburg, FL 33702
(813) 577-6011

Program type: Long-term outpatient, temporary residential for persons 12 to 21

TAMPA

Charter Hospital of Tampa Bay
4004 Riverside Drive
Tampa, FL 33603
(813) 238-8671

Program type: Short-term inpatient for persons 13 to 18; short-term (4-week) inpatient for persons 18 and older

WILTON MANORS

Spectrum
Broward House
2301 Wilton Drive
Wilton Manors, FL 33305
(305) 920-7979

Program type: Outpatient for all ages;
therapeutic community for persons 18
and older

GEORGIA

ATHENS

Charter Winds Hospital
240 Mitchell Bridge Road
Athens, GA 30604
(404) 546-7277

Program type: Short-term (45-to-90-
day) inpatient for persons 13 to 18

ATLANTA

Charter Brook Hospital
3913 North Peachtree Road
Atlanta, GA 30341
(404) 457-8315

Program type: Outpatient and short-
term (3-month average) inpatient for
persons 13 to 18

Charter Peachford Hospital
2151 Peachford Road
Atlanta, GA 30338
(404) 454-2302

Program type: Short-term (6-to-8-week)
inpatient for persons 18 and older

Peachwood Park
2300 Peachford Road
Atlanta, GA 30338
(404) 458-5462

Program type: Outpatient for persons 18
and older

AUGUSTA

Charter Hospital of Augusta
3100 Perimeter Parkway
Augusta, GA 30909
(404) 868-6625

Program type: Outpatient and short-
term (60-day) inpatient for persons 13
to 19

COLUMBUS

Turning Point
1220 Third Avenue
P.O. Box 2299
Columbus, GA 31993
(404) 323-3167

Program type: Short-term (4-week) residential for persons 17 and older

MACON

Charter Lake Hospital
3500 Riverside Drive
P.O. Box 7067
Macon, GA 31209
(912) 474-6200

Program type: Outpatient, short-term
(4-to-6-week) inpatient and short-term
(4-week) alcohol inpatient for persons
13 and older

MARIETTA

Straight
2221 Austrell Road
Marietta, GA 30060
(404) 434-8679

Program type: Long-term outpatient,
temporary residential for persons 12 to
21

SAVANNAH

Charter Hospital of Savannah
1150 Cornell Avenue
Savannah, GA 31404
(912) 354-3911

Program type: Outpatient and short-term inpatient for persons 18 and older

ST. SIMONS

Charter-by-the-Sea Hospital
2927 Demere Road
St. Simons, GA 31522
(912) 638-1999

Program type: Short-term (45-to-55-day) inpatient for persons 12 and older; short-term (6-week) inpatient for persons 18 and older; short-term (30-day) alcohol inpatient for persons 18 and older

ILLINOIS

BELLEVILLE

Gateway Foundation
409 East Main Street
Belleville, IL 62220
(618) 234-9002

Program type: Outpatient for persons 13 and older

BOLLINGBROK

Lifeworks Chemical Dependency
   Program
420 Medical Center Drive
Suite 230
Bollingbrok, IL 60439
(312) 759-5750

Program type: Outpatient for persons 13 to 19

CHICAGO

Charter Barclay Hospital
4700 North Clarendon
Chicago, IL 60640
(312) 728-7100

Program type: Inpatient for persons 12 and older

Gateway Foundation
1706 North Kedzie Avenue
Chicago, IL 60647
(312) 227-6040

Program type: Therapeutic community for men 17 and older, for women 18 and older

Gateway Foundation
3162 North Broadway
Chicago, IL 60657
(312) 929-1865

Program type: Outpatient for persons 13 and older

EAST ST. LOUIS

Gateway Foundation
1509 King Drive
East St. Louis, IL 62205
(618) 397-9720

Program type: Outpatient for persons 13 and older

LAKE VILLA

Gateway Foundation
25480 West Cedarcrest Lane
Lake Villa, IL 60046
(312) 356-8205

Program type: Therapeutic community for persons 13 to 18

Gateway Foundation
815 North 5th Street
Springfield, IL 62702
(217) 522-7732

Program type: Therapeutic community for men 17 and older, for women 18 and older

INDIANA

FORT WAYNE

Charter Beacon Hospital
1720 Beacon Street
Fort Wayne, IN 46805
(219) 423-3651

Program type: Short-term inpatient for persons 13 to 19

KANSAS

OVERLAND PARK

Charter Hospital of Overland Park
8000 West 127th Street
P.O. Box 25870
Overland Park, KS 66225
(913) 897-4999

Program type: Short-term (30-to-45-day) inpatient for persons 13 to 18; outpatient and short-term inpatient for persons 19 and older

TOPEKA

C. F. Menninger Memorial Hospital Alcohol and Drug Abuse Recovery
    Program
P.O. Box 829
Topeka, KS 66601
(913) 273-7500

Program type: Outpatient and short-term inpatient for persons 5 to 17; short-term (4-week-minimum) inpatient for persons 18 and older

WICHITA

Charter Hospital of Wichita
8901 East Orme
Wichita, KS 67207
(316) 686-5000

Program type: Short-term (45-day) inpatient for persons 13 to 18; outpatient and short-term (30-day) inpatient for persons 18 and older

KENTUCKY

LEXINGTON

Charter Ridge Hospital
3050 Rio Doso Drive
Lexington, KY 40509
(606) 269-2325

Program type: Short-term inpatient for persons 12 and older; short-term (3-to-4-week) inpatient for persons 18 and older

LOUISVILLE

Charter Hospital of Louisville
1405 Browns Lane
Louisville, KY 40207
(502) 896-0495

Program type: Short-term (60-day) inpatient for persons 13 to 17; outpatient and short-term (30-day) inpatient for persons 18 and older

PADUCAH

Charter Hospital of Paducah
435 Berger Road
P.O. Box 7609
Paducah, KY 42002-7609
(502) 444-0444

Program type: Short-term (90-day) inpatient for persons 12 to 18; short-term (4-week) inpatient for persons 18 and older

LOUISIANA

LAKE CHARLES

Charter Hospital of Lake Charles
4250 5th Avenue South
Lake Charles, LA 70605
(318) 474-6133

Program type: Short-term (45-day) inpatient for persons 12 to 18; short-term (4-week) inpatient for persons 18 and older

St. Patrick Hospital
524 South Ryan Street
Lake Charles, LA 70601
(318) 433-7872

Program type: Outpatient and short-term (4-week minimum) inpatient for persons 18 and older

NEW ORLEANS

Odyssey House Louisiana
1125 North Tonti Street
New Orleans, LA 70119
(504) 821-9211

Program type: Therapeutic community for persons 14 and older

SHREVEPORT

Charter Forest Hospital
9320 Linwood Avenue
Shreveport, LA 71108
(318) 688-3930

Program type: Short-term (5-to-7-week) inpatient for persons 10 to 18; short-term (4-week) inpatient for persons 19 and older

MARYLAND

ROCKVILLE

Second Genesis
14701 Avery Road
Rockville, MD 20853
(301) 424-8500

Program type: Therapeutic community for persons 14 and older

UPPER MARLBORO

Second Genesis
P.O. Box 668
Upper Marlboro, MD 20772
(301) 568-4822

Program type: Therapeutic community for persons 14 and older

MASSACHUSETTS

SPRINGFIELD

Marathon House
5 Madison Avenue
Springfield, MA 01105
(413) 733-2178

Program type: Therapeutic community for persons 18 and older

Treatment and Counseling

STOUGHTON

Straight
53 Evans Drive
Stoughton, MA 02072
(617) 344-0930

Program type: Long-term outpatient, temporary residential for persons 12 to 21

MICHIGAN

PLYMOUTH

Straight
42320 Ann Arbor Road
Plymouth, MI 48170
(313) 453-2610

Program type: Long-term outpatient, temporary residential for persons 12 to 21

WEST BLOOMFIELD

Maplegrove Youth Treatment Center
6773 West Maple Road
West Bloomfield, MI 48033
(313) 661-6507

Program type: Short-term (6-week) residential for persons 12 to 18

MINNESOTA

PLYMOUTH

Hazelden Pioneer House
11505 36th Avenue North
Plymouth, MN 55441
(800) 559-2022

Program type: Short-term (6-week) residential for persons 14 to 30

ROCHESTER

Mayo Clinic Alcoholism- and Drug-
Dependence Unit
Rochester Methodist Hospital
Rochester, MN 55905
(507) 286-7593

Program type: Short-term (4-week minimum) residential for persons 18 and older

MISSISSIPPI

JACKSON

Charter Hospital of Jackson
East Lakeland Drive
P.O. Box 4297
Jackson, MS 39216
(601) 939-9030

Program type: Outpatient and inpatient for persons 12 and older

MISSOURI

COLUMBIA

Charter Hospital of Columbia
200 Portland Street
Columbia, MO 65201
(314) 876-8000

Program type: Short-term (4-to-8-week) inpatient for persons 12 to 18; short-term (4-week) inpatient for persons 18 and older

KANSAS CITY

Renaissance West
4311 East 58th Street
Kansas City, MO 64130
(816) 333-2311

Program type: Therapeutic community for persons 14 and older

Renaissance West
425 East 63rd Street
Kansas City, MO 64110
(816) 444-0733

Program type: Outpatient for persons 14 and older

ST. LOUIS

Magdala Foundation
4158 Lindell Boulevard
St. Louis, MO 63108
(314) 652-6004

Program type: Outpatient for all ages

NEVADA

LAS VEGAS

Charter Hospital of Las Vegas
7000 West Spring Mountain
Las Vegas, NV 89117
(702) 876-4357

Program type: Short-term inpatient for persons 12 to 17; outpatient and short-term inpatient for persons 18 and older

NEW HAMPSHIRE

DUBLIN

Marathon House
Box C
Dublin, NH 03444
(603) 563-8501

Program type: Therapeutic community for persons 18 and older

NEW JERSEY

MORRISTOWN

Fair Oaks Hospital
Outpatient Recovery Center
20 Community Place
Morristown, NJ 07960
(800) 872-3864

Program type: Outpatient for all ages

NEWARK

Integrity House
103 Lincoln Park
P.O. Box 1806
Newark, NJ 07101
(201) 623-0600

Program type: Outpatient and therapeutic community for persons within three months of 18 and older

PARAMUS

Fair Oaks Hospital
Outpatient Recovery Center
Bergen Medical Center Building
1 West Ridgewood Avenue
Paramus, NJ 07652
(800) 872-3864

Program type: Outpatient for all ages

SUMMIT

Fair Oaks Hospital
19 Prospect Street
Summit, NJ 07901
(800) 526-4494; in New Jersey
(201) 522-7000

Program type: Short-term inpatient for persons 12 and older

Fair Oaks Hospital
Outpatient Recovery Center
2 Broad Street
Summit, NJ 07901
(800) 872-3864

Program type: Outpatient for all ages

NEW MEXICO

ALBUQUERQUE

Charter Hospital of Albuquerque
5901 Zuni S.E.
Albuquerque, NM 87108
(505) 265-8800

Program type: Outpatient and short-term inpatient for persons 8 to 18; outpatient and short-term (30-day) inpatient for persons 18 and older

SAN JUAN PUEBLO

Delancey Street Foundation
P.O. Box 1240
San Juan Pueblo, NM 87566
(505) 852-4291

Program type: Therapeutic community for persons 10 and older

SANTA TERESA

Charter Hospital of Santa Teresa
100 Charter Lane
P.O. Box 6
Santa Teresa, NM 88008
(505) 589-0033

Program type: Short-term (3-to-4-week) inpatient for persons 14 to 17; short-term (4-week-to-45-day) inpatient for persons 18 and older

NEW YORK

BLAUVELT

Daytop Village
523 Route 303
Blauvelt, NY 10913
(914) 353-2730

Program type: Outpatient for all ages

BREWSTER

Delancey Street Foundation
Turkhill Road
Brewster, NY 10509
(914) 278-6181

Program type: Therapeutic community for persons 18 and older

BRONX

Daytop Village
16 Westchester Square
Bronx, NY 10461
(212) 822-1217

Program type: Outpatient for all ages

Phoenix House
1851 Phelan Place
Bronx, NY 10453
(212) 299-3850

Program type: Therapeutic community for persons 18 and older

BROOKLYN

Daytop Village
401 State Street
Brooklyn, NY 11201
(718) 625-1388

Program type: Outpatient for all ages

Phoenix House
55 Flatbush Avenue
Brooklyn, NY 11201
(718) 852-3150

Program type: Therapeutic community
for persons 16 and older

FAR ROCKAWAY

Daytop Village
316 Beach 65th Street
Far Rockaway, NY 11692
(718) 474-3800

Program type: Therapeutic community
entry and reentry for all ages

HARTSDALE

Daytop Village
246 Central Avenue
Hartsdale, NY 10539
(914) 949-6640

Program type: Outpatient for all ages

HUNTINGTON STATION

Daytop Village
2075 New York Avenue
Huntington Station, NY 11743
(516) 351-7112

Program type: Outpatient for all ages

JAMAICA

Daytop Village
166-10 91st Avenue
Jamaica, NY 11432
(718) 523-8288

Program type: Outpatient for all ages

LONG ISLAND CITY

Phoenix House
34-25 Vernon Boulevard
Long Island City, NY 11101
(718) 274-4213

Program type: Therapeutic community
for persons 18 and older

MANHATTAN

Daytop Village
132 West 83rd Street
New York, NY 10024
(212) 595-7855

Program type: Outpatient for all ages

Odyssey House
309–11 East 6th Street
New York, NY 10003
(212) 477-9639

Program type: Therapeutic community
for persons 16 and older

Phoenix House Riverside Center
164 West 74th Street
New York, NY 10023
(212) 595-5810

Program type: Outpatient for persons 16
and older; therapeutic community for
persons 16 and older; short-term therapeutic community for persons 18 and
older

MILLBROOK

Daytop Village
P.O. Box 607
Millbrook, NY 12545
(914) 677-5335

Program type: Therapeutic community
for all ages

PARKSVILLE

Daytop Village
P.O. Box 368
Parksville, NY 12768
(914) 292-6372

Program type: Therapeutic community
for all ages

RHINEBECK

Daytop Village
Fox Hollow Road
Rhinebeck, NY 12572
(914) 876-3050

Program type: Therapeutic community
for all ages

SHRUB OAK

Phoenix House Academy
Stoney Street
P.O. Box 458
Shrub Oak, NY 10588
(914) 962-2491

Program type: Residential high school
for persons 16 and older

STATEN ISLAND

Daytop Village
1915 Forest Avenue
Staten Island, NY 10303
(718) 981-3136

Program type: Outpatient for all ages

SWAN LAKE

Daytop Village
P.O. Box 340
Swan Lake, NY 12783
(914) 292-6880

Program type: Therapeutic community
for all ages

NORTH CAROLINA

GREENSBORO

Charter Hills Hospital
700 Walter Reed Drive
Greensboro, NC 27403
(919) 852-4821

Program type: Short-term (30-day) inpatient for persons 12 and older; short-
term (2-to-3-week) inpatient for persons
18 and older

RALEIGH

Charter Northridge Hospital
400 Newton Road
Raleigh, NC 27615
(919) 847-0008

Program type: Outpatient and short-
term (45-day) inpatient for persons 13
to 18; outpatient and short-term (4-
week) inpatient for persons 18 and older

WINSTON-SALEM

Charter Mandala Hospital
3637 Old Vineyard Road
Winston-Salem, NC 27104
(919) 768-7710

Program type: Short-term (4-week) inpatient for persons 18 and older

OHIO

Straight
6074 Branch Hill
Guinea Pike
Milford, OH 45150
(513) 575-2673

Program type: Long-term outpatient, temporary residential for persons 12 to 21

PENNSYLVANIA

ERIE

Abraxas II
348 West 8th Street
Erie, PA 16502
(814) 459-0618

Program type: Short-term (4-month minimum) therapeutic community for persons 16 to 25

HARRISBURG

Guadenzia Centro De Vida
301 South 13th Street
Harrisburg, PA 17101
(717) 233-6327

Program type: Bilingual outpatient for persons 16 and older

Guadenzia Commonground
2835 North Front Street
Harrisburg, PA 17110
(717) 238-5553

Program type: Short-term (4-week) residential for persons 18 and older

Guadenzia Concept 90
Harrisburg State Hospital
P.O. Box 10396
Harrisburg, PA 17105
(717) 232-3232

Program type: Short-term (90-day) inpatient for persons 15 and older

Guadenzia Youth Outpatient
  Counseling Service
2237 North 3rd Street
Harrisburg, PA 17110
(717) 233-3424

Program type: Outpatient for persons 12 to 21

LANCASTER

Guadenzia Vantage
212–212½ East King Street
Lancaster, PA 17602
(717) 291-1020

Program type: Therapeutic community for women 18 and older with children

MARIENVILLE

Abraxas I/Abraxas School
Blue Jay Village
P.O. Box 59
Marienville, PA 16239
(814) 927-6615

Program type: Therapeutic community for persons 15 to 21; for program's phases two, three, reentry, and outpatient, clients are sent to either Erie, Philadelphia, or Pittsburgh facility

MECHANICSBURG

Guadenzia West Shore
323 West Allen Street

Mechanicsburg, PA 17055
(717) 766-8517

Program type: Outpatient for persons 15 and older

PHILADELPHIA

Abraxas IV
5401 Wayne Avenue
Philadelphia, PA 19144
(215) 848-3220

Program type: Short-term (4-month minimum) therapeutic community for persons 15 to 21

The Bridge
8400 Pine Road
Philadelphia, PA 19111
(215) 342-5000

Program type: Therapeutic community for persons 14 to 19

The Bridge
1912 Welsh Road
Philadelphia, PA 19115
(215) 969-8990

Program type: Outpatient for all ages

Charter Fairmount Institute
561 Fairthorn Street
Philadelphia, PA 19128
(215) 487-4000

Program type: Outpatient and short-term inpatient for persons 13 to 18; outpatient and short-term (4-week) inpatient for persons 18 and older

Guadenzia
1509 West Columbia Avenue
Philadelphia, PA 19121
(215) 235-5200

Program type: Outpatient for employed persons 16 and older

Guadenzia Focus House
701 North 63rd Street
Philadelphia, PA 19151
(215) 477-0063

Program type: Therapeutic community for men 18 to 30

Guadenzia House
1834 West Tioga Street
Philadelphia, PA 19140
(215) 228-0644

Program type: Therapeutic community for persons 16 and older

PITTSBURGH

Abraxas III
936 West North Avenue
Pittsburgh, PA 15233
(412) 323-9221

Program type: Short-term (4-month minimum) therapeutic community for persons 16 to 21

Supervised Independent Living
241 Amber Street
Pittsburgh, PA 15206
(412) 441-5233

Program type: Short-term (4-month minimum) therapeutic community for persons 15 to 18 who can't go home after having been in rehabilitation programs, group homes, or youth development centers

WEST CHESTER

Guadenzia House West Chester
1030 South Concord Road
West Chester, PA 19382
(215) 399-6929

Program type: Short-term (90-day minimum) therapeutic community for persons 16 and older

RHODE ISLAND

COVENTRY

Marathon House
P.O. Box 328
Coventry, RI 02816
(401) 397-7778
Program type: Therapeutic community for all ages

Marathon House
131 Wayland Avenue
Providence, RI 02906
(401) 331-4250

Program type: Outpatient for persons 18 and older, some adolescents

SOUTH CAROLINA

WEST COLUMBIA

Charter Rivers Hospital
2900 Sunset Boulevard
P.O. Box 4116
West Columbia, SC 29171

Program type: Outpatient and short-term (7-to-8-week) inpatient for persons 13 to 18; short-term (4-week) inpatient for persons 18 and older

TENNESSEE

MEMPHIS

Charter Lakeside Hospital
2911 Brunswick Road
Memphis, TN 38134
(901) 377-4700

Program type: Outpatient and short-term (6-to-8-week) inpatient for persons 13 to 18; outpatient and short-term (4-week) inpatient for persons 18 and older

TEXAS

AUSTIN

Charter Lane Hospital
8402 Crosspark Drive
Austin, TX 78761
(512) 837-1800

Program type: Short-term (30-to-60-day) inpatient for persons 14 to 18; outpatient and short-term (4-week) inpatient for persons 18 and older

CORPUS CHRISTI

Charter Hospital of Corpus Christi
3126 Roddfield Road
Corpus Christi, TX 78414
(512) 993-8893

Program type: Short-term inpatient for persons 12 to 18; outpatient and short-term (3-to-6-week) inpatient for persons 18 and older

DALLAS

Charter Hospital of Dallas
6800 Preston Road
Dallas, TX 75024
(214) 964-3939

Program type: Short-term (4-to-6-week) inpatient for persons 12 to 18; short-term (4-week) inpatient for persons 18 and older

Help Is Possible
723 South Peak
Dallas, TX 75223
(214) 827-2870

Program type: Outpatient and therapeutic community for persons 17 and older

FORT WORTH

Cenikor
2209 South Main
Fort Worth, TX 76110
(817) 921-2771

Program type: Therapeutic community for persons 18 and older

Charter Hospital of Fort Worth
6201 Overton Ridge Boulevard
Fort Worth, TX 76132
(817) 292-6844

Program type: Short-term (6-to-7-week) inpatient for persons 12 to 18; short-term (30-day) inpatient for persons 18 and older

HOUSTON

Cenikor
1423 Texas Avenue
Houston, TX 77002
(713) 228-4145

Program type: Therapeutic community for persons 18 and older

St. Joseph Hospital
1919 LaBranch
Houston, TX 77002
(713) 757-1000

Program type: Outpatient for all ages; short-term (1-to-5-week) inpatient for persons 18 and older

KINGWOOD

Charter Hospital of Kingwood
2001 Ladbrook
Kingwood, TX 77339
(713) 358-2273

Program type: Outpatient and short-term (4-to-6-week) inpatient for persons 13 to 18; outpatient and short-term (30-day) inpatient for persons 18 and older

LAREDO

Charter Hospital of Laredo
6062 North Springfield
Laredo, TX 78041
(512) 722-0900

Program type: Short-term inpatient for persons under 18; short-term (4-week) inpatient for persons over 18

LUBBOCK

Charter Plains Hospital
P.O. Box 10560
Lubbock, TX 79408
(806) 744-5505

Program type: Short-term (2-to-3-month) inpatient for persons 13 and older

McALLEN

Charter Palms Hospital
1421 Jackson Avenue
P.O. Box 5239
McAllen, TX 78502
(512) 631-5421

Program type: Short-term (3-week) in-patient for persons 6 to 18; outpatient and short-term inpatient for persons 18 and older

RICHARDSON

Straight
1399 Executive Drive West
Richardson, TX 75081
(214) 644-4357

Program type: Long-term outpatient; temporary residential for persons 12 to 21

SAN ANTONIO

Charter Real Hospital
8550 Huebner Road
San Antonio, TX 78240
(512) 699-8585

Program type: Outpatient and short-term (4-week) inpatient for persons 12 to 18; outpatient and short-term (4-week) inpatient for persons 18 and older

SUGAR LAND

Charter Hospital of Sugar Land
1550 First Colony Boulevard
P.O. Box 1295
Sugar Land, TX 77487

Program type: Short-term inpatient for persons 12 to 17; short-term (4-week) inpatient for persons 18 and older

UTAH

MIDVALE

Charter Summit Hospital
175 West 7200 South
Midvale, UT 84047
(801) 561-8181

Program type: Outpatient and short-term (3-to-4-week minimum) inpatient for persons 10 to 18; outpatient and short-term (3-to-4-week) inpatient for persons 18 and older

OREM

Charter Canyon Hospital
750 North 1350 East
Orem, UT 84050
(801) 225-2800

Program type: Outpatient and short-term (3-to-4-week minimum) inpatient for persons 10 to 18; outpatient and short-term (3-to-4-week) inpatient for persons 18 and older

SALT LAKE CITY

Odyssey House of Utah
68 South 600 East
Salt Lake City, UT 84102
(801) 322-1001

Program type: Therapeutic community for persons 17 and older

Odyssey House of Utah
625 South 200 East
Salt Lake City, UT 84111
(801) 363-0203

Program type: Therapeutic community for persons 13 to 18

VIRGINIA

ALEXANDRIA

Second Genesis
1001 King Sreet
Alexandria, VA 22314
(703) 548-0442

Program type: Therapeutic community for persons 14 and older

CHARLOTTESVILLE

Charter Hospital of Charlottesville
2101 Arlington Boulevard
Charlottesville, VA 22903
(804) 977-1120

Program type: Short-term inpatient for persons 12 and older; short-term (4-week) inpatient for persons 18 and older

NEWPORT NEWS

Charter Colonial Institute
17579 Warwick Boulevard
Newport News, VA 23603
(804) 887-2611

Program type: Short-term (4-to-6-week) inpatient for persons 13 to 18

RICHMOND

Charter Westbrook Hospital
1500 Westbrook Avenue
Richmond, VA 23227
(804) 266-9671

Program type: Short-term (4-week) inpatient for persons 12 and older; outpatient for persons 18 and older

SPRINGFIELD

Straight
5515 Barlick Road
Springfield, VA 22151
(703) 642-1980

Program type: Long-term outpatient, temporary residential for persons 12 to 21

STEPHENSON

Shalom et Benedictus
P.O. Box 309
Stephenson, VA 22656
(703) 667-0875

Program type: Therapeutic community for persons 14 to 18

WEST VIRGINIA

WAVERLY

White Oak Village
Route 2
P.O. Box 56A
Waverly, WV 26184
(304) 679-3621

Program type: Therapeutic community for persons 15 to 21

WISCONSIN

KENOSHA

Meridian House Ltd.
6755 14th Avenue
Kenosha, WI 53140
(414) 654-0638

Program type: Therapeutic community for persons 18 and older

251

WYOMING

CHEYENNE

Pathfinder
803 West 21st Street
P.O. Box 1604
Cheyenne, WY 82001
(307) 635-0256

Program type: Outpatient for all ages

To learn about state laws regarding private health-insurance coverage for alcoholism- and drug-dependency treatment programs, contact:

National Association of State Alcohol
and Drug Abuse Directors
444 North Capitol Street, N.W.
Suite 520
Washington, DC 20001
(202) 783-6868

Other sources: Contact your state's department of insurance, the address and telephone number of which are in the State Government Offices listings of the White Pages, or your state's alcohol- and drug-abuse agency.

If the children you love need the support of a self-help group, or fellowship, for coming to grips with their substance abuse, contact the following organizations' headquarters, to be referred to the chapter nearest you:

Alcoholics Anonymous
P.O. Box 459
Grand Central Station
New York, NY 10163
(212) 686-1100

Narcotics Anonymous
World Service Office, Inc.
P.O. Box 9999
Van Nuys, CA 91409
(818) 780-3951

Cocaine Anonymous
World Services, Inc.
P.O. Box 1367
Culver City, CA 90232
(213) 559-5833

Other sources: In the Yellow Pages, look under "Alcoholism Information and Treatment Centers" and "Drug Abuse and Addiction Information and Treatment"; look alphabetically in the White Pages.

Drugs Anonymous
World Services
P.O. Box 473
Ansonia Station, NY 10023
(212) 874-0700

Treatment and Counseling

For referrals to self-help organizations of any type, contact:

National Self-Help Clearinghouse
33 West 42nd Street
Room 620N
New York, NY 10036
(212) 840-1259

If you or other family members need the support of a self-help group, or fellowship, for coming to grips with a child's substance abuse, contact the following organizations' headquarters, to be referred to the chapter nearest you:

Al-Anon/Alateen
1372 Broadway
New York, NY 10018
(212) 302-7240

Drug-Anon
P.O. Box 473
Ansonia Station
New York, NY 10023
(212) 874-0700

Families Anonymous
P.O. Box 528
Van Nuys, CA 91408
(818) 989-7841

Toughlove
P.O. Box 1069
Doylestown, PA 18901
(215) 348-7090

Other sources: In the Yellow Pages, look under "Alcoholism Information and Treatment Centers" and "Drug Abuse and Addiction Information and Treatment"; look alphabetically in the White Pages.

If you or the children you love need individual or family counseling, contact the following organizations for referrals to professionals in your area. Explain your problem, what type of therapy you are seeking, and if cost is a factor:

American Association for Marriage and
    Family Therapy
1717 K Street N.W.
Suite 407
Washington, D.C. 20006
(202) 429-1825

American Psychiatric Association
1400 K Street N.W.
Washington, D.C. 20005
(202) 682-6000

American Psychological Association
1200 17th Street N.W.
Washington, D.C. 20036
(202) 955-7600

Family Service America
11700 West Lake Park Drive
Park Place
Milwaukee, WI 53224
(414) 359-2111

Appendix A

Minnesota Institute on Black
  Chemical Abuse
2166 Nicolet Avenue South
Minneapolis, MN 55408
(612) 871-7878

National Association of Social Workers
7981 Eastern Avenue
Silver Spring, MD 20910
(301) 565-0333

Other sources: For additional referrals (including low-cost therapy) as well
as information regarding fees and therapists' credentials, contact your state's
mental health office or administration,
the number of which is in the State
Government Offices and/or Community Services Numbers listings of the
White Pages.

*If your child feels temporarily distressed by problems but is uneasy discussing
them with you, have him contact:*

National Adolescent Suicide Hotline
(800) 621-4000

Other sources: For local hotlines,
look in the Community Services Numbers of the White Pages or under "Crisis
Intervention Service" in the Yellow
Pages.

Appendix B

Free Educational Information

For print materials and videotapes on drugs, alcohol, and tobacco (most of which are free), contact:

Families in Action
National Drug Information Center
3845 North Druid Hills Road
Suite 300
Decatur, GA 30033
(404) 325-5799

Just Say No Club Members' Handbook
The Just Say No Foundation
1777 North California Boulevard
Suite 200
Walnut Creek, CA 94596
(800) 258-2766; in California,
(415) 939-6666

National Clearinghouse for Alcohol
and Drug Information
P.O. Box 2345
Rockville, MD 20852
(301) 468-2600

National Council on Alcoholism
12 West 21st Street
Seventh Floor
New York, NY 10010
(212) 206-6770

National Council on Alcoholism
1511 K Street N.W.
Washington, DC 20005
(202) 737-8122

National Federation of Parents for
Drug-Free Youth
8730 Georgia Avenue
Suite 200
Silver Spring, MD 20910
(301) 585-5437
(800) 554-KIDS

National Parents' Resource Institute
for Drug Education
100 Edgewood Avenue
Suite 1002
Atlanta, GA 30303
(800) 241-7946

Parents' Association to Neutralize
Drug and Alcohol Abuse
P.O. Box 314
Annandale, VA 22003
(703) 750-9285

Quitter's Guide: Seven-day Plan to
Help You Stop Smoking Cigarettes
American Cancer Society
90 Park Avenue
New York, NY 10016
(212) 599-8200

Local branches are listed under A
in the White Pages.

What Works: Schools Without Drugs
(handbook)
U.S. Department of Education
400 Maryland Avenue S.W.
Washington, D.C. 20202
(800) 624-0100

For free films and videocassettes:

National Institute on Drug Abuse
Free-Loan Collection
U.S. Department of Health and
Human Services
Public Health Service
Alcohol, Drug Abuse and Mental
Health Administration
Rockville, MD 20857
Order through:
Modern Talking Picture Service
Scheduling Center
5000 Park Street North
St. Petersburg, FL 33709
(813) 541-5763

Other sources: Virtually all drug-rehabilitation programs and self-help
groups will supply parents with free
print information on drugs.

For answers to your questions about alcohol, drugs, and their abuse, contact the
following drug-information hotlines:

Cocaine Hotline
(800) COC-AINE

National Federation of Parents for
Drug-Free Youth
(800) 554-KIDS

National Institute on Drug Abuse
Drug-Referral Helpline
(800) 662-HELP

National Parents' Resource Institute for
Drug Education
Drug Information Line
(800) 241-7946

Parents' Association to Neutralize Drug
and Alcohol Abuse
The Listening Ear
(703) 750-9285

Free Educational Information

For free information on how to form or join one of the approximately seven thousand parents support/drug-education groups, contact:

Committees of Correspondence
57 Conant Street
Room 113
Danvers, MA 01923
(617) 774-2641

Families in Action
National Drug Information Center
3845 North Druid Hills Road
Suite 300
Decatur, GA 30033
(404) 325-5799

Informal Networks, Inc.
200 Ramsay Road
Deerfield, IL 60015
(312) 945-5021

Mothers Against Drunk Driving
669 Airport Freeway
Suite 310
Hurst, Texas 76053
(817) 268-MADD

National Clearinghouse for Alcohol
    and Drug Information
P.O. Box 2345
Rockville, MD 20852
(301) 468-2600

National Federation of Parents for
    Drug-Free Youth
8730 Georgia Avenue
Suite 200
Silver Spring, MD 20910
(301) 585-5437
(800) 554-KIDS

National Institute on Drug Abuse
Drug-Referral Helpline
5600 Fishers Lane
Rockville, MD 20857
(800) 662-HELP

National Parents' Resource Institute for
    Drug Education
100 Edgewood Avenue
Suite 1002
Atlanta, GA 30303
(800) 241-7946

National Self-Help Clearinghouse
33 West 42nd Street
Room 620N
New York, NY 10036
(212) 840-1259

Toughlove
P.O. Box 1069
Doylestown, PA 18901
(215) 348-7090

Other sources: Contact your state's alcohol and drug abuse agency, the address and telephone number of which is contained in Appendix A.

Appendix C

Alternative Activity Groups and Educational Programs for Children

For childrens' drug-free clubs and organizations, contact:

The Just Say No Foundation
1777 North California Boulevard
Suite 200
Walnut Creek, CA 94596
(800) 258-2766; in California,
(415) 939-6666

These clubs, of which there are some fifteen thousand nationally, provide a variety of educational, recreational, and services activities in an atmosphere that encourages leading drug-free lives. They meet in schools, houses of worship, community centers, and other free facilities and are each lead by one adult volunteer plus one or more teens.

The Club's 220-page get-started book costs $10 and contains information on organizing, recruiting, and activities.

Project LEAD (Leadership, Experience and Development)
Quest International
6655 Sharon Woods Boulevard
Columbus, OH 43229
(800) 446-2800

Operating in thirty-five cities, Project LEAD involves children ages twelve through eighteen in school- and community-service projects. For example, students in Michigan produced their own video to help peers contend with teenage violence; in New Mexico, LEAD teams collected and donated toys to a children's home. Two adult mentors assist each group's four student leaders, who are trained through a two-and-a-half-day workshop. Project LEAD enriches kids' lives by instilling self-confidence and leadership abilities.

> Students Against Driving Drunk
> P.O. Box 800
> Marlboro, MA 01752
> (617) 481-3568

SADD was founded by high-school teacher Robert Anasatas in 1981 after two of his students were killed in traffic accidents. Today it encompasses more than seven thousand chapters and millions of members, who band together in the fight against drunk driving by organizing community events designed to heighten public awareness of the problem. Teenagers are encouraged to enter into a Contract for Life with their friends, so that if someone drinks too much or is with an intoxicated driver, he can depend on a ride home, at any time.

> Youth to Youth
> 700 Bryden Road
> Columbus, OH 43215
> (614) 224-4506

Youth to Youth, started in 1982, is a national network of drug-free youth groups. Kids learn about substances' harmfulness, participate in drug-free activities, and support one another's decision to be drug-free.

Other sources: Many county youth boards sponsor free recreational and cultural programs for kids. They are listed in the Community Services Numbers of the White Pages.

Recommended in-school drug-prevention programs:

> Alcohol/Drug Program
> Archdiocese of Louisville
> Office of Catholic Schools
> 1516 Hepburn Avenue
> Louisville, KY 40204
> (502) 585-4158

This program stresses multilevel involvement: High-school juniors and seniors assist teachers in instructing ninth- and tenth-graders about alcohol and drugs. Parents also participate, to varying degrees, on a regular basis.

Hampton Intervention and Prevention Project (HIPP)
Alternatives, Inc.
1520 Aberdeen Road
No. 102
Hampton, VA 23666
(804) 838-2330

Grades kindergarten through twelve are taught substance prevention through a curriculum that incorporates various activities. Junior-high and high-school students are encouraged to join a "Natural Helpers" group, in which they are trained to provide peer support for other students.

"Here's Looking at You, 2000"
Comprehensive Health Education Foundation
20832 Pacific Highway South
Seattle, WA 98198
(206) 824-2907

Operating in more than ten thousand schools, the "Here's Looking at You, 2000" multimedia drug-education program is for kindergartners through twelfth-graders. It engages students in various learning activities, utilizing games, work sheets, more than thirty videotapes, and dozens of filmstrips, books, charts, costumes, posters, scripts, and other reference sources. It can be employed year after year without having to reorder materials.

DARE (Drug Abuse Resistance Education)
Los Angeles Police Department
P.O. Box 30158
Los Angeles, CA 90030
(213) 485-4856

Endorsed by Secretary of Education William J. Bennett, DARE is a sixteen-week kindergarten-through-eighth-grade program. Its effectiveness can be largely attributed to the uniformed police officer instructors; children seem to respond to them enthusiastically. DARE's focus is on drug education, building self-esteem, and encouraging kids to "dare to say no." Originated by the LAPD and the Los Angeles Unified School District in 1983, the program is now replicated in more than thirty-one states.

Project STAR (Students Taught Awareness and Resistance)
The Kauffman Foundation and Marion Laboratories
9233 Ward Parkway
Kansas City, MO 64114
(816) 363-8604

For grades six through twelve, this program teaches and reinforces resistance skills and is based on a successful program developed by the University of Southern California's Behavior Research Institute.

Pros for Kids
1710 South Amphlett
Suite 300
San Mateo, CA 94403
(415) 571-6726

Uses athletes as positive role models to help prevent youthful substance abuse.

REACH America (Responsible Educated Adolescents
Can Help America [Stop Drugs!])
National Federation of Parents for Drug-Free Youth
8730 Georgia Avenue
Suite 200
Silver Spring, MD 20910
(301) 585-5437
(800) 554-KIDS

REACH America is an intensive antidrug program taught by teenagers, who attend a two-day training seminar. There they learn about drugs' effects and how to present lectures, demonstrations, and skits to younger students. Before qualifying, they must pass a test administered at the seminar's conclusion.

"Say No" to Drugs and Alcohol
City of Tempe, Arizona
1801 East Jen Tilly Lane
Suite C-4
Tempe, AZ 85281
(602) 731-8278

Designed for students in grades four through eight, "Say No" has already proved to be effective: Those exposed to the course were found to take a strong antidrug stand during high-school freshman orientation sessions.

Talking With Your Kids About Alcohol
Talking With Your Students About Alcohol
Prevention Research Institute, Inc.
629 North Broadway
Suite 210
Lexington, KY 40508
(606) 254-9489

Appendix C

These programs are as much for instructors and parents as they are for children. Adults learn how to teach kids in grades five through ten about alcohol and alcohol abuse. Both are endorsed by the National Council on Alcoholism.

Other sources: For the addresses and numbers of other in-school substance-abuse prevention programs, contact the National Association of State Alcohol and Drug Abuse Directors, 444 North Capitol Street N.W., Suite 520, Washington, DC 20001, (202) 783-6868.

Bibliography

Adolescent Maltreatment: Issues and Program Models. Washington, D.C.: U.S. Department of Health and Human Services, 1984.

Albrecht, Margaret. *Parents and Teenagers: Getting Through to Each Other.* New York: Parent's Magazine Press, 1972.

Allinson, Russell. *Drug Abuse: Why It Happens and How to Prevent It.* Lower Burrell, PA: Valley Publishing, 1983.

Bell, Ruth, and Leni Zeiger Wildflower. *Talking with Your Teenager.* New York: Random House, 1983.

Baron, M.D., Jason D. *Kids & Drugs: A Parents Handbook of Drug Abuse Prevention.* New York: Perigee Books, 1981.

Chatlos, M.D., Calvin. *Crack: What You Should Know about the Cocaine Epidemic.* New York: Perigee Books, 1987.

Chilnick, Lawrence D., ed. *The Little Black Pill Book.* New York: Bantam Books, Inc., 1983.

Claypool, Jane Miner. *Alcohol and Teens.* New York: Messner, 1984.

Cohen, Susan, and Daniel Cohen. *Teenage Stress.* New York: Evans, 1984.

Cretcher, Dorothy. *Steering Clear: Helping Your Child Through the High-Risk Drug Years.* San Francisco: Winston Press, 1982.

DuPont, Jr., M.D., Robert L. *Getting Tough on Gateway Drugs.* Washington, D.C.: American Psychiatric Publishing, 1984.

263

Elkind, David. *All Grown Up & No Place to Go.* Reading, Mass.: Addison-Wesley Publishing Company, 1984.

Fine, Louis L. *"After All We've Done for Them": Understanding Adolescent Behavior.* Englewood Cliffs, N.J.: Prentice Hall, 1977.

Gardner, James E. *The Turbulent Teens.* San Diego: Oak Tree Publications, Inc., 1982.

Gilbert, Sara. *Feeling Good (A Book about You and Your Body).* New York: Four Winds Press, 1978.

————. *What Happens in Therapy.* New York: Lothrop, Lee & Shepard Books, 1982.

Gold, M.D., Mark S. *The Facts about Drugs and Alcohol.* New York: Bantam Books, 1986.

————. *800-COCAINE.* New York: Bantam Books, 1984.

Gross, Leonard. *How Much Is Too Much?: The Effects of Social Drinking.* New York: Random House, 1983.

Haskins, Jim. *The Child Abuse Handbook.* Reading, Mass.: Addison-Wesley Publishing Company, 1982.

Hatterer, Dr. Lawrence J. *The Pleasure Addicts.* Cranbury, N.J.: A. S. Barnes and Co., Inc., 1980.

Hegarty, Carol. *Alcoholism Today: The Progress and the Promise.* Minneapolis: CompCare Publications, 1979.

Hutchings, Ph.D., Donald. *Methadone: Treatment for Addiction.* New York: Chelsea House Publishers, 1985.

Hyde, Margaret O. *Mind Drugs,* 3rd ed. New York: McGraw-Hill, 1974.

Hyden, Nancy Woodward. *If Your Child Is Drinking . . .* New York: Putnam, 1981.

Jones, Hardin B., and Helen C. Jones. *Sensual Drugs.* London: Cambridge University Press, 1977.

Klagsbrun, Francine. *Too Young to Die: Youth and Suicide.* Boston: Houghton Mifflin, 1976.

Kline, Nathan S., Stewart F. Alexander, and Amparo Chamberlain. *Psychotropic Drugs: A Manual for Emergency Management of Overdose.* Oradell, N.J.: Medical Economics Company, Inc., 1974.

Bibliography

Kolodny, Robert C., Nancy J. Kolodny, Thomas Bratter, and Cheryl Deep. *How to Survive Your Adolescent's Adolescence*. Boston: Little, Brown & Company, 1984.

Kurtz, Ph.D., Ernest. *Professional Education: Shame and Guilt: Characteristics of the Dependency Cycle*. Center City, Minn.: Hazelden Foundation, 1981.

Kuzma, Ed.D., Kay. *Prime-Time Parenting*. New York: Rawson, Wade Publishers, Inc., 1980.

Long, Robert Emmet. *Drugs and American Society*. New York: H. W. Wilson Company, 1986.

Manthe, George L. *Inside Dope*. Port Jefferson, New York: Cube Publications, Inc., 1983.

Marks, Jane. *Help: A Guide to Counseling and Therapy without a Hassle*. New York: Julian Messner, 1976.

McCoy, Kathy. *Coping with Teenage Depression: A Parent's Guide*. New York: New American Library, 1982.

Meyer, Roberta. *The Parent Connection*. New York: Franklin Watts, 1984.

Morgan, H. Wayne. *Drugs in America: A Social History, 1800–1980*. Syracuse, N.Y.: Syracuse University Press, 1981.

Moses, M. D., Donald A., and Robert E. Burger. *Are You Driving Your Children to Drink?* New York: Van Nostrand Reinhold Company, 1975.

Nale, Sharon. *A Cry for Help: Families of Alcohol- and Other Drug-Dependent Persons*. Philadelphia: Fortress Press, 1982.

National Directory of Drug Abuse and Alcoholism Treatment and Prevention Programs. Washington, D.C.: National Institute on Drug Abuse, 1984.

Neff, Pauline. *Tough Love: How Parents Can Deal with Drug Abuse*. Nashville: Abingdon, 1982.

1984 National Strategy for Prevention of Drug Abuse and Drug Trafficking. Washington, D.C.: U.S. Government Printing Office/Drug Abuse Policy Office, Office of Policy Development, The White House, 1984.

Norman, Jane, and Myron Harris. *The Private Life of the American Teenager*. New York: Rawson, Wade Publishers, Inc., 1981.

Otteson, Orlo, John Townsend, Ph.D., and Tim Rumsey, M.D. *Kids & Drugs: A Parent's Guide*. New York: CFS Publishing Corp., 1983.

Bibliography

Physician's Desk Reference 40th ed. Oradell, N.J.: Medical Economics Company, Inc., 1986.

Polson, Beth, and Miller Newton, Ph.D. *Not My Kid: A Parent's Guide to Kids and Drugs.* New York: Arbor House Publishing Co., 1984.

Pursch, Joseph A. *Dear Doc . . .* Minneapolis: CompCare Publications, 1985.

Rice, F. Philip. *The Adolescent: Development, Relationships and Culture.* Newton, Mass.: Allyn & Bacon, 1975.

Ryerson, Eric. *When Your Parent Drinks Too Much.* New York: Facts on File, 1985.

Satir, Virginia. *Conjoint Family Therapy.* Palo Alto, Calif.: Science and Behavior Books, Inc., 1967

Saunders, Ph.D., Antoinette, and Bonnie Remsberg. *The Stress-Proof Child.* New York: Holt, Rinehart and Winston, 1984.

Scott, Sharon. *PPR: Peer Pressure Reversal: How to Say No and Keep Your Friends.* Amherst, Mass.: Human Resource Development Press, 1986.

Seixas, Judith S., and Geraldine Youcha. *Children of Alcoholism: A Survivor's Manual.* New York: Crown Publishers, Inc., 1985.

Weiss, Ann E. *Biofeedback.* New York: Franklin Watts, 1984.

Wood, Abigail. *The Seventeen Book of Answers to What Your Parents Don't Talk to You about and Your Best Friends Can't Tell You.* New York: McKay, 1972.

Young, Lawrence A., Linda G. Young, Marjorie M. Klein, Donald M. Klein, and Dorianne Beyer. *Recreational Drugs.* New York: Berkley Books, 1982.

Youngs, Dr. Bettie B. *Stress in Children.* New York: Arbor House, 1985.

About the Authors

Ken Barun is currently vice-president and executive director of Ronald McDonald Children's Charities and in November 1987 was appointed by President Ronald Reagan to the National White House Conference for a Drug-Free America. Previously he served under First Lady Nancy Reagan at the White House as her director of projects and policy, and was executive assistant to the administrator for the Alcohol, Drug Abuse and Mental Health Administration.

Other positions held include deputy assistant secretary of public affairs/public liaison, U.S. Department of Health and Human Services; and chairman of the board of directors, president, and chief executive officer of Cenikor Foundation, one of the country's largest nonprofit health-care corporations, specializing in drug- and alcohol-abuse rehabilitation. It was at Cenikor that in 1972 he conquered a long-standing heroin addiction.

Barun lives with his wife, Maria, and sons Seth, Adam, and Max in Naperville, Illinois.

Philip Bashe is the author or coauthor of the *Rolling Stone Rock Almanac, Heavy Metal Thunder, Dee Snider's Teenage Survival Guide, That Ain't All, Folks!,* an autobiography of Mel Blanc, and a forthcoming biography of Ricky Nelson. He was editor of *International Musician, Circus, Good Times,* and *Foxtrot* magazines and has written for the *Buffalo Evening News* as well as for several national publications. In addition, Bashe is a former radio and TV announcer.

He lives with his wife, Patty, in Baldwin, New York.